Unwin Critical Library

GENERAL EDITOR: CLAUDE RAWSON

SHAKESPEARE'S SONNETS

Unwin Critical Library
General Editor: Claude Rawson

Shakespeare's Sonnets

KENNETH MUIR

Emeritus Professor of English Literature
The University of Liverpool

London
GEORGE ALLEN & UNWIN
Boston   Sydney

First published in 1979

GEORGE ALLEN & UNWIN LTD
40 Museum Street, London WC1A 1LU

© George Allen & Unwin (Publishers) Ltd, 1979

British Library Cataloguing in Publication Data

Muir, Kenneth
    Shakespeare's sonnets.—(Unwin critical library).
    1.   Shakespeare, William. Sonnets
    I.   Title
    821′.3   PR2848   79–40008

    ISBN 0–04–821042–0

Typeset in 10 on 11 point Plantin by Trade Linotype Ltd, Birmingham
and printed in Great Britain
by Hollen Street Press Ltd, Slough

PREFACE

Unlike many writers on the Sonnets, I do not know the answers to all the problems which are discussed at length in the second volume of the great Variorum edition. Forty years ago, when I collaborated with Sean O'Loughlin on *The Voyage to Illyria*, I thought I knew many of the answers. I no longer have the brash confidence of youth. So the reader must not expect to be told of the identity of Mr W.H., nor whether he was the person to whom the Sonnets were addressed, or merely the procurer of the manuscript. I do not know whether the Dark Lady was Lucy Negro, or Emilia Lanier, the pious author of *Salve Deus Rex Judaeorum*, or someone else, or an imaginary character. I do not know the names of the rival poets. I do not know how far, if at all, the Sonnets were autobiographical. I do not know whether Shakespeare approved or disapproved of their publication.

Some of these questions will necessarily affect our interpretation of the Sonnets, and these will be discussed in the body of the book; but the rest I have relegated to an appendix for the partial satisfaction of those who disagree with Milton's view, expressed in a letter to an unknown friend, that curiosity is a profitless sin. Such questions are necessarily important to biographers, but they are almost irrelevant to criticism of the poems.

Liverpool   KENNETH MUIR

GENERAL EDITOR'S PREFACE

Each volume in this series is devoted to a single major text. It is addressed to serious students and teachers of literature, and to knowledgeable non-academic readers. It aims to provide a scholarly introduction and a stimulus to critical thought and discussion.

Individual volumes will naturally differ from one another in arrangement and emphasis, but each will normally begin with information on a work's literary and intellectual background, and other guidance designed to help the reader to an informed understanding. This is followed by an extended critical discussion of the work itself, and each contributor in the series has been encouraged to present in these sections his own reading of the work, whether or not this is controversial, rather than to attempt a mere consensus. Each volume also contains a historical survey of the work's critical reputation, including an account of the principal lines of approach and areas of controversy and a selective (but detailed) bibliography.

The hope is that the volumes in this series will be among those which a University teacher would normally recommend for any serious study of a particular text, and that they will also be among the essential secondary texts to be consulted in some scholarly investigations. But the experienced and informed non-academic reader has also been in our minds, and one of our aims has been to provide him with reliable and stimulating works of reference and guidance, embodying the present state of knowledge and opinion in a conveniently accessible form.

University of Warwick

ACKNOWLEDGEMENTS

Acknowledgements are due, for permission to quote copyright trans-
lations, to Miss L. Zaina, to George R. Kay and Penguin Books, to
James Michie and Rupert Hart-Davis, and to Rolfe Humphries and
Indiana University Press.

A NOTE ON ABBREVIATIONS AND TEXTS

ABBREVIATIONS

The usual abbreviations are used for the titles of Shakespeare's plays. Other abbreviations of journals, etc.:

CHEL	=	Cambridge History of English Literature
EA	=	Etudes anglaises
EC	=	Essays in Criticism
EngSt	=	Englische Studien
NQ	=	Notes and Queries
OHEL	=	Oxford History of English Literature
RES	=	Review of English Studies
ShJ	=	Shakespeare Jahrbuch
SQ	=	Shakespeare Quarterly
SS	=	Shakespeare Survey
SSt	=	Shakespeare Studies
TLS	=	Times Literary Supplement

TEXTS

Peter Alexander's one-volume edition is used for all Shakespeare's works, but his text of the Sonnets has occasionally been altered after comparison with the 1609 Quarto and other editions. The editions of other sonneteers are listed in the Select Bibliography.

CONTENTS

CHAPTER 1

Preliminaries

In this first chapter, I shall discuss briefly three inter-related topics – the dates when the Sonnets were written, the nature of the text, and whether the order is Shakespeare's own.

(a) DATE

The only certainties about the dates of the Sonnets are that some, though not necessarily the ones we have, were written by 1598 when Francis Meres wrote *Palladis Tamia* and spoke of Shakespeare's sugared sonnets which were circulating among his friends; that two of the 'Dark Lady' sonnets were written by 1599, and probably before that, whenever the first edition of *The Passionate Pilgrim* was published – the title-page of the only extant copy is missing; and that the whole collection was published in 1609. Five methods have been used, singly or in combination, to date the composition more precisely.

(i) Those critics who believe they know to whom the Sonnets were addressed are able to fix the date within a few years. If Leslie Hotson was right in thinking that they were addressed to William Hatcliffe, some at least of the Sonnets were written as early as 1588[1]; if Southampton was the recipient, they must have been composed, for the most part, in the early nineties; and, if Pembroke was the man, they could not have been written before 1596; and, if CXLV was really addressed to Anne Hathaway, that must have been written before she became Mrs Shakespeare in 1583.[2]

(ii) A similar method is used by many of the same critics: to date the Sonnets by identifying the Rival Poet. If, for example, Marlowe was the rival, the relevant sonnets must have been written before 1593, when he was stabbed to death in a Deptford tavern. But many other rivals have been proposed, usually after the critics have decided on the identity of the recipient. It is, in any case, by no means certain that the main rival's work has survived, or whether Shakespeare's admiration was sincere or ironical.

(iii) A number of sonnets contain what purport to be topical allusions, but there is no general agreement about their application. Sonnet CVII, for example, was thought by Hotson to refer to the defeat of the Spanish Armada in 1588; but not everyone agrees that 'the mortal moon' refers to the crescent formation of the Armada, or that a poet would then believe that peace proclaimed 'Olives of endless age'.[3] Ten or eleven other dates have been proposed for this sonnet, of which the favourites are 1596 when Elizabeth I survived her grand climacteric, 1601 when she survived the Essex rebellion, and 1603 when James I peacefully succeeded her. There are similar disagreements about the identity of 'the fools of time' in CXXIV 'Which die for goodness, who have lived for crime'. One suspects that critics have just decided on the identity of W.H. and then searched for events to which the allusions might refer. (Hotson, it should be said, was not guilty of this error of method.)

(iv)　A method which appears to be more promising is by the listing of parallels between the Sonnets and Shakespeare's other works. In the tables compiled by Isaac and Davis, set out conveniently by Claes Schaar in 1962, it is immediately apparent that the largest number of parallels are with works written between 1593 and 1595.[4] But the peaks on the graph represented by *Venus and Adonis, Lucrece, Love's Labour's Lost* and *Romeo and Juliet* may be explained by the congruity of the content of those works with that of the Sonnets. Romeo's unreturned love for Rosaline, for example, is a classic sonnet situation; the nobles in *Love's Labour's Lost* are sonneteers; and Venus addresses arguments to Adonis which are not unlike those used by Shakespeare in the first seventeen sonnets. It is noticeable that some plays written in these same years – *Titus Andronicus, The Taming of the Shrew* and *Richard II* – have very few parallels. Among the later plays, there are few parallels with *Coriolanus* and *Timon of Athens*, and more with *Cymbeline* and *The Winter's Tale* – and this is what we should expect.

We should also bear in mind that one or two certain parallels outweigh a score of vaguer resemblances, and that by some trick of memory a phrase or an image can be called up years later. Bassanio's meditation on wigs – to take one example – is clearly connected with Sonnet LXVIII, but it may have been written years after or (as Baldwin believed) before the sonnet. Schaar rightly points out that the theme of false hair taken from corpses is not peculiar to Shakespeare.[5]

(v)　The last method of dating is by the examination of echoes of other writers in the Sonnets, or of the Sonnets in the works of others since they could have been read in manuscript. The most detailed and persuasive application of this method is by Claes Schaar.[6] It is seldom possible to be sure whether Shakespeare or the other writer is the debtor; but a notoriously derivative poet such as Samuel Daniel seems more likely to have imitated Shakespeare, as he did many other poets. Even here there are doubts, for Shakespeare clearly echoed Daniel in *Romeo and Juliet, Richard II* and *Antony and Cleopatra*. Michael Drayton, Barnabe Barnes and Bartholomew Griffin were also derivative. The best

of this trio, Drayton, did not develop into an impressive sonneteer until
he had learnt some valuable lessons from Shakespeare. On the other
hand, two of Shakespeare's sonnets (XXXI, CVI) may be indebted to
Constable's *Diana*. The first of these may be compared with Constable's
dedicatory sonnet:

> Grace full of grace though in these verses heere
> My love complaynes of others then of thee
> Yet thee alone I lov'd and they by mee
> (Thow yet unknowne) only mistaken were
> Like him which feeles a heate now heere now there
> Blames now this cause now that untill he see
> The fire indeed from whence they caused bee
> Which fire I now doe knowe is you my deare
> Thus diverse loves dispersed in my verse
> In thee alone for ever I waite
> But follie unto thee more to rehearse
> To him I flye for grace that rules above
> That by my Grace, I may live in delight
> Or by his grace never more may love.

So Shakespeare tells his friend:

> Thou art the grave where buried love doth live,
> Hung with the trophies of my lovers gone,
> Who all their parts of me to thee did give;
> That due of many now is thine alone:
>   Their images I lov'd I view in thee,
>   And thou (all they) hast all the all of me.

The basic idea is the same; but the two poets could have thought of it
independently, or Constable may here be indebted to Shakespeare. The
other comparison is with the Constable sonnet which begins:

> Miracle of the world I never will denye
> That former poets prayse the beautie of theyre dayes
> But all those beauties were but figures of thy prayse
> And all those poets did of thee but prophecye.

So Shakespeare, reading descriptions of 'ladies dead and lovely knights',
declares:

> I see their antique pen would have express'd
> Even such a beauty as you master now.
> So all their praises are but prophecies
> Of this our time, all you prefiguring. . . .

Once again, it looks as though one poet had read the other; and, since Constable's sonnet was sent to his mistress with a copy of Petrarch, it is likely to have been written first. Constable, however, appears to have imitated XCIX in one of his best pieces:

My Ladies presence makes the roses red.

Whatever doubts we may have about priority in individual cases, by using this method Schaar claims that 'the vast majority of the sonnets . . . seem to have been written between 1591-2 and 1594-5'.[7] Quite properly, Schaar is cautious. We do not know when some poems were written (e.g. Marlowe's *Hero and Leander*), and resemblances between poems may sometimes be due to the fact that both have been influenced by an unidentified source. Yet Schaar's arguments about what Baldwin called the 'literary genetics' of the Sonnets are much more convincing than Baldwin's own. I accept Schaar's dating as the most probable.

It is true that many of the Sonnets seem maturer in style than the plays written during those years; but it often happens that poets succeed with shorter poems before they achieve comparable success with longer ones – one has only to think of Keats.

On the other hand, both Beeching and Dover Wilson, in comparing lines from *Venus and Adonis* with some of the Sonnets, seem to exaggerate the comparative weakness of the former, which may be due, in any case, to other considerations.[8]

(b) TEXT

Two of the 'Dark Lady' sonnets (CXXXVIII, CXLIV) were printed in *The Passionate Pilgrim* (see Appendix E), and the text contains a number of variants. One of them (CXLIV.6) enables us to correct the unrhyming 'sight' of the Quarto. It is difficult to tell whether the others are due to compositors or transcribers and which, if any, were Shakespearian first shots.

The Quarto (1609) provides the basis for all modern texts of the Sonnets since the *Poems* of 1640, in which most were reprinted, has no authority. The Quarto is badly printed, but editors have tended to exaggerate its badness. A check of the most recent edition containing the Sonnets – the Riverside – shows that it departs from the text of the first fifty sonnets in some 125 readings; but more than a hundred of these are corrections of spelling and punctuation, and only eighteen of the remainder are certain improvements.

We do not know who provided T[homas] T[horpe] with the copy for the volume. Dover Wilson's conjecture that it was the Dark Lady seems unlikely on psychological grounds.[9] That 'the onlie begetter' (see

Appendix A) was not the man to whom the Sonnets were addressed – as nearly everyone supposes – but the man who procured them for the publisher involves a strained use of language, but cannot be entirely ruled out.[10] William Harvey, who married Southampton's mother, has been suggested and presumably he might have had access to the manuscript if, and only if, they were addressed to Southampton. Neither W.H., whose vices are exposed, nor Shakespeare, a self-confessed adulterer, is likely to have allowed the Sonnets to be made public to readers who would probably assume they were autobiographical. It was another matter to have them circulating among one's private friends (as Meres recorded), and we must assume that one of the private friends made a copy which he, or one of his friends, gave or sold to Thorpe.

Shakespeare was the most popular playwright of his day, and *Venus and Adonis* was a bestseller. It is therefore odd that the Sonnets were not reprinted during the seventeenth century – other than in the 1640 collection. It has been surmised that by 1609 the sonneteering craze had burnt itself out, and that by the time Shakespeare's volume appeared it was already somewhat old-fashioned. But, as very few copies are extant, it seems possible that the volume was suppressed. Some have supposed that Shakespeare was outraged by the publication of his most intimate thoughts and feelings, although the promise of immortality through his powerful rhyme could hardly be substantiated without publication at some time. Others have pointed out that the publisher would not have withdrawn a profitable volume because of complaints by the author, but he would doubtless have succumbed to pressure from a member of the aristocracy. On the whole it seems likely that the volume was withdrawn.[11]

Some of the Quarto spellings may be authorial, but there is no certain evidence that it was printed from Shakespeare's own manuscript.[12] Indeed, the most careful study of the habits of the compositors makes it seem unlikely that the poet's punctuation or spelling has survived.[13]

One bibliographical fact has aroused controversy. Thirty-five words in the volume are printed in italics. '*Will*' is italicised eleven times to call attention to the quibbles on Shakespeare's name and on the sexual connotations of the word. Another ten are classical names (e.g. '*Mars*', '*Adonis*', '*Hellen*', '*Saturne*', '*Cupid*'). This is in accordance with the custom of Elizabethan printers. The remainder are less easy to explain. '*Quietus*' and '*Interim*' are italicised in *Hamlet* and *Macbeth* respectively. '*Alcumie*' is italicised in one sonnet, but not in another. There seems to be no special reason for italicising '*Autumne*' (but not the other seasons), '*statues*', '*abisme*' and '*satire*' (unless the compositor assumed it meant '*satyr*'). '*Heretick*' and '*Informer*' may call attention to topicalities. But the controversy centres on the remaining words – '*Rose*' (1.2), '*Hews*' (XX.7), '*Alien*' (LXXVIII.3), which may conceivably conceal the identity of W.H. or of the Rival Poet. But the erratic italics may be due to the aberrations of compositors. We need not suppose, with Oscar Wilde, that W.H. was William Hughes or that '*Rose*' is a quibble on Wriothesley.

(c) ORDER

At first sight, the order of the Sonnets in the 1609 edition appears to be somewhat confused. It is true that the first seventeen, in which the poet is urging his friend to marry in order to perpetuate his beauty, have a thematic unity. The 'Dark Lady' sonnets (CXXVII–CLII) likewise belong together, although the actual order in the group appears to be unnatural. The sonnet which expresses most consciousness of sin is sandwiched between two which are quite light-hearted (CXXVIII–CXXX), and the sonnet which most clearly reveals the seduction of the poet's better angel by his worser spirit (CXLIV) is sandwiched between two trivial love-poems. The narrative line, both here and in the main sequence, is erratic. It is therefore to be expected that many critics and most editors should believe that Sonnets XLI and XLII, and possibly others in the sequence, refer to the same seduction of friend by mistress as that described in the Dark Lady sequence:

> Take all my loves, my love, yea take them all. . . .

> And when a woman woos, what woman's son
> Will sourly leave her till she have prevailed?
> Ay me, but yet thou mightst my seat forbear. . . .

This argument makes a number of assumptions for which proof is inevitably lacking. First, that the Sonnets are autobiographical; secondly, that the first 126 sonnets are addressed to one, and only one, man; thirdly, that the poet had only one mistress; fourthly, that, even if all these assumptions were justified, the order would be improved by the insertion of the Dark Lady sonnets in the sequence addressed to Mr W.H. But the sequence, which is concerned with a friendship which lasted at least three years, would be seriously impaired by this alteration, for it would make a transient episode outweigh in importance the rest of the main series.

If we assume, as I think we should, that the Sonnets, although not directly autobiographical, do at least reflect the poet's experience – that he loved and lusted – the order of events, the line, as Lady Bracknell said, is immaterial. However much we shuffle the pack, we have the same basic facts: that the poet loved a younger man, probably of aristocratic birth; that he urged him to marry and then claimed that he would immortalise him in his verse; that other poets shared his friend's patronage and favour; that at some time the poet's dark-haired mistress seduced the friend; that the young man's character had serious faults, as the poet was reluctantly forced to acknowledge.

Sonnet sequences from the time of Petrarch to the age of Auden have never been narrative poems in fourteen-line stanzas. Even Sidney's *Astrophil and Stella,* in which there is a beginning, a middle and an end, and which has more of a story than the sequences of Spenser, Daniel or Drayton – not to mention Ronsard and Desportes – is not a narrative poem. Even if we could rearrange Shakespeare's sugared sonnets so as to turn them into a novel in verse, we should be violating the spirit of the genre; but happily this is impossible.

None of the proposed rearrangements has given much satisfaction, except to its originator. The favourite method, summarised in the Variorum edition, is to juxtapose sonnets with common rhymes, so that the whole sequence is linked in this way. It can easily be shown that several pairs of sonnets, which no one would dream of separating, do have common rhyme-words, or at least common rhymes, and sometimes more than one. In the last four lines of XLIV, for example, two of the four elements are mentioned:

> But that, so much of earth and water wrought,
> I must attend time's leisure with my moan,
> Receiving nought by elements so slow
> But heavy tears, badges of either's woe.

The next sonnet begins:

> The other two, slight air and purging fire. . . .

The two sonnets are indivisible; and XLV repeats rhyme-words from the previous sonnet ('thee' and 'gone'). In the same way CXXXV and CXXXVI share the rhymes 'still' and '*Will*'. There are other manifest pairs which echo the rhymes but not the identical words. Nor is this surprising. A poet composing a sonnet may think of a number of possible rhymes, the discarded ones coming in handy a few hours, or days, or weeks later.

It is quite possible to arrange the Sonnets so that each is linked by common rhymes to those immediately before and immediately after. The difficulty is that the number of possible arrangements is enormous. Even if we assume that the sonnets counselling marriage come first – as they probably do – there are a large number of permutations even in these caused by the repetition of the poet's favourite rhymes. The very first sonnet has rhyme-links with twelve of the next sixteen; Sonnet IV has links with nine of the same group; and Sonnet VIII with eight. It

would be supererogatory to examine links with the whole sequence, but
an indication of the extent of the possible linkage can be obtained by
considering at random Sonnets L–LX, C–CX. Sonnet I has links with
twelve of these, Sonnet IV with nine, and Sonnet VII with fourteen.
The number of permutations, it would seem, exceeds a million.

Some of these possible arrangements can doubtless be ruled out on
other grounds. Despite the rhymes, one would not wish to juxtapose
'Shall I compare thee to a summer's day?' (XVIII) and 'Th'expense of
spirit in a waste of shame' (CXXIX), nor even with 'Poor soul, the
centre of my sinful earth' (CXLVI). Yet, when all is said, the rearrangements according to rhyming, by Bray and others, do not give greater
coherence to the sequence; and, if they did, they might make the story
less autobiographical – for life is never as tidy as art.

Quite the most successful attempt to rearrange the Sonnets is that of
Brents Stirling.[14] It is less drastic and was psychologically plausible. He
is wise enough not to attempt to make all the pieces of the jig-saw fit.
Instead, he assumes that Shakespeare wrote intermittently over a number
of years. The whole collection can be divided into thirty-five poems,
ranging from single sonnets (XX, LXXVII) to a sequence of fourteen,
urging the young man to marry (I–XIV). But Stirling distinguishes
between the poems which are complete in themselves (e.g. XXV–XXVI
or XXIX–XXXI) and those which are linked with others, as XV–XVII
are clearly linked with the first fourteen. Shakespeare turns from the
straightforward injunction to marry to three sonnets in which he
promises a double immortality, by breed and by verse. Stirling thus
divides the Sonnets into five groups of poems and six other poems. He
does not, I think, imply that the groups were written in strictly chrono-
logical order, though the first group, showing less intimacy than the rest,
was certainly written first.

Stirling does not use rhyme-links and he has only occasional references
to other editors. He relies on logical and thematic connections. For
example, he associates XCI–XCIII, LXIX–LXX, XCV–XCVI and
XCIV, in that order. The sonnets adjacent in the Quarto are plainly
inseparable. The link between XCIII, LXIX and LXX is that they have
parallel phrases in the concluding couplets: 'answer not thy show',
'matcheth not thy show', 'masked not thy show'. Although theoretically
XCIII could have been written some weeks or months after LXX, the
link is fairly conclusive. Similarly, XCV contains the same image of
canker in the rose as LXX; and (Stirling argues) must be misplaced
because festering lilies should not be followed by 'the fragrant rose' of
XCV. He puts XCIV at the end of this series because

> Its couplet, far more decisive and disquieting than the others, now
> caps not only a sonnet but the poem as a whole. And its reference

back to previous sonnets – to their opposition of sweetness and corruption imaged in decaying 'flower', 'rank smell', 'odor', 'weeds', 'deeds' – is definitive.

In a similar way Stirling links XXIV and XLVI, LXI and XXVII, XLIX and LXXXVII, XXXII and LXXXI, XXIII and CII. Not all these juxtapositions are equally convincing; but it is fair to say that Stirling generally produces a more logical order than that of the Quarto. Whether a more logical order is necessarily the right order is another question; but what Stirling has done undoubtedly required acuteness, sensitiveness and immense patience. Later critics may wish to modify the details, but it is a real achievement.

This may well be how the Sonnets were written. Nevertheless, the Quarto order, with its division into two sequences, can be supported by a number of powerful arguments. In the first place, it should be mentioned that there are no less than fourteen adjacent sonnets in the Quarto with identical pairs of rhymes (I, II 'eyes'/'lies'; III, IV 'be'/ 'thee'; XVI, XVII 'rhyme'/'time'; XXXIII, XXXIV 'face'/'disgrace'; XXXVI, XXXVII 'spight'/'delight', 'thee'/'me'; XXXVIII, XXXIX 'me'/'thee'; XLVI, XLVII 'heart'/'part'; CVI, CVII 'time'/'rhyme'; CXIII, CXIV 'you'/'true'; CXXXII, CXXXIII 'me'/'be'; CXXXIV, CXXXV 'will'/'still'; CXL, CXLI 'thee'/'be'; CXLI, CXLII 'thee/'be'; CLIII, CLIV 'love'/'prove'). There are forty-seven sonnets which repeat a rhyme-word from the previous one, and eight of them repeat two such words (XXVII, XXVIII 'thee', 'night'; XLIV, XLV 'thee', 'gone'; LIII, LIV 'show', 'made'; LXXIV, LXXV 'away', 'life'; LXXXIV, LXXXV 'more', 'you'; CXVI, CXVII 'minds', 'love'; CXXXI, CXXXII 'heart', 'face'; CXXXVII, CXXXVIII 'lies', 'be'). There are four other sonnets which repeat a singular or plural form of a rhyme-word used in the previous sonnet. There are many examples of sonnets which echo a rhyme, but not the identical words, from the previous one (e.g. VI, VII 'one', 'son'; XII, XIII 'grow', 'know'; XXVIII, XXIX 'rest', 'possess'd') and a number of cases where a word used in one sonnet, but not as a rhyme, is used as a rhyme in the next (e.g. V, VI 'distill'd'). There are other cases where the reverse process takes place, a rhyme-word of one sonnet being used internally in the sonnet following. There are, of course, some gaps in the sequence which are not bridged in any of these ways, but many of the gaps are bridged not by rhyme, but by reason, an obvious congruity of sense (e.g. X, XI; LXXXI, LXXXII; LXXXIII, LXXXIV). It is not at all surprising that in a sequence that covers a period of more than three years, including periods when, on the poet's own confession, no sonnets were being written, there should be gaps; the remarkable thing is that so many of the sonnets as printed in 1609 are closely linked.

The second defence of the Quarto order is numerological. Alastair Fowler, following Adrian Benjamin, suggests that several other Elizabethan sonnet sequences are carefully organised.[15] Sidney's *Astrophil and Stella* consists of 108 sonnets to remind us of *The Odyssey*, in which Penelope (Stella's real name) had 108 suitors. Both Constable's *Diana* and Drayton's *Idea* in their final forms contained 63 sonnets, 63 being the age of the grand climacteric. It is well known that Spenser's 'Epithalamion' was constructed on numerological lines;[16] and Fowler argues that the volume in which it appeared, containing the *Amoretti* and some anacreontics, was also numerologically designed.

With this background, it is not surprising that Fowler should seek for evidence that Shakespeare, with his small Latin and less Greek, also made use of number symbolism in the Sonnets. By the omission of CXXXVI (because it contains the injunction 'Then in the number let me pass untold') Fowler was left with 153 sonnets. These can be arranged as an equilateral triangle with a base of 17. The three irregular poems in the sequence (XCIX with an extra line, CXXVI with twelve lines and CXLV in octosyllabics) are so placed that they are at the left of the bases of triangles of 55, 28 and 10 sonnets respectively (the eighth, eleventh and fourteenth lines counting from the bottom, the fourth, the seventh and the tenth counting from the top of the large triangle).

Nor is this all. If we omit these three poems and CXXXVI (for the reason given), we are left with 150 sonnets, a significant number because there are 150 Psalms. There are a number of refinements in Fowler's argument – including a numerological defence of the authenticity of 'A Lover's Complaint' – but we are concerned here only with the justification of the 1609 order. It may be added that the first seventeen sonnets – those concerned with procreation – form the base of Fowler's triangle.

In the same essay, if with some reservations, Fowler supports Leslie Hotson's theory that there were echoes of the first five Penitential Psalms in the corresponding sonnets.[17] One would find this more convincing if there were echoes of the other two Penitential Psalms, and, indeed, if the suggested echoes were somewhat closer. 'My bones consumed away through my daily complaining' is not particularly close to 'When that churl Death my bones with dust shall cover' (Psalm 32.3, Sonnet XXXII.2), the bones of the sonneteer being in the grave. Hotson quotes two verses from Psalm 102.7, 20):

I have watched, and am even as it were a sparrow that sitteth upon the housetops . . . That he might hear the mournings of such as are in captivity.

This he compares with the nightingale's mournful song:

> As Philomel in summer's front doth sing,
> And stops her pipe in growth of riper days;
> Not that the summer is less pleasant now
> Than when her mournful hymns did hush the night.

Even the parallel with Psalm 6 seems insubstantial. 'My beauty is worn away because of mine enemies' (v. 7) is compared with the enemies of beauty in the sonnet (ll. 1, 2, 4, 14): winter and death. It could be supported, however, by an additional parallel:

> For in death no man remembreth thee (v. 5)
> Then what could death do, if thou shouldst depart (l. 11)

The parallels with Psalms 38 and 51 are more striking:

> One that is dumb, who doth not open his mouth (v. 13)
> For who's so dumb that cannot write to thee (l. 7)

> According to the multitude of thy mercies do away mine offences (v. 1)
> Thus can my love excuse the slow offence (l. 1)

More significant, perhaps, is the parallel between the 'mortal moon' sonnet and the corresponding psalm:

> Not mine own fears, nor the prophetic soul
> Of the wide world, dreaming on things to come,
> Can yet the lease of my true love control,
> Suppos'd as forfeit to a confin'd doom.
> The mortal Moon hath her eclipse endur'd,
> And the sad Augurs mock their own presage;
> Incertainties now crown themselves assur'd,
> And peace proclaims Olives of endless age.
> Now with the drops of this most balmy time
> My love looks fresh, and Death to me subscribes,
> Since, spite of him, I'll live in this poor rhyme,
> While he insults o'er dull and speechless tribes;
>   And thou in this shalt find thy monument
>   When tyrants' crests and tombs of brass are spent.

It will be recalled that Hotson believes that this sonnet was written in 1588 and that it refers to the destruction of the Spanish Armada. He quotes a number of contemporary descriptions of the crescent formation of the Armada ('a half moone', 'a Moone cressant', 'a horned Moone'). He shows that there were three eclipses in 1588 and that there were predictions that 1588 years after the birth of Christ was regarded as a particularly dangerous time. Not all critics have accepted Hotson's dating of this sonnet; but it is certainly true that the corresponding psalm celebrates a series of unexpected deliverances from trouble and distress, with its repeated 'we cried unto the Lord in our trouble and he delivered us out of our distress'.

There are a number of other links between Psalms and Sonnets, which appear to be as significant as those to which Hotson called attention. It will be convenient to tabulate them in parallel columns. (Numbers in the left-hand column refer to psalm *and* corresponding sonnet; bracketed numbers in the right-hand column are line-numbers in the relevant sonnet).

Psalms	*Sonnets*
1 The righteous man is compared with a tree 'that bringeth forth his fruit in due season'; and he is contrasted with the barren evil man.	The poet exhorts his friend to marry and increase and (as we learn later) not to be guilty of self-love, murder, avarice and waste.
18 death . . . wind . . . fire	death (12), winds (3), too hot (5)
21 gold	gold (12)
22 heart . . . garments . . . darling . . . sword	heart (6), raiment (6), babe (12), slain (13)
40 sacrifice . . . poor	The poet sacrifices his mistress to his friend and speaks of his poverty (10)
41 The psalmist's 'own familiar friend whom he trusted' has laid in wait for him.	The poet complains of his friend's treachery.
46 wars	war (1)
50 beast	beast (5)
65 earth . . . sea . . . raging crowns the year with his goodness	earth . . . sea (1) . . . rage (3) summer (5)
104 trees	forests (4)

Some of these parallels are obviously more significant than others, and some may well be fortuitous; but it is difficult not to believe that Shakespeare was aware of the links with the Psalms. It is arguable, however, that at one stage the links were closer than they are now. This is suggested by the fact that in several of the sonnets there are echoes of the adjacent psalm. The 'fountain' mentioned in Psalm 36 appears in Sonnet XXXV, the 'idol' of Psalm 106 in Sonnet CV; and, more remotely, the 'lion' of Psalm 17 appears two sonnets later, in XIX.

If this is so, it may be suggested that the last of the Penitential Psalms, 143, is much closer to Sonnet CXLIV than to CXLIII. There is nothing penitential about the housewife who sets down her baby in order to pursue a chicken, while in CXLIV the Poet speaks of his good and evil spirits and guesses 'one angel in another's hell' (the sexual organ of the friend in the sexual organ of his mistress). The Psalmist declares, although without the sexual innuendo:

> My spirit is vexed within me . . . My spirit waxeth faint; hide not thy face from me, lest I be like unto them that go down into the pit . . . Let thy loving spirit lead me forth into the land of righteousness.

Similarly, it may be suggested that Psalm 130, the *De profundis*, has no relation to the light-hearted ironical sonnet, 'My mistress' eyes are nothing like the sun', which ends with the complimentary couplet:

> And yet, by heaven, I think my love as rare
> As any she belied with false compare.

But the Poet's own *De profundis*, in which he laments his slavery to lust, is surely CXXIX, 'Th'expense of spirit in a waste of shame'.

Professor Fowler suggests that Shakespeare may have used the links with the Psalms as an initial scaffolding and that he afterwards adjusted the original order.[18] This is possible; but, as there are several indications that the Sonnets are not printed in the order of composition, it seems more likely that the sonnets linked with the psalms were inserted in their appropriate places at some later stage. The occasional dislocations may have been caused by a copyist (as happened with Constable's sonnets[19]) or by the compositor.

We are not here concerned with what some may regard as the excessive and irrelevant ingenuity displayed by Shakespeare in matching sonnet with psalm, but merely with the strong evidence it provides that the 1609 order was Shakespeare's own.

CHAPTER 2

The Vogue of the Sonnet

There is no evidence that Shakespeare was directly influenced by the *Rime* of Francesco Petrarca, but any account of the vogue of the sonnet in the last years of the sixteenth century must start with the 'Rerum vulgarium fragmenta' (as Petrarch called them) which were a dominating influence two centuries later on the poets of western Europe. In the last years of his life Petrarch rearranged the poems he had written for Laura during her life and after her death in 1348. The collection included *canzoni* and other poems not in the sonnet form, and many of his imitators followed this practice.

Although Chaucer inserted a translation of one of Petrarch's sonnets into *Troilus and Criseyde*, expanding it into three stanzas (bk I, ll. 400 *ff.*), Sir Thomas Wyatt seems to have been the first to introduce the actual form of the sonnet into England. His first diplomatic mission had been in Italy; he had come across the work of French Petrarchans during his travels; and in Italy, or soon after his return to England, he began translating a number of Petrarch's sonnets. Nearly all his own sonnets were translations, or adaptations, from the Italian; and even those for which no source has yet been discovered are not necessarily original. As Patricia Thomson has demonstrated, Wyatt had studied the commentaries in an edition of Petrarch, and when he departed from the original, as he often did, it was not due to incompetence.[1] Even if we may doubt whether his version of 'Una candida cerva' was to express his realisation that the King's interest in Anne Boleyn made his own highly dangerous, there is no doubt that he adopted Petrarch's lament for the death of his patron to suit his own grief on the execution of Thomas Cromwell:

> Rotta è l'alta colonna e 'l verde lauro
> che facean ombra al mio stanco pensero:
> perduta ò quel che ritrovar non spero
> dal borea a l'austro o dal mar indo al mauro.
>
> Tolto m'ài, morte, il mio doppio tesauro
> che mi fea viver lieto e gire altero,
> e ristorar nol po terra né impero,
> né gemma oriental né forza d'auro.

Ma se consentimento è di destino,
che posso io più se no aver l'alma trista,
umidi gli occhi sempre e 'l viso chino?

O nostra vita ch'è sì bella in vista,
com' perde agevolmente in un mattino
quel che 'n molti anni a gran pena s'acquista!

[Shattered is the high column and the green Laurel which cast shade
for my tired thoughts; I have lost what I do not hope to find again
from Boreas to Auster, from the Indian sea to the Mauritanian. You
have taken my double treasure from me, Death, which made me go
about so lightsome and proud; and the earth cannot, nor empire, nor
eastern gem, nor power of gold, make good my loss. But if this is with
the consent of fate, what can I do but bear a sad soul, wet eyes and
bent head for ever? O our life which is so fair outwardly, how easily
does it lose in a morning what in many years with great struggling is
gained. (trans. George R. Kay)]

This is Wyatt's version:

The pillar pearisht is whearto I lent,
  The strongest staye of myne vnquyet mynde;
  The lyke of it no man agayne can fynde,
  Ffrom East to West, still seking thoughe he went.
To myne vnhappe! for happe away hath rent
  Of all my ioye the vearye bark and rynde;
  And I (alas) by chaunce am thus assynde
  Dearlye to moorne till death do it relent.
But syns that thus it is by destenye,
  What can I more but have a wofull hart,
  My penne in playnt, my voyce in carefull crye,
  My mynde in woe, my bodye full of smart,
  And I my self, my self alwayes to hate,
  Till dreadfull death do ease my dolefull state?

Henry Howard, Earl of Surrey, Wyatt's friend and disciple, translated
a number of Petrarch's sonnets, with smoother versification, but with
much less power and originality. These appeared, along with Wyatt's,
at the end of Mary's reign in Tottel's miscellany of *Song and Sonnets*.
Surrey was given pride of place, partly because an earl is superior to a
knight, partly because his smoothness was more acceptable than Wyatt's
strength – as Denham and Waller were preferred to Donne after the
Restoration – and partly because Wyatt's son had recently been executed
after the suppression of his rebellion. In one respect Surrey was more
influential than Wyatt: although he sometimes linked his quatrains by

using the same rhymes in each, he invariably ended his sonnets with a rhymed couplet – a practice followed by most Elizabethan poets. Here is one example:

> When Windesor walles susteyned my wearied arme,
> My hande my chin, to ease my restlesse hed:
> Ech pleasant plot reuested green with warme,
> The blossomed bowes with lusty Ver yspred,
> The flowred meades, the wedded birdes so late
> Mine eyes discouered. Than did minde resorte
> The ioilly woes, the hatelesse shorte debate,
> The rakehell lyfe that longes to loues disporte.
> Wherewith (alas) myne heauy charge of care
> Heapt in my brest breakes forth against my will,
> In smoky sighes, that ouercast the ayer.
> My vapord eyes suche drery teares distill,
>   The tender spring to quicken where they fall,
>   And I have bent to throwe me downe withall.

Oddly enough, despite the many editions of Tottel's Miscellany, the sonnets of Wyatt and Surrey had few imitators. In the various anthologies which appeared during the first thirty-five years of Elizabeth I's reign – anthologies with glamorous titles and mostly drab contents – there were hardly any sonnets.[2]

Thomas Watson's *Hecatompathia* (1582), the next landmark in the history of the sonnet in England, consists of a hundred poems, mostly imitated from the Italian, but with the sonnet expanded to fill three six-line stanzas. A characteristic example, imitated confessedly from Aeneas Silvius and *Orlando Furioso*, was later to be utilised by Shakespeare in writing of his very different lady:[3]

> Harke you that list to heare what sainte I serve:
> Her yellowe lockes exceede the beaten goulde;
> Her sparkeling eies in heav'n a place deserve;
> Her forehead high and faire of comely moulde;
>   Her wordes are musicke all of silver sounde;
>   Her wit so sharpe as like can scarse be found.
> Each eybrowe hanges like *Iris* in the skies;
> Her *Eagles* nose is straight of stately frame;
> On either cheeke a *Rose* and *Lillie* lies;
> Her breath is sweete perfume, or hollie flame;
>   Her lips more-red than any *Corall* stone;
>   Her neck more white, than aged *Swans* yat mone;
> Her brest transparent is, like *Chrystall*-rocke;
> Her fingers long, fit for *Apolloes* Lute;
> Her slipper such as *Momus* dare not mocke;
> Her virtues all so great as make me mute:

> What other partes she hath I neede not say
> Whose face alone is cause of my decaye.

This volume preceded the publication, if not the composition, of Sidney's *Astrophil and Stella* (as we must now call it); but it was Sidney who began the real vogue of sonneteering in England. This was due partly to his popularity and heroic death, and partly to the superiority of his poems to nearly everything written during the reign of Elizabeth – the only exception being Sackville's great 'Induction' in *A Mirror for Magistrates*. Sidney and Spenser hoped to do for England what the poets of the Pléiade had done for France; and, as Ronsard and his fellows had been inveterate sonneteers, Sidney, Spenser and Greville naturally wrote collections of sonnets – *Astrophil and Stella, Amoretti* and *Caelica.* Of the three, Sidney's is the most impressive. Spenser, although the greatest poet of the three, did not in his sonnets reach the heights of 'Epithalamion,' published in the same volume. The sonnets are well wrought, elegant and melodious, but only a few are memorable. Greville, at his best, has a knotty and individual style, he is admirable as a commentator on moral and psychological complexities, but he is never at his best as a love-poet. Sidney is the only one of the three to produce not merely a collection of sonnets but a unified work of art.

Astrophil and Stella was printed posthumously in 1591 in a dreadfully bad and unauthorised text; but Thomas Nashe, who provided a preface, had the wit to recognise the dramatic quality of the sequence. He called it 'a tragi-comedy of love . . . performed by starlight . . . the argument, cruel chastity; the prologue, Hope; the epilogue, Despair'. When the official edition appeared (1598), the songs were inserted in their correct places in the sequence, not lumped all together. Just as Petrarch had interspersed his sonnets with other kinds of poem, so Sidney, Greville, Spenser, Daniel and Barnes followed suit.[4] The presence of 'A Lover's Complaint' at the end of Shakespeare's Sonnets – as Daniel's *Complaint of Rosamond* was published with *Delia* – may belong vestigially to the same tradition.

The other quality, besides the dramatic, which distinguishes Sidney from his followers is akin to it: namely, the greater naturalness and colloquiality of his style:

> How then? even thus: in *Stella's* face I reed,
> What Love and Beautie be. . . . (3)

> I do confesse, pardon a fault confest,
> My mouth too tender is for thy hard bit. (4)

> Alas poore wag, that now a scholler art
> To such a schoole-mistresse. (46)

'What he?' say they of me, 'now I dare sweare,
He cannot love: no, no, let him alone.' (54)

Fy, schoole of Patience, Fy, your lesson is
Far far too long to learne it without booke:
What, a whole weeke without one peece of looke,
And think I should not your large precepts misse? (56)

Your words my friend (right healthfull causticks) blame
My young minde marde, whom Loue doth windlas so:
That mine owne writings like bad seruants show
My wits, quicke in vaine thoughts, in vertue lame:
That *Plato* I reade for nought, but if he tame
Such coltish gyres, that to my birth I owe
Nobler desires, least else that friendly foe,
Great expectation, weare a traine of shame.
But since mad March great promise made of me,
If now the May of my yeares much decline,
What can be hopd my harvest time will be?
Sure you say well, your wisedome's golden mine
    Dig deepe with learnings spade: now tell me this,
    Hath this world ought so faire as *Stella* is? (21)

During the remainder of the sixteenth century imitations of *Astrophil and Stella* poured from the presses. Some of Daniel's had been included in the piratical edition of Sidney's sequence, and in the following year he published a revised and expanded collection, entitled *Delia*. In the same year, 1592, also appeared the first edition of Henry Constable's *Diana*. In 1593 there were four collections: *Phillis* by Thomas Lodge, *The Tears of Fancie* by Thomas Watson, *Licia* by Giles Fletcher, and *Parthenophil and Parthenophe* by Barnabe Barnes. Other volumes followed: in 1594 *Celia* by William Percy, *Ideas Mirrour* by Michael Drayton, and the anonymous *Zepheria*; in 1595 *Cynthia* by Richard Barnfield – containing twenty sonnets – *Amoretti* by Spenser, and *Emaricdulfe* by E.C.; in 1596 *Fidessa* by Bartholomew Griffin, *Diella* by Richard Linche, and *Chloris* by William Smith; in 1597 Robert Tofte's *Laura*, resembling Petrarch more in title than in content. In addition to these volumes of love-sonnets, there were also collections devoted to religious themes, the best of them, by Constable, not published until the nineteenth century. Donne's were written and published after Shakespeare's death.

Although some sequences, including Daniel's, have a number of closely linked sonnets, only one, *The Tears of Fancie*, seems to consist throughout of linked sonnets. The first two sonnets, for example, described the poet's scorn of Cupid. Sonnet 2 ends '*Venus* sweetly smiled' and Sonnet 3 begins 'Shee smild', and to pacify Cupid she agrees to let him have his revenge. In Sonnet 4, Cupid fails to wound the Poet, until in Sonnet 6 'he coucht himselfe within my Ladies eies' and the Poet duly falls a victim.

Some of the sonneteers translated directly from French or Italian sonnets. Spenser acknowledged that his *Ruines of Rome* was translated from Joachim du Bellay's *Antiquités de Rome* and that *The Visions of Petrarch* was translated, probably via Marot's version, from the original *canzone*. Giles Fletcher, likewise, acknowledged on the title-page of *Licia* that his sonnets were written 'to the imitation of the best Latin Poets, and others'. The versions include twenty-four from Angerianus, and others from Marullus, Muretus and Gruterus. Many of Lodge's sonnets were translated from Ronsard, Ariosto and Desportes. He does not mention the fact, but there is no reason to think that he hoped to conceal it, and Sir Sidney Lee's attack on him for dishonesty is absurd. The real question is not whether the sonnets were original or translations, nor even whether Lodge's versions were accurate, but whether the results are good English poems. The following is a typical example, based on Ariosto's

> Non senza causa il giglio e l'amaranto,
> l'uno di fede e l'altro fior d'amore,
> del bel leggiadro lor vago colore,
> vergine illustre, v'orna il sacro manto.
>   Candido e puro l'un mostra altro tanto
> in voi candore e purità di core;
> all'animo sublime l'altro fiore
> di constanzia real dà il pregio e il vanto.
>   Come egli al sole e al verno fuor d'usanza
> d'ogni altro germe, ancor che forza il sciolga
> dal natio umor, sempre vermiglio resta,
>   così vostra alta intenzïon onesta,
> perché Fortuna la sua ruota volga,
> com'a lei par, non può mutar sembianza.[5]

[It is not without cause that the lily and amaranth, one the flower of faith and the other the flower of love, ornament your sacred mantle with their beautiful light and lovely colour, O illustrious virgin. The one is white and pure and shows forth in you an equal candour and purity of heart. The other flower gives a sublime soul the prized quality of regal constancy. Just as it (the amaranth), unlike any other flower sprouts both in the sun and in winter, and remains red even if removed by force from its native humour, so your high upright intent cannot change its aspect because Fortune turns her wheel as best pleases her. (trans. L. A. Zaina)]

> Not causelesse were you christned (gentle flowers)
> The one of faith, the other fancies pride,

> For she who guides both faith and fancies power,
> In your faire coloures wrapes hir Iuory side:
> As one of you hath whitenes without staine,
> So spotlesse is my loue and neuer tainted:
> And as the other shadoweth faith againe,
> Such is my lasse, with no fond chaunge acquainted:
> And as nor tirant sonne nor winter weather,
> May euer chaunge sweet *Amaranthus* hew:
> So she tho loue and fortune ioyne together,
> Will neuer leaue to bee both faire and true:
> > And should I leaue thee then thou prettie elfe?
> > Nay first let *Damon* quite forget himselfe.

Apart from the feeble couplet, Lodge succeeds in reproducing the spirit of the original.

Lee extended his accusations of plagiarism to embrace all the Elizabethan sonneteers. But he was unable to point to a single translation in *Astrophil and Stella, Idea* or *Amoretti*. The editors of these three volumes have quoted possible sources of occasional phrases and lines, but nothing very substantial.

Renwick has some admirably sane remarks in his edition:

> Still more labour has been spent on the 'sources' of the *Amoretti*, and these provide an interest – for those who are interested – that is almost endless. The difficulty here does not lie in the paucity of evidence, but in its superabundance. The Petrarchan convention was so universally accepted all over Western Europe that nothing is easier than to collect 'parallels' and nothing more difficult than to fix upon 'sources'. . . . Spenser . . . was an imitator, but not a translator like Wyatt or Watson, was right inside the convention and used it freely. He rarely takes more than a hint. Even where he begins from another man's work he seldom fails to give it a new turn, either original or by combination with another commonplace.[6]

Shakespeare, as we shall see, owed less than Spenser or Sidney to earlier sonneteers, and Lee, in trying to prove his conventionality, takes refuge in vague generalities.

Most Elizabethan sonnets were mediocre, and many were positively bad. Not much can be said in favour of *Celia, Diella, Laura* and *Emaricdulfe*,[7] volumes which no one would have bothered to reprint if they had not been thought to throw an obscure and smoky light on the better sonneteers. *Zepheria*, on the other hand, has been unjustly attacked. It was never intended to be good poetry, but rather a parody of bad sonnets, written (to judge by the legal jargon) by a student at one of the Inns of Court:

How often hath my pen (mine heart's Solicitor!)
Instructed thee in Breviat of my case! (20)

When last mine eyes dislodged from thy beauty,
Though served with Process of a parent's Writ,
A *Supersedeas* countermanding duty,
Even then, I saw upon thy smiles to sit! (37)

From the revenue of thine eyes' Exchequer,
My faith his Subsidy did ne'er detract!
Though in thy favour's book, I rest a debtor;
Yet, 'mongst accountants who their fame have crackt,
My name thou findest not irrotulate! (38)

'Mongst Delian nymphs, in Angels' University,
Thou, my Zepheria, liv'st matriculated! (25)

The sonnets are filled with ink-horn terms which must have been written
with tongue in cheek – 'hyperbolised trajections', 'thesaurize', 'the heart's
hermaphrodite', 'love's sweet souvenance'. The sonnets are not less absurd
than Sir John Davies's gulling sonnets; and, as one of these refers to
Zepheria, it may be suggested that he himself was the author of the
volume he ostensibly parodies.

The other gulling sonnets have a more general target:

> The Lover under burthen of his mistress' love,
> Which like to Ætna did his heart oppress,
> Did give such piteous groans that he did move
> The heavens at length to pity his distress
> But for the Fates in their high court above
> Forbade to make the grievous burthen less,
> The gracious powers did all conspire to prove
> If miracle this mischief might redress;
> Therefore regarding that the load was such
> As no man might with one man's might sustain,
> And that mild patience imported much
> To him that should endure an endless pain,
>   By their decree, he soon transformed was
>   Into a patient burden-bearing Ass.

The outpouring of sonnets by poetasters inevitably led to parody and
satire. John Eliot, for example, in his conversation manual, *Ortho-epia
Gallica*, which Shakespeare appears to have read,[8] has an amusing
portrait of a young man smitten by the Petrarchan germ:[9]

Jeronimo Pierruche is miserably enamoured of a pretty wench. . . .
This Jeronimo you know him well, fat slave, cherry-cheeked, fair and

well-liking, with a slick face, pleasant-disposed, and a tratling companion: Now he is lean, wan, pale-looking like one half dead, weak,
ugly, dreaming, loving to be alone, and cares for nobody's company:
so that none of those that had seen him before could know him again.
. . . Now he is mad; he is foolish: oftentimes he walketh alone: but
will never speak to anybody: always mumbling or recording something in English verse, that he hath made to his sweetheart and minion.
. . . One while you shall see him feign a sea of tears, a lake of miseries,
wring his hands and weep, accuse the heaven, curse the earth, make
an anatomy of his heart, to freeze, to burn, to adore, to play the
idolator, to admire, to feign heavens, to forge hells, to counterfeit
Sisyphus, to play the Tantalus, to represent Titius' tragedy. And by
and by he exalteth in his verses that Diana whom he loveth best: her
hair is nothing but gold wire, her brows arches and vautes of Ebenus:
her eyes twinkling stars like Castor and Pollux, her looks lightning:
her mouth coral; her neck orient pearl; her breath balm, amber and
musk; her throat of snow: her neck milk-white: her dugs that she
hath on her breast, mountains or apples of alabaster. All the rest of
her body is but a prodigality and treasure of heaven and of nature,
that she had reserved to work the perfection of his mistress and dear.

The satirist reads a letter by the lover, and his friend comments: 'He
understands already the courtisan rhetoric; the poor boy is blind, and
out of his best wit.'

Before the end of the century, John Donne was writing his witty,
sensuous, anti-Petrarchan poems; and by the time Shakespeare's sonnets
were published the form was no longer fashionable. Yet Shakespeare
himself, as we shall see, satirised in his plays, and even in his own sonnets,
the conventional attitudes of third-rate sonneteers. To poke fun at
excesses and aberrations does not imply a rejection of the genre, nor
does it impugn the sincerity of its practitioners. Poetic 'sincerity' is, of
course, a different thing from autobiographical accuracy. Drayton's *Idea*
may have been inspired by his long-standing, well-documented affection
for Lady Rainsford, whose beauty was mentioned in the case-book of
Shakespeare's son-in-law, Dr John Hall,[10] even though we do not know
whether any of the incidents recorded in the sequence actually happened.
Spenser's *Amoretti* served as a wedding-present to his bride, Elizabeth
Boyle, although it is generally thought that some of the poems in the
collection had originally been addressed to other women. Daniel's Delia
is so shadowy a figure that the change in the colour of her hair in later
editions may not be due to a wig or dye, or even to her being a different
woman. Sidney's Stella – as we can tell from puns on Rich – was the
poet's name for Lady Rich, the former Penelope Devereux. The events
of the sequence were partly fictional, no doubt. Stella refuses Astrophil

because she is chaste; Lady Rich, who cuckolded her husband with another man, probably refused Sidney for other reasons. But only Sir Sidney Lee believes that the sonnets were merely exercises of a well-read man and that Sidney was unacquainted with love.[11] It is true that protestations of sincerity and complaints of the artificiality of other poetry were the stock-in-trade of sonneteers, but all the internal and external evidence goes to show that the sequence had some basis in fact.

Apart from Sidney, the best Elizabethan sonneteers were Daniel, Spenser, Drayton and Constable. Daniel tinkered with his sonnets over a period of some twenty years, eliminating feeble lines and some of his weaker poems, but there is no great difference in quality between the original *Delia* of 1594 and the sequence as it appeared in his collected poems, published posthumously in 1623. He did not develop as a sonneteer as Drayton and Constable did. He was without much originality, and many of the finest sonnets are imitative, even though Sir Sidney Lee exaggerated the extent of his borrowings. According to him, the opening of one of the best sonnets is adapted from Desportes' *Hippolyte*:

> Sommeil, paisible fils de la nuit solitaire,
> Père-alme, nourricier de tous les animaux,
> Enchanteur gracieux, doux oubli de nos maux,
> Et des esprits blessés l'appareil salutaire,
> O frère de la mort. . . .

> Care-charmer sleepe, sonne of the Sable night,
> Brother to death, in silent darknes borne:
> Relieue my languish, and restore the light,
> With darke forgetting of my cares returne.

In fact, the idea of death and sleep being brothers is a commonplace; sleep is often regarded as the son of Night, and also as the balm of hurt minds: and, even if Daniel owed a debt to Desportes in these lines, the the rest of his sonnet diverges completely.

Daniel's best sonnets are on the transitoriness of beauty, and a group of four (34–7 in the final edition) are all derived from Tasso – the first two from *Gerusalemme Liberata*, XVI, and the others from his *Rime Amorose*. Daniel ingeniously links the four sonnets together by the repetition of the last lines of the first three as the first lines of the last three. The first two may be compared with Spenser's imitation of the same stanzas in *The Faerie Queene*, book II, canto xii, stanzas 74–5.

> – Deh mira – egli cantò – spuntar la rosa
> dal verde suo modesta e verginella,
> che mezzo aperta ancora e mezzo ascosa,
> quanto si mostra men, tanto è più bella.

Ecco poi nudo il sen già baldanzosa
dispiega; ecco poi langue e non par quella,
quella non par che desiata inanti
fu da mille donzelle e mille amanti.

Così trapassa al trapassar d'un giorno
de la vita mortale il fiore e 'l verde;
né perché faccia indietro april ritorno,
si rinfiora ella mai, né si rinverde.
Cogliam la rosa in su 'l mattino adorno
di questo dì, che tosto il seren perde;
cogliam d'amor la rosa: amiamo or quando
esser si puote riamato amando.–

The whiles some one did chaunt this lovely lay;
Ah see, who so faire thing doest faine to see,
In springing, flowre the image of thy day.
Ah see the Virgin Rose, how sweetly shee
Doth first peepe forth with bashful modestee,
That fairer seemes, the lesse ye see her may;
La see soone after, how more bold and free
Her bared bosome she doth broad display;
Loe see soone after, how she fades, and falles away.

So passeth, in the passing of a day,
Of mortal life the leafe, the bud, the flowre,
No more doth flourish after first decay,
That earst was sought to decke both bed and bowre,
Of many a Ladie, and many a Paramoure;
Gather therefore the Rose, whilest yet is prime,
For soone comes age, that will her pride deflowre:
Gather the Rose of love, whilest yet is time,
Whilest loving thou mayst loved be with equall crime.

In Tasso and Spenser the theme of 'Gather ye rosebuds while ye may'
is the expression of temptation: in Spenser, indeed, as the last word
of the passage shows, it is an invitation to crime. In Daniel's sonnets,
as in Ronsard's warning to Hélène – 'Cueillez aujourd'hui les roses de la
vie' – there is no suggestion that rose-gathering is to be deplored.

Looke DELIA how w'esteeme the halfe blowne Rose,
The image of thy blush and Sommers honor:
Whilst yet her tender bud doth vndisclose
That full of beauty, time bestowes vpon her.
No sooner spreads her glory in the ayre,
But straight her wide blowne pomp comes to decline:
She then is scornd that late adornd the Fayre;
So fade the Roses of those cheeks of thine.

No Aprill can reuiue thy withered flowres.
Whose springing grace adorns thy glory now:
Swift speedy Time, feathred with flying houres,
Dissolues the beauty of the fairest brow.
  Then do not thou such treasure wast in vaine,
  But loue now whilst thou maist be lou'd againe.

But loue whilst that thou maist be lou'd againe,
Now whilst thy May hath fild thy lap with flowers,
Now whilst thy beauty beares without a staine;
Now vse the Sommer smiles, ere Winter lowers.
And whilst thou spreadst vnto the rising sunne,
The fairest flowre that euer saw the light,
Now ioy thy time before thy sweet be done.
And (DELIA) thinke thy morning must haue night,
And that thy brightnes sets at length to West,
When thou wilt close vp that which now thou show'st,
And thinke the same becomes thy fading best,
Which then shall most inuaile and shadow most.
  Men do not wey the stalke for that it was,
  When once they find her flowre her glory pas.

Daniel is not so much translating as composing variations on the same theme – a theme which, *mutatis mutandis*, was one of Shakespeare's favourites.

The form of Spenser's sonnets is an attempt to combine the quatrains of the characteristic English sonnet with the tighter structure of the Italian. This he does by linking the quatrains by common rhymes – ABABBCBCCDCDEE. He thus uses only five rhymes instead of the Shakespearian seven. It has the effect of linking the sextet to the octave and of preserving the epigrammatic flavour of the final couplet. One is seldom conscious of the difficulty of finding the additional rhymes. Spenser, as always, is a careful craftsman. The fourteen lines convey the idea of each sonnet without undue compression or padding. If the imagery is seldom or never original, it is expressed with consistent artistry. Here, for example, is a sonnet on the immortalising effect of poetry:

One day I wrote her name upon the strand,
  but came the waves and washed it away:
  agayne I wrote it with a second hand,
  but came the tyde, and made my paynes his pray.
Vayne man, sayd she, that doest in vaine assay,
  a mortall thing so to immortalize,
  for I my selue shall lyke to this decay
  and eek my name bee wyped out lykewise.
No so, (quod I) let baser things deuize,

to dy in dust, but you shall live by fame:
my verse your vertues rare shall eternize,
and in the hevens wryte your glorious name.
Where whenas death shall all the world subdew
our love shall live, and later life renew.

Spenser has one of the best ears of any English poet, and almost any
of his sonnets could be used to illustrate his subtle use of alliteration and
vowel music.

After long stormes and tempests sad assay,
which hardly I endured heretofore:
in dread of death and daungerous dismay,
with which my silly barke was tossed sore.
I doe at length descry the happy shore,
in which I hope ere long for to arryue,
fayre soyle it seemes from far and fraught with store
of all that deare and daynty is alyue.

Nevertheless, one gets the impression that, skilful as he is, Spenser in
these sonnets looks at life through the spectacles of books. Keats remarked
that poetry should surprise by a fine excess, and not by singularity.[12]
We can admire Spenser's lack of singularity but miss any trace of fine
excess. His development of a theme is nearly always predictable. When
we read the opening lines of Sonnet XXVI –

Sweet is the Rose, but growes upon a brere;
sweet is the Iunipere, but sharpe his bough;
sweet is the Eglantine, but pricketh nere;
sweet is the firbloome, but his braunches rough.
Sweet is the Cypresse, but his rynd is tough,
sweet is the nut, but bitter is his pill;
sweet is the broome-flowre, but yet sowre enough;
and sweet is Moly, but his root is ill.

– we can be certain that the poem will conclude with a passage about the
pains and pleasures of love, as indeed it does.

Drayton is a much more uneven writer than Spenser. His early sonnets
give no promise of his later excellence. This can be seen particularly by
comparing *Ideas Mirrour* with the final version of *Idea* twenty-seven
years later. Although Drayton included revised versions of some of the
early sonnets in his latest recension, all his best examples were added in
1599 or later – Sonnets 10, 11, 20, 23 in 1599; 14 and 37 in 1602; 43
and 51 in 1605; and 1, 6 and 61 in 1619. The development is extraordinary. In place of the tired poeticisms of *Ideas Mirrour*, its unoriginal
and forced conceits, and its artificial diction, we have power and

simplicity. It is hardly too much to say that Drayton acquired his new mastery by his reading of Shakespeare's sonnets in manuscript. The contrast can be seen by comparing *Ideas Mirrour*, 11, with any of the later sonnets:

> Thine eyes taught mee the Alphabet of loue,
> To con my Cros-rowe ere I learn'd to spell;
> For I was apt, a scholler like to proue,
> Gaue mee sweet lookes when as I learned well.
> Vowes were my vowels, when I then begun
> At my first Lesson in thy sacred name:
> My consonants the next when I had done,
> Words consonant, and sounding to thy fame.
> My liquids then were liquid christall teares,
> My cares my mutes, so mute to craue reliefe;
> My dolefull Dypthongs were my liues dispaires,
> Redoubling sighes the accents of my griefe:
> My loues Schoole-mistris now hath taught me so,
> That I can read a story of my woe.

One of the later sonnets (14), 'If hee from heaven that filch'd that living fire', is based on an equally extravagant conceit, but with much greater effectiveness, ending with the couplet:

> Yet old *Prometheus* punish'd for his Rape.
> Thus poore Theeues suffer, when the greater scape.

It is certain that Drayton had read some of Shakespeare's sonnets in manuscript. Sonnet 20, which begins

> An evill spirit your beautie haunts me still
> Wherewith (alas) I have beene long possest.
> Which ceaseth not to tempt Me to each Ill,
> Nor gives Me once, but one poor minutes rest

was probably influenced by one of the Dark Lady sonnets. But more significant than the echoing of a particular sonnet is the change of style which appears to be due to Shakespeare's influence – a greater restraint, the avoidance of false poeticisms, the cultivation of the speaking voice. This is apparent in passages like the following:

> This new rich Novice, lauish of his chest,
> To one Man giues, doth on another spend,
> Then heere he riots, yet amongst the rest,
> Haps to lend some to one true honest Friend. . . . (10)

> Deare, why should you command me to my Rest,
> When now the Night doth summon all to sleepe?
> Me thinkes this Time becommeth Louers best;
> Night was ordayn'd, together Friends to keepe. . . . (37)

By 1619 Drayton had acquired a touch of Shakespearian sublimity when writing on a Shakespearian theme on the immortalising of the recipient by means of his verse.

> How many paltry, foolish, painted things,
> That now in Coaches trouble eu'ry Street,
> Shall be forgotten, whom no Poet sings,
> Ere they be well wrap'd in their winding Sheet?
> Where I to thee Eternitie shall giue,
> When nothing else remayneth of these dayes,
> And Queenes hereafter shall be glad to liue
> Vpon the Almes of thy superfluous prayse.

Drayton could also dramatise an incident in superbly restrained diction:

> Since there's no helpe, Come let vs kisse and part,
> Nay, I haue done: You get no more of Me,
> And I am glad, yea glad withall my heart,
> That thus so cleanly, I my Selfe can free,
> Shake hands for euer, Cancell all our Vowes,
> And when we meet at any time againe,
> Be it not seene in either of our Browes,
> That We one iot of former Loue reteyne;
> Now at the last gaspe of Loues latest Breath,
> When his Pulse fayling, Passion speechlesse lies,
> When Faith is kneeling by his bed of Death,
> And Innocence is closing vp his Eyes,
>   Now if thou would'st, when all haue giuen him ouer,
>   From Death to Life, thou might'st him yet recouer.

If Shakespeare influenced some of his contemporaries, his own sonnets, as we shall see in the next chapter, owed comparatively little to those of his contemporaries. Two of Constable's may have left their mark on two of Shakespeare's;[13] and one critic, Katharine Wilson, has maintained that many of Shakespeare's were written as parodies.[14] This is an interpretation which 'reason without miracle/Shall never plant in me'. J. B. Leishman in his excellent book analysed how Shakespeare treated some of the same themes as previous poets – Italian, French and Latin – but in the process he demonstrated the distinctiveness of Shakespeare's attitudes and method.[15]

With nearly all previous sonneteers we have a series of unrelated poems, excellent in the best, unmemorable in most. Although Spenser's

Amoretti leads on naturally – after a few feeble anacreontics – to the celebration of his marriage, the sequence has no narrative interest. Drayton did not merely add to and subtract from his collection – he rearranged it continually; but in no edition is there any development. These and the sequences of Daniel and Constable are collections of disparate poems. Only in *Astrophil and Stella*, as we have seen, are the individual sonnets subordinated to the effect of the whole. Despite many abortive attempts to rearrange Shakespeare's sonnets, they are closest to Sidney's in this respect, as also in the feeling we get of a man speaking to men. This is not surprising as Shakespeare alone among the English sonneteers was a professional dramatist.[16]

What tension there is in most Elizabethan sequences – and there isn't much – is provided by the woman's inaccessibility, because she is either married or 'cruel', which is almost a synonym for 'chaste'. Shakespeare's beloved in the main series belongs to a different class and to the same sex; and in the subordinate series the beloved belongs to a different sex, but she is married and promiscuous. When the two beloveds meet, the situation contains the potentials of both comedy and tragedy.

Although previous sonneteers had addressed affectionate poems to people of their own sex, especially to patrons, the only Elizabethan sonnets at all comparable are the twenty included in Richard Barnfield's *Cynthia*, addressed to a boy. In *The Affectionate Shepheard*, published in the previous year, Barnfield had written a poem inspired by Virgil's second eclogue; and the Ganymede sonnets are variations on the same theme, sugary, sentimental and vaguely bisexual.[17]

CHAPTER 3

Tradition and the Individual Talent

The curious change of heart undergone by Sir Sidney Lee with regard to Shakespeare's Sonnets has been mentioned by Hyder E. Rollins and S. Schoenbaum.[1] He began by claiming that Mr W.H. was William Herbert and ended by asserting with equal vehemence that he was the Earl of Southampton. But this volte-face was less surprising than the extraordinary difference between his article in the *Dictionary of National Biography* as it appeared in England in 1897 and the version published in America in the same year. English readers were assured that the Sonnets were autobiographical; American readers were informed with equal confidence that they were 'to a large extent . . . literary exercises'. We may suspect that the original article was drafted before the trial of Oscar Wilde in 1895 and that the retraction was designed to establish Shakespeare's heterosexual orthodoxy. Lee spent much of the rest of his life in attempting to prove that all Elizabethan sonneteers were slavish imitators of foreign models rather than men in love. If Sidney (as Lee thought) was unacquainted with love, Shakespeare could be cleared of the more serious charge of loving one of his own sex: he wrote his sonnets to flatter his patron for financial reward.

Now, it is perfectly true, as we have seen, that the lesser poets translated Tasso, Petrarch, Desportes, Ariosto, Ronsard, Du Bellay and others; but when Lee came to the three major poets – Sidney, Spenser and Shakespeare – he had to take refuge in generalities. Of course, all three were writing within a tradition and they took hints from their predecessors, but the nearest approach to a translation is the pair of sonnets at the end of Shakespeare's sequence, which are alternative versions of a Latin poem, itself imitated from a poem in the Greek Anthology. This is so unlike Shakespeare's normal method of working that some critics have doubted his authorship.[2]

As no one has read all the 300,000 sonnets which, it is estimated, were written in the sixteenth century, and few scholars (it is safe to say) have read all the 326 volumes of sonnets published in Italy alone between 1575 and 1600, one cannot state categorically that none of *Astrophil and Stella* or of *Amoretti* is directly translated. It may well be that Sidney would not have written a sonnet about Stella on the

Thames, if Petrarch had not written one about Laura on the Rhône; but this does not prove that Astrophil was not in love with Stella, that Sidney was never in love with Penelope Rich, or even that he never saw her on the Thames. Elizabethan sonneteers wrote within a tradition – and, of course, Lee was right to stress this fact – but this has little to do with the absence or presence of 'sincerity' and still less to do with their biographies.

Lee tried very hard to find analogues to Shakespeare's sonnets – of those urging the recipient to marry, of those celebrating a friend's beauty, of those concerned with rivals, and those about the Dark Lady – but he came up only with some dubious parallels. He concluded – but not in accordance with the evidence – that 'Many a phrase and sentiment of Petrarch and Ronsard, or of English sonneteers who wrote earlier than he, gave the cue to Shakespeare's noblest poems.'³

How far Shakespeare was indebted to earlier English sonneteers is not easy to determine. It depends partly on dating. We know that some of the sonnets were circulating among his friends well before the end of the sixteenth century, and Leslie Hotson argued that most were written before 1590, but many critics believe they were written much later. Some of the poets doubtless read each other's work in manuscript, so that we cannot go by the dates of publication; and even where one poet may be echoing another it is often impossible to say which was the borrower.

Let us consider a few examples of the difficulties. John Dover Wilson accepted the view that Sonnet CV was influenced by a poem by Nicholas Breton published in 1600 in a volume entitled *Melancholick Humours*.'⁴

> Lovely kind, and kindly loving,
> Such a mind were worth the moving:
> Truly fair, and fairly true,
> Where are all these, but in you?
>
> Wisely kind, and kindly wise,
> Blessed life, where such love lies:
> Wise, and kind, and fair, and true,
> Lovely live all these in you.
>
> Sweetly dear, and dearly sweet,
> Blessed, where these blessings meet:
> Sweet, fair, wise, kind, blessed, true,
> Blessed be all these in you.

The relevant lines of the sonnet are:

> Fair, kind, and true, is all my argument.
> Fair, kind, and true, varying to other words,
> And in this change is my invention spent
> Three themes in one, which wondrous scope affords.
> Fair, kind, and true, have often lived alone,
> Which three till now never kept seat in one.

Breton is just as likely to have echoed Shakespeare as the other way round. But it is by no means certain that either poet is indebted to the other. Any poet enumerating the real or supposed virtues of a friend or mistress is bound to praise beauty, goodness, constancy, kindness and wisdom, or a selection of these. The song in praise of Silvia in *The Two Gentlemen of Verona*, probably written before the sonnet, and certainly before Breton's poem, will illustrate this:

> Who is Silvia? What is she,
>   That all her swains commend her?
> Holy, fair and wise is she;
>   The heaven such grace did lend her,
> That she might admired be.
>
> Is she kind as she is fair?
>   For beauty lives with kindness.

Holy, fair, wise and kind comes as close as Breton's poem to Shakespeare's sonnet.

There are some striking resemblances between Sidney's sixty-fourth sonnet and Shakespeare's twenty-ninth.[5] Sidney's begins:

> Let fortune lay on me her worst disgrace;
> Let folk . . . against me cry. . . .

So Shakespeare writes:

> When in disgrace with fortune and men's eyes. . . .

Both poets weep and feel themselves to be outcasts; but thereafter the sonnets diverge. Whereas Shakespeare envies other men,

> Desiring this man's art, and that man's scope,

Sidney declares that, if he is allowed to love, he does not envy Aristotle's wit or Caesar's fame. Nevertheless, it seems probable that Shakespeare remembered Sidney's sonnet when he wrote his own.

Another of Sidney's sonnets, 'Leave me, O Love', which used to be regarded as a kind of epilogue to *Astrophil and Stella*, but which Ringler showed was written earlier, has been compared with CXLVI.

Leave me ô Love, which reachest but to dust,
And thou my mind aspire to higher things;
Grow rich in that which never taketh rust:
What ever fades, but fading pleasure brings.
Draw in thy beames, and humble all thy might,
To that sweet yoke, where lasting freedomes be:
Which breakes the clowdes and opens forth the light,
That doth both shine, and give us sight to see.
O take fast hold, let that light be thy guide,
In this small course, which birth draws out to death,
And thinke how evill becommeth him to slide,
Who seeketh heav'n, and comes of heav'nly breath.
   Then farewell world thy uttermost I see,
   Eternal Love maintaine thy life in me.

Sidney is saying farewell to earthly love and following the scriptural injunction to lay up treasure in heaven where neither moth nor rust doth corrupt. Shakespeare's sonnet does not mention love, although in the context of the Dark Lady sonnets it is natural for the reader to suppose that a farewell to lust is implied:

Poor soul, the centre of my sinful earth,
[Foil'd by] these rebel powers that thee array,
Why dost thou pine within and suffer dearth,
Painting thy outward walls so costly gay?
Why so large cost, having so short a lease
Dost thou upon thy fading mansion spend?
Shall worms, inheritors of this excess
Eat up thy charge? Is this thy body's end?
Then, soul, live thou upon thy servant's loss,
And let that pine to aggravate thy store;
Buy terms divine in selling hours of dross:
Within be fed, without be rich no more:
   So shalt thou feed on death, that feeds on men,
   And death once dead there's no more dying then.

Although the two sonnets are on similar themes, and although Shakespeare had probably read Sidney's, there would seem to be no direct influence. On the other hand, there are obvious links between this sonnet of Shakespeare's and one by Bartholomew Griffin, published in 1596, thirteen years before Shakespeare's *Sonnets.*[6] This begins:

Well may my soul, immortal and divine,
That is imprison'd in a lump of clay,
Breathe out laments until this body pine,
That from her takes her pleasures all away.
Pine then, thou loathed prison of my life!
Untoward subject of the least aggrievance!
O let me die! Mortality is rife!

The sonnet ends with a compliment to Fidessa, which clashes awkwardly with the religious resignation of the opening lines. Griffin is not saying farewell to love or life, but paying a tribute to his cruel mistress; yet his actual phrasing is close to Shakespeare's, his 'lump of clay' paralleling Shakespeare's 'earth', and both poets use the word 'pine' twice and 'divine' once. Moreover, Griffin's preceding sonnet begins with the words 'Poor worm', while Shakespeare begins with 'Poor soul' and mentions worms in line 7. The following sonnet begins:

> Earth! take this earth wherein my spirits languish!
> Spirits leave this earth. . . .

This may be compared with another of Shakespeare's sonnets (LXXIV):

> The earth can have but earth, which is his due;
> My spirit is thine, the better part of me.
> So then thou hast but lost the dregs of life
> The prey of worms, my body being dead.

If Shakespeare's sequence was dedicated to William Herbert, Griffin could not have been echoing Shakespeare in 1596. We should then have to suppose that sometime after 1596 Shakespeare echoed three adjacent sonnets in Griffin's *Fidessa* in two widely separated sonnets of his own. But, as Melchiori and others have pointed out, Shakespeare's sonnet owes a good deal to familiar Pauline texts and (we may suggest) to one or two passages from the book of Job.[7]

> When this corruption hath put on incorruption, and this mortal hath put on immortality, then shall be brought to pass the saying that is written, Death is swallowed up in victory. Death where is thy sting? (1 Cor., 15)

> If ye be risen again with Christ, seek those things which are above. . . . Mortify therefore your earthly members. . . . (Col., 3)

> I shall say to corruption, Thou art my father, and to the worme, Thou art my mother and my sister. . . . And though . . . wormes destroy this body, yet in any flesh shall I see God. (Job, 17. 19)

As the biblical influence is direct in Shakespeare's sonnets and indirect in Griffin's, we can be sure that Griffin had read Shakespeare's in manuscript.

Shakespeare doubtless wrote sonnets because most of his fellows were doing it. But there is no evidence that he had read Petrarch, except the translations of Wyatt and Surrey and the adaptations by Watson. He began to write before the publication of any of the sonnet sequences; and, although there is an unmistakable echo of *Astrophil and Stella* in *Romeo and Juliet* and a mention of Petrarch in the same play, Romeo's affected love for the cruel Rosaline is much closer to the Petrarchan spirit than anything in the Sonnets. The themes of Shakespeare's sonnets, if not unique, are rare. Many poets wrote enthusiastic dedicatory sonnets to patrons, but no one had made his affection for a young aristocrat the subject of over a hundred poems. Others had written anti-Petrarchan sonnets on dark ladies, but they are unlike Shakespeare's. As far as I know, there is no other group of sonnets consisting of persuasions to marry. Considering the wearisome sameness of most Elizabethan sonnets, the independence of tone in Shakespeare's is remarkable. Instead of writing of a hard-hearted mistress, Shakespeare is concerned with the nature of love and friendship, with jealousy – not merely of a sexual kind – with the enslavement of lust, with the destructive power of time and how it may be resisted or overcome, with the difficulties caused by difference of age and class, with what Hubler has expressively called 'the economy of the closed heart'.[8]

I am not arguing that tradition is unimportant for our understanding and interpretation of Shakespeare's sonnets, but that he was never wholly absorbed in the Petrarchan tradition. In reading Daniel and Drayton, even Spenser and Sidney, one continually encounters familiar topics, images and themes. Not so with Shakespeare. He seems almost to have shared Mercutio's scorn of Petrarch's imitators or John Eliot's ridicule of the conventional Petrarchan lover.[9]

I propose, then, to consider some of the main themes of Shakespeare's sonnets and with the help of numerous commentators to attempt to outline the relationship of the poet to some of his predecessors, other than previous sonneteers.[10]

The first group of seventeen sonnets, in which the poet urges his friend to perpetuate his beauty by marriage, may be considered together, as variations on a theme of Erasmus:

Non moritur, qui vivam sui reliquit imaginem.[11]

The seventeen sonnets are linked not merely by the common theme, but also by the use of common sources – Erasmus, Ovid, Sidney – and by the linking of sonnet to sonnet by shared rhymes. Unlike the rest of the sequence, this group might almost be regarded as a single poem in seventeen stanzas.

There are two other relevant Erasmian passages. One is in the colloquy entitled *Proci et Puellae*, in which a girl is advised to marry rather than preserve her virginity – and we know from several echoes in the early plays that Shakespeare had read this particular colloquy.[12] The other passage is more substantial and more relevant since it is addressed to a man. It is one of the model letters in *De Conscribendis Epistolis* advising a young man to get married. Apart from the fact that Shakespeare used the letter on banishment in connection with Bolingbroke in *Richard II*, the letter connected with these sonnets was familiar to all educated Elizabethans from the complete translation provided in Wilson's *Art of Rhetoric*.[13] Erasmus uses the image of ploughing to mean sexual relations:

> If that manne be punished, who little heedeth the maintenance of his Tillage . . . what punishment is he worthie to suffer, that refuseth to plow that lande which beyng Tilled, yeldeth children.

So Shakespeare tells his friend:

> Thou dost beguile the world, unbless some mother,
> For where is she so fair, whose unear'd womb
> Disdains the tillage of thy husbandry? (III)

Erasmus declares that celibacy is a kind of murder:

> You shall be compted a *Parricide* or a murtherer of your stocke.

Shakespeare similarly speaks of the 'murderous shame' (IX) and of the 'murderous hate' (X) which possess his friend. Erasmus quibbles on the double meaning of 'house', as family and residence:

> Seyng also you are a man of grate landes and revenues by your ancestors, the house whereof you came beyng both right honourable and right anciente, so that you could not suffer it to perishe, without your great offence and great harme to the common weale. You notwithstandyng can not want great rebuke, seeyng it lieth in your handes to keep that house from decaie, whereof [you're] lineally descended, and to continue still the name of your ancestors.

Shakespeare likewise complains that, by not marrying, his friend is

> Seeking that beauteous roof to ruinate,
> Which to repair should be thy chief desire. (X)

And he asks:

> Who lets so fair a house fall to decay,
> Which husbandry in honour might uphold
> Against the stormy gusts of winter's day
> And barren rage of death's eternal cold? (XIII)

It should be mentioned that there are a number of parallels between a passage in *Hero and Leander* (ll. 234–66) and this group of sonnets. Leander is trying to persuade Hero:

> Then treasure is abus'de,
> When misers keepe it; being put to lone,
> In time it will returne us two for one. . . .
> Who builds a pallace and rams up the gate,
> Shall see it ruinous and desolate.
> Ah simple *Hero*, leave thy selfe to cherish,
> Lone women like to emptie houses perish.
>   . . . his golden earth remains,
> Which after his disceasse, some other gains.
> But this faire iem, sweet in the losse alone,
> When you fleet hence, can be bequeath'd to none. . . .
> Wilt thou live single still? one shalt thou bee,
> Though never-singling *Hymen* couple thee. . . .
> Base boullion for the stampes sake we allow,
> Even so for mens impression do we you. . . . (sestiad I, ll. 234–66)

L. C. Martin and others have shown that the argument and some of the imagery of these lines is echoed in Sonnets IV, VIII, X, XI and XII. Shakespeare could have seen the manuscript of *Hero and Leander* before he wrote these sonnets; or Marlowe could have read the sonnets in manuscript before he wrote his poem. It seems more likely that both poets were drawing on the same commonplaces, whether in Erasmus or elsewhere. Judith Weil, in *Christopher Marlowe* (1977), stresses his considerable acquaintance with Erasmus' writings.

The parallels between these sonnets and Sidney's *Arcadia* were pointed out by the Chartist poet, Gerald Massey. In book III, chapter 5, Cecropia tries to persuade the captive Philoclea to marry her son, Amphialus, who has already been refused. T. W. Baldwin thinks that Cecropia's long speech influences seven of the sonnets (III–IX), although there are only three close parallels. Cecropia asks:

> Have you ever seen a pure Rosewater kept in a christal glas; how fine it lokes, how sweet it smels, while that beautifull glasse imprisons it? Breake the prison and let the water take his owne course, doth it not imbrace dust, and loose all his former sweetenesse, and fairenesse? Truly so are we, if we have not the stay, rather than the restraint of christalline mariage.

In sonnets V and VI Shakespeare uses the rosewater image for a different purpose, as a symbol not directly of marriage but of the perpetuation of beauty in one's children; but he retains the idea of imprisonment in a glass vial:

Then were not summer's distillation left,
A liquid prisoner pent in walls of glass,
Beauty's effect with beauty were bereft,
Nor it nor no remembrance what it was.
  But flowers distill'd, though they with winters meet,
  Leese but their show: their substance still lives sweet.

Then let not winter's ragged hand deface
In thee thy summer ere thou be distill'd:
Make sweet some vial; treasure thou some place
With beauty's treasure ere it be self-kill'd

Sidney's rosewater image was probably suggested by a passage in the Erasmus colloquy mentioned above in which one of the speakers argues:

Ego, rosam existimo feliciorem, quae marescit in hominis manu, delectans interim et oculos et nares, quam quae senescit in frutice.

[I think that the rose is happier which begins to droop in a man's hand, delighting meanwhile both eyes and nose, than that which withers on the bush.]

This was a well-known passage. Robert Greene, the picker up of unconsidered trifles, quotes it in *Mamillia*.[14] Shakespeare, too, was familiar with it, since it is echoed in Theseus' advice to Hermia to marry Demetrius:

> But earthlier happy is the rose distill'd
> Than that which, withering on the virgin thorn,
> Grows, lives, and dies in single blessedness.[15]

It seems likely, therefore, that in his rosewater image Shakespeare blended memories of Erasmus with those of Sidney. The other close Sidney parallel is with Cecropia's words:

And is a solitary life as good as this? then can one string make as good musicke as a consort.

So Shakespeare in VIII uses the same musical image to signify the blessedness of marriage:

> Mark how one string, sweet husband to another,
> Strikes each in each by mutual ordering
> Resembling sire, and child, and happy mother,
> Who all in one one pleasing note do sing.

The pleasures of family life are described in an earlier passage in Cecropia's speech, derived in part from Erasmus' colloquy:

> Nature, when you were first borne, vowed you a woman, and as she made you child of a mother, so to do your best to be mother of a child: she gave you beautie to move love; she gave you wit to know love; she gave you an excellent body to reward love: which kind of liberal rewarding is crowned with unspeakable felicitie. For this, as it bindeth the receiver, so it makes happy the bestower: this doth not impoverish, but enrich the giver. O the sweet name of a mother: O the comfort of comforts, to see your children grow up, in whom you are (as it were) eternized: if you could conceive what a hart-tickling joy it is to see your own little ones, with awful love come running to your lap, and like little models of your selfe, stil carry you about them, you would thinke unkindnes in your own thoughts, that ever they did rebell against the meant unto it.

The other parallels with Sidney are less striking; but Cecropia's complaints of her widowhood may have coloured Sonnet IX.

> O widow-nights, beare witnes with me of the difference. How often alas do I . . . with teares acknowledge, that I now enjoy such a liberty as the banished man hath.

The sonnet begins:

> Is it for fear to wet a widow's eye,
> That thou consum'st thyself in single life?
> Ah, if thou issueless shalt hap to die,
> The world will wail thee like a makeless wife,
> The world will be thy widow and still weep.

The Ovidian influence is less pervasive in this group of sonnets than it is later in the sequence; but there are allusions to the stories of Narcissus and Phaethon, and a number of comparisons of the ages of man's life to the four seasons probably derived from the last book of Ovid's *Metamorphoses*.

> The age of man, departes itself in quarters fowre? first bayne
> And tender in the spring it is,.even like a sucking babe.
> Then greene, and voyd of strength, and lush, and foggye is the blade,
> And cheeres the husbandman with hope. Then all things florish gay.
> The earth with flowres of sundry hew then seemeth for too play,
> And vertue small or none too herbes there dooth as yit belong.
> The yeere from springtyde passing foorth too sommer, wexeth strong,

Becommeth lyke lusty youth. For in our lyfe through out
There is no tyme more plentifull, more lusty hote and stout.
Then followeth Harvest when the heate of youth growes sumwhat cold,
Rype, meeld, disposed meane betwixt a yoongman and an old,
And sumwhat sprent with grayish heare. Then ugly winter last
Like age steales on with trembling steppes, all bald, or overcast,
With shirle thinne heare as whyght as snowe. . . .[16]

In Sonnet I, the Poet's friend is described as 'only herald to the gaudy
spring'; in II, VI and XII age is compared with winter; in III the Poet
refers to his friend's mother's April; in V he speaks of summer and
winter with reference to man's life; and in VII he writes of the ages of
man as Ovid had done.

It has often been pointed out that the arguments used by Venus in
her attempted seduction of Adonis are not merely similar to those used
by Leander, but even closer to those used by Shakespeare in the first
seventeen sonnets. It has even been suggested that *Venus and Adonis* was
part of the same campaign to persuade Southampton to marry, that the
Sonnets are a private version of the public poem. The objection to this
theory is that Venus is predatory and lustful, while Adonis, if narcissistic,
is also chaste. We may sympathise with Venus, but we are not meant to
give her moral approval. This said, it must be admitted that Venus and
Shakespeare use some of the same arguments. Adonis is compared with
Narcissus (ll. 161–2); he is told that it is his duty to breed (ll. 168–71);
that only by so doing can his likeness remain after his death (l. 174);
and that if he does not have children his body is

> but a swallowing grave
> Seeming to bury that posterity. (l. 758)

Celibacy is a kind of suicide or murder (ll. 765–6) and (as in Sonnet IV)
gold should be put to use. The arguments both here and in the Sonnets
are those of Erasmus.

Of course, as we are dealing with commonplaces it is impossible to
be dogmatic about Shakespeare's actual sources. Hankins has written a
book to prove Shakespeare's indebtedness to Googe's translation of
Palingenius. In the same book he argues that some phrases in those
sonnets are derived from La Primaudaye, another repository of commonplaces. In XV, for example, the lines

> Holds in perfection but a little moment. . . .
> When I perceive that men as plants increase . . .
> Then the conceit of this in constant stay

seem to echo La Primaudaye's 'little moment of life', 'increasing . . .
until he hath placed them in perfection', and 'stand a while at stay'.

Possibly, too, 'Fall to decay' (XIII) may be echoed from 'falleth to
decay' in the same context.

Another tradition in which Shakespeare was writing is in the long
line of poets who have boasted of the immortality of their work and
promised immortality to the people they celebrate. For Elizabethans
this tradition goes back to Horace. In the last ode of book III he boasted
– I quote in Michie's translation –

> More durable than bronze, higher than Pharaoh's
> Pyramids is the monument I have made,
> A shape that angry wind or hungry rain
> Cannot demolish, nor the innumerable
> Ranks of the years that march in centuries.
> I shall not wholly die: some part of me
> Will cheat the goddess of death, for while High Priest
> And Vestal climb our Capitol in a hush,
> My reputation shall keep green and growing. . . .
> Be proud, Melpomene, for you deserve
> What praise I have, and unreluctantly
> Garland my forehead with Apollo's laurel.

Here Horace is concerned only with his own glory; and even in two
odes in book IV, addressed to Censorinus and Lollius, he assures them
that it is only his poetry which will keep alive their reputations.

Shakespeare certainly knew some of Horace's work. He echoes one of
the odes and one of the epistles in the third act of *King Lear*.[17] But his
favourite Latin poet was Ovid, and the confident claim of literary
immortality at the end of the *Metamorphoses* left its mark on at least
one of the Sonnets:

> Now have I brought a woork too end which neither *Ioues* feerce wrath,
> Nor swoord, nor fyre, nor freating age with all the force it hath
> Are able too abolish quyght. Let comme that fatall howre
> Which (saving of this brittle flesh) hath over mee no powre,
> And at his pleasure make an end of myne uncerteyne tyme.
> Yit shall the better part of mee assured bee to clyme
> Aloft above the starry skye. And all the world shall never
> Be able for too quench my name. For looke how farre so ever
> The Romane Empyre by the ryght of conquest shall extend,
> So farre shall all folke reade this woork. And tyme without all end
> (If Poets as by prophesie about the truth may ame)
> My lyfe shall everlastingly bee lengthened still by fame.

Shakespeare picks up Horace's 'non omnis moriar' in several of his
sonnets and the sword and fire of Ovid's exordium in LV. (Baldwin
quotes a comment by Regius on the Ovidian boast: 'Verissimus autem
fuit vates Ovidius cum enim hactenus tot bellorum incendiis quibus

priora secula arserunt absumptum non fuerit.'[18] Ovid was a very accurate prophet, for there have up till now been so many fires of war which burst out in former ages, but Ovid's work was not destroyed.) So Shakespeare writes:

> Not marble, nor the gilded monuments
> Of princes shall out-live this powerful rhyme,
> But you shall shine more bright in these contents
> Than unswept stone, besmeared with sluttish time.
> When wasteful war shall statues over-turn
> And broils root out the work of masonry,
> Nor Mars his sword, nor war's quick fire shall burn
> The living record of your memory.
> 'Gainst death and all-oblivious emnity
> Shall you pace forth, your praise shall still find room
> Even in the eyes of all posterity
> That wear this world out to the ending doom.
>   So till the judgement that your self arise,
>   You live in this, and dwell in lovers' eyes.

The influence of Ovid is apparent, but the tone of Shakespeare's sonnet is completely different. He is not concerned with his own posthumous fame, but with the immortalising of his friend.[19]

Some critics have suggested that Shakespeare resembles Petrarch in this respect. As Leishman says, both poets 'never speak of their own poetry other than as a thing wholly dedicated, wholly subordinated, to the person it professes to honour'.[20] Both poets in this respect may be contrasted with Ronsard, who is much more concerned with his own glory than with Cassandra's or Hélène's. Indeed, he tells Hélène that, if he had not loved her, she would be forgotten. Several Elizabethan poets touched on the same traditional theme of immortalisation but, apart from one of Spenser's sonnets, the best treating this theme were probably written after Shakespeare's, as when Drayton boasts that

> . . . Queenes hereafter shall be glad to live
> Vpon the Almes of thy superfluous prayse.

The third topic which is of major importance in Shakespeare's sonnets is linked in one way to the topic we have been discussing – for immortalisation by means of poetry is one method of defeating the arch-enemy Time.

There are, indeed, more references to Time in Shakespeare's sonnets than in those of Sidney, Spenser, Daniel and Drayton rolled into one – more than sixty in all – and in his other works there are more than a thousand. Many of these are of no special significance; but the long tirade of Lucrece after her rape, the speech of Ulysses in *Troilus and Cressida* when he tells Achilles that love and friendship are Time's subjects, and Macbeth's obsession with Time, so well analysed by Stephen Spender – all these are, in their various ways, dramatically appropriate, and so is the treatment of Time in the Sonnets. As we can see from Renaissance iconography, Time was depicted both as the destroyer and as the revealer, Truth being Time's daughter. In the Sonnets, Shakespeare is concerned only with Time the destroyer – the enemy of youth, beauty and love. He found the imagistic material for his continuous struggle with Time in the last book of *Metamorphoses*, in which the ideas of Pythagoras are expounded. (I quote in Rolfe Humphries' translation since I do not share Ezra Pound's aberrant view that Golding was a better poet than Milton.)

> Nothing is permanent in all the world.
> All things are fluent; every image forms,
> Wandering through change. Time is itself a river
> In constant movement, and the hours flow by
> Like water, wave on wave, pursued, pursuing,
> Forever fugitive, forever new.
> That which has been, is not; that which was not
> Begins to be; motion and movement always
> In process of renewal.
>
> Nature shaped us, brought us forth, exposed us
> To the void air, and there in light we lay,
> Feeble and infant, and were quadrupeds
> Before too long, and after a little wobbled
> And pulled ourselves upright, holding a chair,
> The side of the crib, and strength grew into us,
> And swiftness; youth and middle age went swiftly
> Down the long hill towards age . . . Time devours all things.

From these two passages – on the waves of time and on the lifetime of man – Shakespeare derived his Sonnet LX. But, whereas Pythagoras contemplates Time's effects with equanimity, Shakespeare is profoundly disturbed.

> Like as the waves make towards the pebbled shore,
> So do our minutes hasten to their end;
> Each changing place with that which goes before,
> In sequent toil all forwards do contend.
> Nativity, once in the main of light,
> Crawls to maturity, wherewith being crown'd,
> Crooked eclipses 'gainst his glory fight,
> And Time that gave doth now his gift confound.
> Time doth transfix the flourish set on youth,

And delves the parallels in beauty's brow,
Feeds on the rarities of nature's truth,
And nothing stands but for his scythe to mow.
    And yet to times in hope my verse shall stand,
    Praising thy worth, despite his cruel hand.

A later Ovidian passage provided Shakespeare with the imagery of another sonnet, LXIV. Ovid tells how

> I have seen oceans
> That once were solid land, and I have seen
> Lands made from ocean.

This is the basis of Shakespeare's second quatrain:

When I have seen by Time's fell hand defaced
The rich proud cost of outworn buried age;
When sometime lofty towers I see down-rased,
And brass eternal slave to mortal rage;
When I have seen the hungry ocean gain
Advantage on the kingdom of the shore,
And the firm soil win of the wat'ry main,
Increasing store with loss, and loss with store;
When I have seen such interchange of state,
Or state itself confounded to decay;
Ruin hath taught me thus to ruminate –
That Time will come and take my love away.
    This thought is as a death, which cannot choose
    But weep to have that which it fears to lose.[21]

I have been stressing the fact that Shakespeare was more indebted to Erasmus, Ovid and Sidney's *Arcadia* than he was to Petrarch or to his imitators in French, Italian and English. The differences between Shakespeare's sonnets and those of his predecessors are more significant than the resemblances; and when we find Elizabethan sonnets which remind us of Shakespeare's it appears probable that the other poets took Shakespeare as their model. Yet Shakespeare's choice of the sonnet form was dictated by its popularity in the last decade of the sixteenth century. If he had been born a generation earlier or a generation later, he would not have written sonnets. No one was writing sonnets in 1560, and by 1620 they had become old-fashioned.

CHAPTER 4

Commentary

As we have seen, there is reason to believe that the order of the Sonnets in the 1609 Quarto is Shakespeare's own. But this does not mean that there is a straightforward narrative, or that there will not be strange juxtapositions. In the present chapter the Sonnets have been divided into a number of sections, although it will often be found that the last sonnet in one section has closer affinities with the first sonnet of the next than adjacent sonnets in the same section do.

(a) I – XVII

The first seventeen sonnets, urging the young man to marry so as to perpetuate his beauty, employ, as we have seen, traditional arguments in favour of marriage – some of the imagery, as well as the arguments, being borrowed from Erasmus and Sidney.[1] These sonnets are closely linked by the repetition of rhymes in adjacent, or nearly adjacent, poems. The apparent exception, VIII, has rhyme-links with VII ('son'/'none') and VI ('bear'/'fair'), but not with IX or X; yet the idea of the family group in VIII – 'sire, and child, and happy mother' – leads on quite naturally to that of the childless widow in IX. There is much to be said for Brents Stirling's view, shared by most editors, that this group of sonnets was written first, and written as a single poem. We need not, however, assume that these seventeen sonnets are rhetorical exercises, written perhaps to order, in contrast to the sonnets in which the Poet is speaking for himself. (To distinguish between Shakespeare and his persona, it will be convenient to call the latter 'the Poet'.)

All seventeen sonnets constitute variations on the same theme – how Time's threat to youth, beauty and even life itself may be countered by the reproduction of the parent's beauty in his offspring and by the continuation of the family line. It can be seen, moreover, that one sonnet is often developed from a previous one – as, for example, when the scent of the flowers in V leads on to a different use of the distillation idea in VI.

In the last three sonnets of this group there is a change: the Poet offers an alternative kind of immortality – that afforded by the permanence of great poetry. The persuasions to marry continue, if perfunctorily, in XVI and XVII, but are dropped thereafter. The change has been heralded in X when the Poet appeals to the young man to marry and beget children, not as a duty, to posterity or to his family, but 'for love of me', and in XIII where the recipient is called 'love' for the first time. It has been suggested that the persuasions to marry were written at the request of the young man's parents or relations, or alternatively that they were a spin-off from the arguments used by the goddess in *Venus and Adonis*; but, even if the sonnets were entirely fictional, the increasing involvement of the Poet – from aesthetic admiration to love – would have been a perfectly natural, an almost inevitable, result of the imagined situation.

How closely the seventeen sonnets are linked, so that each one can be regarded as a stanza of a 238-line poem, will be brought out by a brief examination of the whole. The first sonnet enunciates the central theme:

> From fairest creatures we desire increase,
> That thereby beauty's Rose might never die.

The recipient – whom we shall, without prejudice, call W.H. – ought to perpetuate his beauty by begetting children in his image. To refrain from marriage is to be guilty of narcissism, and of cruelty to future generations. The young man is called 'tender churl' ('dear young miser', as Dover Wilson paraphrases), and his hoarding is a shameful waste. The idea is repeated in later sonnets by the use of such words as 'thriftless' (II), 'unthrifty' (IV) and 'unthrifts' (XIII), as well as by the echo of 'niggarding' in 'niggard' (IV) and by 'profitless usurer' (IV). The image of gluttony, eating 'the world's due' (I.12–14), was perhaps suggested by the Ovidian 'tempus edax' which Shakespeare later echoes more directly.[2]

In II, Time, the enemy, is depicted as the besieger of a city and, by a shift in the use of the image, the trenches he digs are the wrinkles W.H. will have when he reaches the age of forty:

> When forty winters shall besiege thy brow,
> And dig deep trenches in thy beauty's field. . . .

It is characteristic of the Sonnets – and, indeed, of Shakespeare's other poetry – that the operation of Time should be symbolised by 'winters' rather than by 'years'. The contrast between the 'proud livery' and the 'tatter'd weed' may have been suggested (as Ingram and Redpath note) by the contrast between the livery of a nobleman's servant and the tattered clothes of a beggar, through which, as Lear reminds us, 'small vices do appear'. But 'livery' as in *Lucrece* (l. 1054) meant the outward appearance, contradicting the inner reality, and there is the same implication in the line in 'A Lover's Complaint' –

Did livery falseness in a pride of truth (l. 105)

– and Isabella, referring to Angelo's hypocrisy, exclaims:

O, 'tis the cunning livery of hell.

In the sonnet the 'proud livery' means primarily the outward beauty of W.H., which is liable to be lost by the operation of Time. The 'all-eating shame' (8) was doubtless suggested by the last line of the previous sonnet:

To eat the world's due, by the grave and thee.

The triple repetition of 'beauty' echoes 'beauty's Rose', and it leads on to the use of the same word or of its synonyms in successive sonnets, while 'beauty's use' contrasts with the disuse of niggarding or miserliness, deplored throughout the sequence. Finally, the winters of the first line contrast with 'only herald to the gaudy spring' (I.10) and lead on to allusions to the winter of life in later sonnets (IV, V).

In III the image of the mirror ('Look in thy glass') and the reference to self-love (8) recall the story of Narcissus; but the mirror image is repeated in 'Thou art thy mother's glass', and she is able to see in her son what she was like in 'the lovely April of her prime'; while he, in his turn, will in old age be able to see in his children what he was like in his 'golden time'. By remaining celibate he would lose the mirror of his youth. There is an effective quibble on 'husbandry', relating both to 'husband' and 'husbandman'. There is also some exquisite phrasing. 'What is a lovely phrase?' Virginia Woolf asked. 'One that has mopped up as much truth as it can hold.' Nevertheless, the sonnet is open to some objections. It is undesirable, perhaps, to use 'thee' twice as a rhyme-word; and there is an awkward departure from the natural order of words in the line:

But if thou live rememb'red not to be.

The imagery of IV is derived from last wills and testaments, and it is easy to see how it could have been suggested by references to death in previous sonnets – 'grave' (I.14) and 'die' (III.14) – and now developed in 'legacy' (2), 'bequest' (3), 'audit' (12), 'tomb'd' (13) and 'executor' (14). J. Q. Adams suggested that in this and other sonnets Shakespeare was alluding to the parable of the talents, the same parable to which Milton returned again and again when he measured his achievements against the responsibilities of genius.[3] I cannot follow Booth, who thinks that 'traffic' (9) suggests masturbation.[4]

Shakespeare develops in V the comparison of the four seasons with the stages of man's life, implied already in 'forty winters'. It was a commonplace, to be found in Palingenius as well as in Ovid.[5] The hours are called tyrants, as Time is later called a 'bloody tyrant' (XVI.2), and winter, as nearly always with Shakespeare, is regarded with horror. Phelps remarked solicitously that the poet must have suffered terribly from the English climate; but it will be recalled that the winter song at the end of *Love's Labour's Lost* embodies a merry note while the spring offers only a 'word of fear'. The lines describing winter in this sonnet pack into fourteen words the essence of the season:

> Sap check'd with frost and lusty leaves quite gone,
> Beauty o'er-snow'd and bareness everywhere.

Equally effective, with its subtle mingling of *p*s and *l*s is the line:

> A *l*iquid *p*risoner *p*ent in wa*ll*s of g*l*ass

The next sonnet, VI, is a development of the same image. It is joined to V by its first word, 'Then', and by the echo of 'distill'd' (2). Tucker thought that the 'vial' (3) was the child embodying the beauty of the father; but a more probable meaning is that it refers to the womb of the mother.[6] Some have thought that the repetition of 'treasure' in successive lines (3, 4) is due to textual corruption; but Shakespeare delighted in the rhetorical device of repeating a word in a different sense.[7] The lines which follow develop the idea of usury and they depend on the contrast between the two meanings of breed, one natural, and the other interest on capital, condemned by the Church, but reluctantly legalised in 1571. Even as late as 1596 an attack on it could be sure to win applause. Antonio, the Merchant of Venice, it will be remembered, asked Shylock:

> When did friendship take
> A breed for barren metal of his friend?

The Poet in this sonnet shows that ten children in the image of their father would make him ten times happier:

> Ten times thy self were happier than thou art
> If ten of thine ten times refigur'd thee. . . .

This kind of breeding is natural and not theologically dubious; and by its means W.H. would live on after his actual death. The final words of the sonnet

> Be not self-will'd, for thou art much too fair
> To be Death's conquest and make worms thine heir.

hark back to the conclusion of IV and to the question in CXLVI:

> Shall worms, inheritors of this excess,
> Eat up thy charge?

In VII human life is compared with the passage of the sun from sunrise to sunset, and the description is apparently influenced by Ovid's account of Phaethon's ill-fated journey, but the basic idea probably came[8] from 'Plures adorant solem orientem quam occidentem' – a proverb which those familiar with court news, 'who's in, who's out', would have proved upon their pulses. Elizabeth I, in refusing to name her successor, remarked that 'Men use to worship the rising sun'.[9]

The musical image in VIII is based, as we have seen, on Cecropia's temptation of Philoclea.[10] The marriage of sounds in a consort of viols is make to symbolise the union of father, mother and child. The image is reinforced by the chime of rhymes, both internal and external, on '*sing*' (12) – '*sing*leness' (8), '*string*' (9), 'order*ing*' (10) 'resembl*ing*' (11), 'pleas*ing*' (12), 'seem*ing*' (13), '*sing*s' (14) and '*sing*le' (14). It is possible that the viols were suggested by the vial of perfume in VI.[11]

In the next sonnet (IX) the Poet imagines W.H. objecting to this picture of married bliss since it ignores the possibility that he might die young, leaving behind a widow and fatherless children. To this the Poet answers, first, that a widow would at least have children to remind her of her dead husband's appearance and, secondly, that by declining to marry the young man will make not one woman but the whole world his widow and, moreover, without the ordinary widow's compensation. He will be guilty of murdering his potential progeny. This is, perhaps, one of the few sonnets in which Shakespeare indulges in excessive alliteration. There are seventeen words beginning with *w*, as in the lines:

> The world will wail thee, like a makeless wife,
> The world will be thy widow and still weep. . . .

Shakespeare might have said with Holofernes: 'I will something affect the letter, for it argues facility.'[12] The 'murd'rous shame' of the last line is picked up at the beginning of the next sonnet:

> For shame! deny that thou bear'st love to any. . . .
> For thou art so possess'd with murd'rous hate. . . .

Shakespeare now introduces a familiar argument in favour of marriage – that one should not allow a house to fall into decay. The house is both a building and a family line, and this makes the analogy a powerful one.[13] But Shakespeare seems to be referring less to the family line – in which W.H.'s hypothetical relations would be chiefly interested – than to the preservation of the friend's beauty in his offspring. By this point the Poet can claim W.H. as a friend who reciprocates his love to some degree:

> Make thee another self for love of me. . . .

Next the Poet thinks of his friend as an archetype, carved by Nature herself (XI), and it was his manifest duty to take more impressions from it. So to act is 'wisdom, beauty and increase'; not to do so is 'folly, age, and cold decay'.

Dowden described XII as 'a gathering into one' of V, VI and VII; but it could rather be regarded as a restatement of the first seven sonnets – the use of procreation to defeat Time. It is, indeed, one of the finest of the early sonnets. The subtle balancing of phrases, the use of cross-alliteration, as in the line

> And summer's green all girded up in sheaves

the near-repetition of sound, for example:

> Borne on the bier with white and bristly beard

the perfection of phrasing throughout the sonnet and, as Caroline Spurgeon pointed out, the vivid succession of colours make this an acknowledged masterpiece.[14] Only Ransom oddly complained of the 'insignificant violet' – a complaint which Wordsworth's 'violet by a mossy stone' should have precluded. Keats quoted the second quatrain in a letter to John Hamilton Reynolds (22 November 1817), prefixed with the words:

> One of the three Books I have with me is Shakespeare's Poems: I neer found so many beauties in the sonnets – they seem to be full of fine things said unintentionally – in the intensity of working out conceits – Is this to be borne?

The question does not mean, as Professor Booth supposed,[15] that Keats was 'shocked' by the passage, but that he was lost in admiration and despairing of ever writing anything as good. This is made doubly clear by his next comment, 'He has left nothing to say about nothing or anything', and by his quotation of several other phrases he admired.

In XIII Shakespeare recapitulates. He takes up the image of the house (X), the legal terminology (IV, VI), winter as the manifestation of Time (II, VI), 'unthrifts' (II, IV), and the double meaning of husbandry (III). The form of the sonnet is unusual in that it compromises between the

English and Italian rhyme-schemes, the first two quatrains being linked
by common rhymes. It should also be mentioned that for the first time
the Poet addresses W.H. as 'you'. Dowden, who pointed this out, thought
that 'you' sometimes expressed 'intimate affection' while 'thou' expressed
'respectful homage'; but he had to admit that the choice of pronouns was
sometimes dictated by rhyme or euphony. We may go farther and say that it
is impossible to detect any consistency in the use of either pronoun. In
the first fifty sonnets, for example, five are not addressed directly to
W.H. and of the remaining forty-five only four use 'you'. It cannot be
seriously pretended that these (XIII, XV, XVI, XVII) express more
intimate affection than many of the 'thee' sonnets (e.g. XVIII, XX,
XXX). Nor is it legitimate to rearrange the Sonnets so as to introduce
greater consistency in this respect. Bray, for example, argued that the
'*thou*-sonnets are Shakespeare's earlier, the other sonnets Shakespeare's
later and more mature work'.

The next two sonnets (XIV, XV) make use of astrological ideas, one
accepting the familiar conceit of the beloved's eyes as stars,[16] the other
accepting the view that the stars do influence human life. One line in
XIV –

> But from thine eyes my knowledge I derive

is clearly related to Berowne's defence of falling in love:

> From women's eyes this doctrine I derive,
> They sparkle still the right Promethean fire;
> They are the books, the arts, the academes,
> That show, contain, and nourish, all the world.

It has been observed that Shakespeare's evil characters, such as Edmund,
scoff at planetary influence as 'an admirable evasion' of reality by
'whoremaster man'.[17] Cassius is playing the role of tempter when he tells
Brutus that the reason why we are slaves 'is not in our stars'. Shakespeare's
good characters, on the other hand, admit that

> It is the stars,
> The stars above us, govern our conditions.

Helena, nevertheless, while allowing that the stars do influence us,
claims that human beings have 'free scope'. The sky

> only doth backward pull
> Our slow designs when we ourselves are dull.

Here, as always, Shakespeare's own opinion is difficult to determine:
the various opinions expressed are dramatically relevant and appropriate

to the characters who utter them. We should expect the superstitious
Gloucester to blame the stars; we should expect Othello to seek to
mitigate his guilt by speaking of Desdemona as 'ill-starred'; and it is
natural for Helena, hoping to marry out of her own class, to believe she
has free will. In the sonnet the 'huge stage' looks forward to Lear's
'great stage of fools'; but after the first quatrain the stars are forgotten
– they are merely auxiliary to the metamorphosing power of Time. Then,
in the last line, the Poet suggests for the first time that his verse is an
alternative way of preserving the beauty of his friend. He declares that
he is warring against Time because of his love; but in XVI, much less
confident of the power of his poetry to grant immortality, he reverts to
his former advice – marry and beget children:

> But wherefore do not you a mightier way
> Make war upon this bloody tyrant Time,
> And fortify your self in your decay
> With means more blessed than my barren rhyme?

– barren, presumably, not because it is bad in itself, but because it lacks
the natural fertility of marriage. Neither verse, nor painting, however
skilful, can provide as satisfactory a reproduction of the 'inward worth'
or 'outward fair' as children would be.

In the final sonnet of the procreation series, the Poet argues that his
verse is liable to seem as extravagant as a eulogy on a tomb, and that
people in future ages will assume that his praise of W.H. is merely

> a poet's rage,
> And stretched metre of an antique song

– the exaggerations of *furor poeticus* combined with a versification which
would seem as halting as Chaucer's did to the Elizabethans. The only
proof that he was telling the exact truth would be the existence of a
descendant as beautiful as W.H.

The fact that the Poet speaks of his 'pupil pen' does not necessarily
mean that these sonnets were written in the days of his apprenticeship,
any more than Shakespeare, in dedicating his highly sophisticated poem,
Venus and Adonis, to the Earl of Southampton, really believed that his
lines were rude and unpolished. Yet to assume, as Dover Wilson did,[18]
that these seventeen sonnets were written for Herbert's seventeenth
birthday in 1597 makes 'pupil pen' refer to one which had already been
responsible for two long narrative poems and sixteen plays – some
40,000 lines. Not so odd, however, if we abandon the idea that the
Poet of the Sonnets is identical with Shakespeare the man.

Although this chapter will be concerned with other groups of sonnets,
it will be apparent that there is no other group which forms as unified
a sequence.

(b) XVIII – XXXII

After the Poet's reference to his pupil pen and his barren rhyme, XVIII, with its boast that his lines will be eternal, comes as a surprise. But these sudden contrasts are one of the means by which he convinces us that the Sonnets are genuine expressions of his feelings from day to day, and from year to year. In the same way, as Maurice Morgann so brilliantly demonstrated,[19] the conflicting impressions set up in the minds of readers and audiences convince them that the characters of Shakespeare's plays are 'real' (Morgann, despite the oft-repeated criticism of his work, was never in danger of confusing art and life.[20]) At first sight the hyperboles of XVIII and XIX seem to conflict with the Poet's scorn of rival sonneteers who compare their mistresses

> With sun and moon, with earth and sea's rich gems,
> With April's first-born flowers, and all things rare. . . .

Is he not doing precisely what he complains of in others?

> Shall I compare thee to a summer's day?
> Thou art more lovely and more temperate.
> Rough winds do shake the darling buds of May,
> And summer's lease hath all too short a date.

This exaggeration, however, is not precisely the same. Here the Poet is not pretending to describe what W.H. invariably is, but what he will seem to be ages hence, caught in a moment of perfection in the Poet's eternal lines. In this case he may well be described as more lovely and more temperate than a summer's day. Bernard Shaw remarked of Rosalind that she 'is not a complete human being: she is simply an extension into five acts of the most affectionate, fortunate, delightful five minutes in the life of a charming woman'.[21] So the friend, permanently beautiful and everlastingly young, is captured by the Poet, like the lovers on the Grecian Urn. The same thought is repeated at the end of XIX.

> My love shall in my verse ever live young.

But, whereas in XVIII the Poet concentrates on W.H.'s temporary perfection, in XIX he is more concerned, as in the first seventeen sonnets, with Time's threat. In both sonnets the three quatrains form a single sentence; but in both the sentence hinges on the 'But' at the beginning of the third quatrain.[22] If XVIII is often regarded as the first indisputable masterpiece and a favourite of anthologists, the first quatrain of XIX is often quoted for its musical perfection and was indeed echoed in the year of its publication.[23]

In the next sonnet, XX, there is another complete change of tone and style. It uses feminine rhymes throughout, suggested perhaps by the androgynous nature of the man described. Rollins calls the poem 'filthy', presumably because of the pun on 'prick' in the penultimate line. It is the only sonnet in the first sequence which depends on bawdy; and it is, moreover, the first sonnet not to be concerned, by one means or other, with the conquest of Time. It is a poem which has caused a good deal of unnecessary embarrassment. Steevens and Rollins are by no means the only critics who have felt disgust and indignation. The Poet recognises frankly that his love is erotic as well as spiritual; yet there seems to be no thought in his mind of the possibility of a physical consummation of his love, or even that he would have been tempted if the possibility had existed. Unlike Marlowe, who wrote about homosexual relationships in two of his plays, and who in conversation, if only to shock his hearers, advocated paederasty, Shakespeare was predominantly heterosexual in his feelings despite his adoration of W.H.'s beauty. On the one occasion when he depicted a full homosexual relationship, he treated it with Thersites-like distaste. The love of Antonio for Sebastian, and of the other Antonio for Bassanio, is much closer to that of the Poet of the Sonnets for W.H. Like him they accept the fact that Nature has picked their beloveds for women's pleasure, not for men's.[24]

Despite the italicising of '*Hews*', there is no need to think that Shakespeare was quibbling on Hughes, for (as Baldwin and Melchiori have shown) the line is perfectly intelligible without. Both critics quote from Hoby's translation of Castiglione about the ideal courtier, who had to have noble birth, wit,

> a comely shape of persone and countenance, but also a certayne grace, and (as they saie) a hewe, that shall make him at the first sight acceptable and lovyng unto who so beholdeth him. (*The Book of the Courtier*, 1928 edn, p. 33)

In another passage, quoted by Baldwin, Castiglione writes of love at first sight, when the man seeing a beautiful and virtuous woman 'wotteth well that his hewe hath an agreement with herres'.[25] Melchiori is thus able to give several meanings of 'all Hews in his controlling' – 'a model for all other appearances', 'dominating, well above all other men for handsomeness', 'setting the rules of beauty for everybody' and 'conquering all women, whatever their colour'. It also means, I suspect, 'sexually attractive to everyone'. At this stage in the Poet's relationship with W.H. the spiritual nature of his friendship can be contrasted with the physical relationship which W.H. would have with women, a contrast which was later to be duplicated by the Poet's two loves of comfort and despair. Nor does the avoidance of the physical mean that the friendship was exempt from jealousies, misunderstandings and estrangement.[26]

The first sonnet concerned with a rival poet (XXI) is couched in general terms and it does not imply that the rival has been well received by W.H. It is not necessarily connected with the later group (LXXVIII–XC), in which the Poet is deeply hurt by his friend's encouragement of a particular rival. The subject of XX had been painted by Nature herself; but in XXI the feminine subject uses cosmetics which the Poet, like Hamlet, strongly dislikes. The point of the sonnet is simply that the Poet's own method is marked by restraint, plainness and sincerity –

> as true as truth's simplicity
> And simpler than the infancy of truth

– whereas the other poet indulges in inflated rhetoric. The repetition of 'heaven's air' has persuaded one or two critics that the sonnet is either textually corrupt or un-Shakespearian.[27] This is, however, characteristic of his style, and not merely in his early work. A similar repetition is to be found in this very sonnet when 'fair' (4) reappears as a rhyme-word six lines later. The criticism of the rival, referred to as 'that Muse', is similar to that made by Sidney – that too much hyperbole and artificiality leaves the reader feeling that the poets do not mean what they say and that they are not really in love:

> But truly many of such writings as come under the banner of irresistable love, if I were a mistresse, would never perswade me they were in loue: so coldly they applie firie speeches, as men that had rather redde louers writings, and so caught up certaine swelling phrases. . . . Now for the outside of it, which is words, or (as I may tearme it) *Diction*, it is euen well worse: so is it that hony-flouring Matrone *Eloquence*, apparrelled, or rather disguised, in a courtisanelike painted affection.

> You that poore *Petrarch's* long deceased woes,
> With new-borne sighes and denisend wit do sing;
> You take wrong waies, those far-fet helpes be such,
> As do bewray a want of inward tuch.[28]

Sidney's own recipe for love-poetry – 'looke in thy heart and write' – was essentially Shakespeare's. Both poets possessed the 'inward touch', but both, of course, knew that art was equally necessary. They criticised their contemporaries for being bad artists more than for a lack of sincerity. The method of pretended understatement was a rhetorical device they both knew how to exploit. In the sonnet under discussion, 'fair/As any mother's child' is praise enough for anyone. To say more, Shakespeare declares, is to indulge in sales talk.[29] 'I will not praise' is not to be taken literally: the whole sonnet is a eulogy which pretends to be a cool assessment.

The next sonnet (XXII) might almost be taken as an example of the kind of love-poem to which Sidney took exception. It is based on the conceit that the Poet's heart is in his friend's breast, and his friend's heart in his. Such a conceit can be put to charming use, as in Sidney's own song:

> My true love hath my hart, and I have his

– charming because it is not taken too seriously; but in Shakespeare's sonnet it appears forced.[30]

In XXIII the Poet uses a theatrical image for the first time – of the poor player who forgets his lines through nervousness. For the first time, too, the Poet appears to doubt whether his love is returned. If that proved to be the case, his love would be what Ficino called 'Amor simplex':

> When the beloved does not love the lover. In this case the lover is completely dead for, as we have shown, he does not live in himself, nor in the beloved, since his love is repulsed. Where then does he live? In the air, in the water, in the fire, in the earth, or in the body of an animal? No, for the human soul does not live in a non-human body. But can he live in the body of another man, not the beloved? No, once more, for if he does not live in the one in whom he desires so ardently to live, how would he be able to live in another?[31]

The words 'that tongue, that more hath more express'd' seem to indicate that a rival, using the sort of style castigated in XXI, has debased the coinage of praise – the Gresham's Law of eulogy – so that Shakespeare's constraint seems somewhat grudging. The first two lines of the sonnet –

> As an unperfect actor on the stage,
> Who with his fear is put besides his part

– are linked with the first two of the second quatrain –

> So I, for fear of trust, forget to say
> The perfect ceremony of love's rite

– and the third and fourth lines of the sonnet are linked with the corresponding lines of the second quatrain. The abundance which is a source of weakness parallels the excess of love which makes the Poet tongue-tied.[32] The doubt underlying the poem contrasts with the confidence displayed in the previous sonnet; but its humility is close to that of XXVI.[33]

The conceit in XXIV is skilfully developed, but too clever to be very satisfying. In XXV the Poet contrasts those who are Fortune's favourites, and liable to fall at any time without warning, with himself, permanently happy (as he thinks) in his love. The structure of the sonnet is another example of the way Shakespeare varied his method. Here the first quatrain enunciates the contrast. The other two provide examples of the inconstancy of Fortune. As Hamlet warned Rosencrantz and Guildenstern, good fortune can be overturned at the whim of a prince; and a general who is defeated after a thousand victories at once loses his reputation. Everything is subject to 'envious and calumniating time', except (as the final couplet claims) a constant and reciprocated love.[34]

The sleeplessness of lovers was a favourite theme of sonneteers – there are notable English examples by Sidney and Daniel, and feebler ones by Barnes, Griffin and Lynch – but Shakespeare varies the topic in XXVII and XXVIII by introducing the weariness caused by travel. The two sonnets, linked by common rhymes, form a single poem. This has been tacitly recognised by every one of the rearrangers except Bray.

In the next sonnet (XXIX), the greatest of poets, and one renowned for his 'gentleness' and affability, makes his persona think of himself as unlucky, disgraced, friendless, and envious of the art of others. It is an impressive catalogue of the ills and misfortunes of life, splendidly dispersed by the image of the lark at break of day who 'sings hymns at heaven's gate',[35] as the thought of the Poet's friend compensates for the evils he has lamented. The double use of 'state' as a rhyme may be justified, in order to bring out the stark contrast between the Poet's apparently outcast state and the state of joy described in the third quatrain.

Another great sonnet (XXX) is similar in theme. Once again the sorrows of human existence are set in the scales against the Poet's love. In the legal metaphor with which the poem opens, Shakespeare embedded a phrase from Ecclesiasticus, already used by Wyatt and Blundeville in their translations of Plutarch – 'remembrance of things past'.[36] It is one of the most highly wrought of all the sonnets, with an extraordinary complexity, of sound-patterns:

> When to the sessions of sweet silent thought
> I summon up remembrance of things past,
> I sigh the lack of many a thing I sought,
> And with old woes new wail my dear time's waste:
> Then can I drown an eye, unus'd to flow,
> For precious friends hid in death's dateless night,
> And weep afresh love's long since cancell'd woe,

And moan th'expense of many a vanish'd sight:
Then can I grieve at grievances foregone,
And heavily from woe to woe tell o'er
The sad account of fore-bemoaned moan,
Which I new pay as if not paid before.
   But if the while I think on thee, dear friend,
   All losses are restored and sorrows end.

Mark Van Doren complained that the final couplet was unworthy of the rest of the poem:

> The first twelve lines are an introduction to the last two, which make the statement to which the sonnet has apparently been tending. But only apparently. The twelve lines with their burden of woe and their slow mournful movement through foregone sorrows which it is both dreadful and delicious to remember, and their music so skilfully constructed on the ground bass of the letter "O" – those are the lines that Shakespeare has been interested in writing. Not the two others which run with such perfunctory and absurd rapidity to fabricate a concluding statement. The sonnet was not written to say what they say, at any rate by the great poet in Shakespeare. That poet is truly personal in the body of the poem; he is dealing with what interests him, namely his own flowing sorrows and the sweetness of still thought.[37]

The question of the couplets will be discussed in the next chapter. Meanwhile, to Van Doren's admirable appreciation of the music of the first twelve lines may be added a reference to the subtle cross-alliteration and the echoes of 'precious' (6) in 'afresh' (7), of 'grieve' in 'grievances' (9), and of 'foregone' (9) in 'o'er' (10).

In this sonnet the Poet grieves for 'precious friends hid in death's dateless night'; but in XXXI he rejoices that the friends who were buried are now in W.H.'s bosom – an idea to be found in Constable's *Diana* and treated again by Shakespeare in XXXII. The thought of the death of friends makes him think of W.H. surviving him and reading the sonnets years hence. He reverts to the idea that his poems will seem old-fashioned to a future generation, 'poor rude lines', and that they will be compared with the better poems of the new age. Ronsard's well-known sonnet to Hélène imagines her rereading the poems he had written to her when she was young; but characteristically he does not suppose that they will ever seem old-fashioned, nor does he beg Hélène to excuse the crudity of his lines because they were the expression of his love. Her glory was to have been Ronsard's subject; Shakespeare's glory, on the contrary, was to have been a friend of W.H., as Fulke Greville reckoned his friendship with Sidney to have been his chief title to be remembered. It would be easy to suspect that there was an element of mock modesty in Shakespeare's attitude; but we should bear in mind once again that the Poet of the Sonnets should not be entirely equated with Shakespeare. An Elizabethan reader, moreover, would find Chaucer archaic; and to a Jacobean, properly excited by the Metaphysicals, even the best Elizabethan poets might seem old-fashioned.

(c) XXXIII – XLII

The next group of sonnets records a temporary estrangement, caused apparently by the seduction of W.H. by the Poet's mistress.[38] The situation is revealed to us only gradually. In XXXIII, for reasons unspecified, the Poet feels he has lost his friend, 'but one hour mine'. It had been only a dream of friendship – the phrase is used in *Timon of Athens* – and the Poet compares the delusion of permanency, of which he had boasted in XXV, with the mountain-tops 'flattered' by the rising sun. The references to 'basest clouds', 'ugly rack', 'stealing', 'disgrace' and, above all, 'stain' in the last line make it clear that W.H. had been guilty of a serious fault, a moral lapse. The weather metaphor is carried on into the next sonnet – some critics absurdly suppose that the drenching was not metaphorical – and the fact that W.H. professes to be sorry for what he has done 'heals the wound, and cures not the disgrace'. The scar, as Wyatt said, remains.[39]

> Th' offender's sorrow lends but weak relief
> To him that bears the strong offence's cross.

Nevertheless, the friend's tears 'ransom all ill deeds', and in XXXV the Poet forgives the culprit, even defending his 'sensual fault' (9) and in so doing corrupting himself (7) and becoming an accessory

> To that sweet thief which sourly robs from me

– the 'sweet' being neatly antithetical to 'sourly'. In XXXVI the Poet accepts the burden of his friend's guilt as well as his own.[40]

The shock sustained by the Poet was due only partly to the fact that he had been betrayed. He had idolised W.H. and idealised the relationship, assuming that outward beauty guaranteed a corresponding inner truth. This had proved to be a delusion, and the realisation of this was the cross he had to bear – one of the rare Christian symbols used in the Sonnets.

These four sonnets are linked in various ways. The sun hidden by the region cloud (XXXIII) leads on to the shower of rain (XXXIV) and the clouds (XXXV); and the disgrace and shame of these three, and the 'stealing' of the last, are linked with 'blots', 'guilt' and 'steal' of XXXVI. There are also rhyme-links, XXXIII and XXIV sharing one rhyme ('face'/'disgrace') and XXXV and XXXVI two. Professor Stephen Booth has a perceptive analysis of the connections between the first three of these sonnets:

> The simultaneous connection and division of the three poems that is made by simultaneously realized likenesses and differences among them is akin in its paradox to a general quality of the three sonnets that only becomes overt in line 10 of 35. . . . The relationship of the three poems is like the relationship they describe, and its operation is like the operation of the terms of the description. The metaphor of the sun for the beloved and its relationship to the storm-threatened and then storm-beaten lover is constant in 33 and 34, but when in 34 the beloved breaks through the clouds to smile on the speaker, the reversal of attitude is mirrored in a reversal of the application of terms in which the incident has been described: in the metaphor the beloved's displeasure fell upon the speaker as rain; at the end of the poem the beloved's contrition is demonstrated in tears.[41]

In the next three sonnets there is a dramatic change. The friend's faults are forgotten as though they had never been. He is hailed as the tenth Muse, worth ten times more than the other nine. The Poet himself, 'made lame by Fortune's dearest spite',[42] acknowledges that his friend is 'all the better part' of him (XXXIX) and that he basks in his reflected glory (XXXVIII):

> Oh, give thy self the thanks if aught in me
> Worthy perusal stand against thy sight. . . .

The three sonnets are inserted at this point, we may suppose, to give the maximum contrast between the adored and idealised friend and the selfish and lascivious boy of the surrounding sonnets.

In the three sonnets that follow (XL–XLII), the Poet does not merely forgive W.H.; he relinquishes his mistress to him.

It is natural to assume, though it is only an assumption, that these sonnets, as well as XXXIV–XXXVI, refer to the same situation as that of the Dark Lady sequence. It is not unknown for a victim of one betrayal to suffer another, but it would be poetically wrong. Whereas the first sequence (I–CXXVI) is concerned exclusively with the Poet's relationship with his friend, the second sequence concentrates on his relationship with a woman, and the effect on that relationship of her seduction of his friend. Here in the first sequence we are not concerned with the character or appearance of the woman, nor even with the precise nature of her relationship with the Poet. We are not told that she is both adulterous and promiscuous, and there is no immediate suggestion that she took the initiative in seducing the friend.

The basic situation is a familiar one in literature, and one that has been treated in a variety of ways, though usually to show that the claims of friendship between men are superior to those of heterosexual love. In *Euphues*, for example, Lucilla is disloyal to Philautus, the hero's friend, and then deserts him for a third suitor, thus enabling Euphues and Philautus to be reconciled. In what was the classic story on the conflict between love and friendship, recounted by Sir Thomas Elyot, Titus falls desperately in love with the betrothed of his friend Gysippus. Gysippus makes him reveal the cause of his depression and arranges for him to sleep with his bride and so claim her as his wife. The girl is not aware of the plot. The story for Elyot is not a horrible story of exploitation and betrayal, but a splendid example of unselfish friendship. Shakespeare himself in *The Two Gentlemen of Verona* provides another variation. Proteus attempts to rape Silvia and is not merely forgiven by the besotted Valentine but is offered the lady as a proof of his forgiveness. The Poet, too, resigns his mistress to his rival because he values his friendship more than his love:

> Take all my loves, my love, yea take them all.

But Shakespeare varies the theme in several important respects. First, it is the woman who takes the initiative and seduces the friend:

> And when a woman woos, what woman's son
> Will sourly leave her till she have prevailed?

The Poet is able to put himself in the position of W.H. and, since he knows his friend is fashioned for woman's pleasure, he can, in a sense, identify with the woman. Secondly, there is no suggestion of marriage, as in the three versions mentioned above. Thirdly, the renunciation comes after the friend has been seduced. The Poet experiences the 'greater grief' of bearing 'love's wrong' – not the woman's inconstancy, but the friend's betrayal of friendship – and of recognising the 'lascivious grace' of his friend. In spite of his forgiveness, the Poet cannot refrain from reproaching W.H. for breaking 'a twofold truth' (XLI.12) and for not forbearing from occupying his 'seat'. In XLII he tries to excuse both W.H. and the woman by arguing that, since he and his friend are one, the lady in loving his friend is really loving him alone. The excuse is a hollow one, as the Poet admits by calling it 'flattery' (14) or self-deception. He forgives the robbery of the 'gentle thief' (XL.9),[43] while remaining aware that his friend is not the paragon of virtue which his appearance had seemed to promise.

(*d*) XLIII–LVIII

The next sonnet (XLIII) is somewhat mannered, with curious repetitions
and juxtapositions, as the following list will make clear. 'Mine eyes' (1)
is repeated in line 9 and 'eyes' in line 12; 'see' (1) is echoed in 'unseeing'
(8) and twice in line 13; 'day' (2) is echoed in lines 7, 10 and 14 and
as 'say' (9), 'day' (10), 'stay' (12) and 'day' (14); 'dream' (3) is echoed in
line 14; 'sleep' (3) in line 12; 'darkly bright . . . bright in dark' is echoed
in 'bright' (5), 'light' (7), 'night' (11), '*sight*less' (12), 'nights' (13) and
'night's bright' (14); 'shadow shadows' (5) is echoed in 'shadow' (6);
'show' (6) in line 14; 'clear' in 'clearer' (7), and 'shade' (8) in 'made' (9).
There are, moreover, three rhyme-links with the next sonnet (XLIV) –
'so'/'slow', 'stay'/'stay', 'thee'/'thee'. Sonnets XLIV and XLV consist
of a single poem on the *four* elements, the first dealing with the heavier
ones, earth and water, the second with air and fire. The rhyme of XLIV.6
is repeated in XLV.6, and another rhyme, 'gone' (10), is repeated in
XLV.5.[44] There are the same kinds of repetition as in XLIII, though
much less obtrusive. For example, 'space' (3) is echoed in 'place' (8), 'sea'
(7) in 'be' (8), 'wrought' (11) in 'nought' (13), and 'thought' (1) is
repeated in line 7 and twice in line 9. The next two sonnets (XLVI,
XLVII) are another pair, one dealing with a stock theme of war between
the eye and the heart, and the other with an alliance between them.
Critics have compared sonnets by Watson, Constable, Drayton and
Barnes, not to mention Ronsard and Petrarch.[45] It has been suggested
that the sonnets were inspired by a portrait – presumably a miniature –
of W.H., with which the Poet had been presented. This is possible, but
the Poet may simply be contrasting the actual and imaginary appearance
of his friend. Yet if these four sonnets were written in absence, while the
Poet was on a journey, or imagining himself on one, it would be natural
for the friend to give him a portrait – if his affection was even only a
fraction of the Poet's. All these five sonnets are ingenious, but it may
be suspected that they were written (to vary his own phrase) 'to witness
duty and to show his wit'.

Then in XLVIII the Poet's fears about his friend's conduct during
his absence, particularly about his constancy, give the impression of much
greater involvement, of greater seriousness. He contrasts the careful way
in which he locked up his jewels before his departure with his inability
to safeguard his friend, 'left the prey of every vulgar thief' – that is,
his fear that someone will steal his affections. This fear is repeated in
a different form in XLIX (doubly linked by rhymes with XLVIII).
Now the Poet humbly – too humbly, many feel – declares that, if W.H.
were to cast him off, he would not blame him at all, but acknowledge
that he was fully justified in his action,

Since why to love I can allege no cause.

It is a carefully structured poem, each quatrain beginning with the same phrase – 'Against that time' – the first two describing his friend's future desertion, and the third defending it.

A pair of sonnets on travelling away from, and toward, his friend are variations on a theme of Sidney's;[46] but the Poet recovers his form in the sonnets which follow. He bravely attempts to prove that the infrequency of meetings is a blessing in disguise since 'the fine point of seldom pleasure' (LII.4) is thereby left unblunted. Juvenal and Montaigne had expressed the same idea, and Prince Hal remarks that 'nothing pleaseth but rare accidents'.[47]

In LIII the Poet celebrates the beauty of W.H. by comparing it with that of classical figures:

> Describe Adonis and the counterfeit
> Is poorly imitated after you,
> On Helen's cheek all art of beauty set,
> And you in Grecian tires are painted new.

There is an implied contrast between the bounty and constancy of his friend and Adonis' lack of bounty and Helen's inconstancy, but there may also be an allusion to the male-female, master-mistress complexity of XX. The doubts expressed in previous sonnets appear to be forgotten, perhaps because W.H. has not, after all, begun to cool. J. J. Chapman described the sonnet as 'cruelly artificial';[48] it seems rather to be both subtle and complex, and fully to justify the subtle and complex analysis given by Stephen Booth. Commenting, for example, on the first quatrain –

> What is your substance, whereof are you made,
> That millions of strange shadows on you tend?
> Since every one hath, every one, one shade,
> And you, but one, can every shadow lend

– he remarks:

> There are three meanings of *shadow* in the quatrain, and as the reader moves from word to word, his mind jumps from one pattern of understanding to another; the jumps are small ones, but there are many of them. The reader's mind is in the state of constant motion appropriate not to paradoxes or poems but to the actual experience of a paradoxical situation.[49]

The three meanings to which he refers are silhouette; picture, reflection or symbol; and ghost. There are similar ambiguities with regard to 'substance', 'tires' (attires or headdresses) and 'blessed shape'; and 'counterfeit' has an undertone of falsity as 'all art of beauty set' suggests the use of cosmetics.

In LIV Shakespeare reverts to the rosewater image of V and VI; but instead of symbolising offspring it now stands for the poetry which will immortalise W.H.'s truth and constancy. This develops the idea of 'constant heart' from the last line of LIII. Indeed, the poems are linked by two identical rhyme-words – 'show' and 'made'. (Despite this the sonnets have been separated in eight of the proposed rearrangements.) The memory of the earlier sonnets is revealed by the contrast between the canker-blooms that 'live unwoo'd' and 'Die to themselves' and 'sweet roses':

> Of their sweet deaths are sweetest odours made:
> And so of you, beauteous and lovely youth,
> When that shall vade, by verse distills your truth.

This leads on to the Poet's most confident assertion of the immortality which will be conferred by his powerful rhyme (LV). The theme, as we have seen, had been treated by many poets, but nearly all of them were concerned with their own fame in the future; Shakespeare uniquely thinks of the survival of his verse simply as a means to an end – the glory of his friend. Almost, one is inclined to say, he would not greatly mind if his own name were to be forgotten.[50]

After the ringing confidence of LV, there is an inevitable reaction. The 'sad interim' is not merely that of enforced absence: it includes a fear that W.H. has become less affectionate, although this is camouflaged by the Poet's own feelings of apathy, and his injunction to love to renew its force. The apprehension and fear of change are more apparent in LVI, but still not explicit. Accepting the rôle of slave – a rôle obviously inappropriate to a friend – the Poet says he dare not 'chide the world-without-end hour' because he cannot see W.H. as often as he would like. The final couplet shows that he has not been able to hoodwink himself:

> So true a fool is love, that in your will,
> Though you do anything, he thinks no ill.

In the light of this confession, LVIII is bound to seem equally ambiguous. Although it begins

> That God forbid that made me first your slave
> I should in thought control your times of pleasure

and goes on to say he will not crave a reckoning of how W.H. spends his time, and although he resolves to tame patience and suffer his friend's liberty without accusing him of injury, it is apparent that he does feel injured:

> I am to wait, though waiting so be hell.[51]

(e) LIX – LXXV

The general theme of the next group of sonnets is Time. The Poet is concerned first with the idea that there is nothing new under the sun; but even though he considers this possibility he is not convinced, for

> Whether we are mended, or whe'er better they,
> Or whether revolution be the same,
>   Oh sure I am the wits of former days
>   To subjects worse have given admiring praise.

The 'subjects worse', we may remember, include Helen and Adonis.

Several of the following sonnets are concerned with the effects of Time on the Poet himself, on his friend, and on the world. Dr Turner has pointed out that if

> we are to pursue Shakespeare's ideas about time, we must do it largely through the images he uses. Shakespeare thinks in symbols and in emotional and moral intuitions. He tests an idea not by its internal logical coherence but rather by its appeal to his imagination, his heart, and his moral sense; and by its applicability in a real situation or a concrete image.[52]

This, I believe, is true, although, as we have seen, some of the imagery was taken directly from Ovid, and some of the ideas indirectly from Pythagoras. There is no reason to believe that Shakespeare had made a study of philosophy, but certain philosophical ideas had become common property and were known to educated Elizabethans from translations of Cicero's *Tusculan Disputations* and other classical and medieval writings. Shakespeare is known to have read Montaigne, Erasmus, Elyot, and Plutarch's *Moralia*, for example; and, although he had not read Ficino, he could have acquired some knowledge of neo-Platonism from Hoby's translation of Castiglione or from Spenser's *Fowre Hymnes*. Morals and philosophy were never segregated, and the appeal of an idea to Shakespeare's imagination, heart and moral sense, guided as all three were by his knowledge of Christian teachings, often may have led him to positions which philosophers arrived at by other routes.

Recalling the ceaseless movement of the waves as described by Ovid, Shakespeare writes of the way 'our minutes hasten to their end' (LX) and how Time 'delves the parallels on beauty's brow'; but he trusts that his poems will remind future ages of his friend's 'worth' – no longer, as in XIX, promising to make him 'ever live young'. Nevertheless, he again promises, when W.H. is 'with Time's injurious[53] hand crush'd and o'erworn' (LXIII), to immortalise his beauty and youth. In the next sonnet it is not so much the threat to beauty that perturbs the poet as the general destructiveness of Time, making 'brass eternal slave to mortal rage', the land swallowed by the ocean, the decline and fall of empires, and, above all, the thought that he may lose his friend –

> That Time will come and take my love away

– not by death, for the 'thought is *as* a death', but by the withdrawal of his friendship.

Professor Grivelet points out that there is an ambiguity in the poet's attitude to time:

> To a sober unimpassioned mind there is truly no tyranny, and there-fore no sorrow in the fact that 'swift-footed Time' is 'never-resting'. . . . It is to the eyes and heart of a lover that the universal operation of time appears as fearful and iniquitous.[54]

On this we may comment that the poet, as well as the lover, is neither sober nor unimpassioned; and since we have all been in love, and since (as Blake said) the poetic genius is the true man, and we are all potential poets, only years will bring the philosophic mind – which is not often conducive to the writing of good poetry. We may say, therefore, that it was not merely as a lover but also as a lover of beauty, and even as a man, that Shakespeare hated Time the Destroyer.

In LXV, one of the greatest sonnets, the Poet again returns to the power of verse to ensure immortality;[55] but now the hope of achieving this is more tentative, depending on a miracle – 'unless this miracle have might' – of preserving his love in black ink. He is referring both to W.H. and to his love for him expressed in the sonnets.[56] In the corres-ponding phrase in LXIII, the 'black lines' preserve the beauty of the friend, and only indirectly the Poet's friendship.

Interspersed with these sonnets on Time are others that reveal different aspects of the Poet's relationship with his friend. He knows that W.H.'s love, 'though much', is not so great as his own (LXI.9). He speaks of himself as

> Beated and chopp'd with tann'd antiquity

– a line that implies a considerable gap between the age of himself and that of his friend. It makes it seem unlikely that the Sonnets were written when Shakespeare was under twenty-five years of age (i.e. before 1590), unless they were more largely fictional than most critics are prepared to believe.

In another sonnet, in which the Poet sings of 'human unsuccess/In a rapture of distress', he declares that he would wish to die, were it not that by his death he would leave his love alone (LXVI). He is thinking of the grief his friend would feel, not primarily of his own love as a compensation for the evils of life. (But an alternative explanation of the last line –

> Save that to die I leave my love alone

– is 'Except that, if I were to die, I should simply be leaving my love'.) Ten of the lines of this sonnet begin with 'And', and each of them enumerates one of the evils from which different people suffer in this life, though no one suffers from them all. Hamlet referred to some of them in the lines

> The insolence of office, and the spurns
> That patient merit of the unworthy takes. . . .

One of the evils listed in the sonnet must have been especially bitter to a dramatist: '. . . art made tongue-tied by authority'.

> Tired with all these, for restful death I cry,
> As, to behold desert a beggar born,
> And needy nothing trimm'd in jollity,
> And purest faith unhappily forsworn,
> And gilded honour shamefully misplaced,
> And maiden virtue rudely strumpeted,
> And right perfection wrongfully disgraced,
> And strength by limping sway disablèd,
> And art made tongue-tied by authority,
> And folly, doctor-like, controlling skill,
> And simple truth miscall'd simplicity,
> And captive good attending captain ill:
>> Tired with all these, from these would I be gone,
>> Save that, to die, I leave my love alone.

The next four sonnets (LXVII–LXX) exhibit considerable anxiety about W.H.'s associates, his presence gracing impiety (LXVII.2), although the Poet still believes, or professes to believe, that 'his rose is true' – that there is a real contrast between his natural beauty and imitations of it in his society. W.H. resembles the beauty of olden days before the use of cosmetics and false hair (LXVIII); but the Poet admits (LXIX) that, although even W.H.'s enemies praise his appearance,

> those same tongues that give thee so thine own,
> In other accents do this praise confound
> By seeing farther than the eye hath shown.

The fact that the men he consorts with are dissipated leads observers to assume that he shares their vices, on the proverbial ground of 'birds of a feather'.

> To thy fair flower add the rank smell of weeds.
> But why thy odour matcheth not thy show
> The soil is this, that thou dost common grow.

These lines suggested the devastating final couplet of XCIV.[57]
The Poet nevertheless declares (LXX) that slander is an oblique tribute to his friend's beauty; that it is an example of 'right perfection wrongfully disgrac'd'; that W.H. is pure and unstained; that he has

> pass'd by the ambush of young days,
> Either not assail'd, or victor being charg'd.

In view of the Poet's previous criticisms, one is bound to suspect that he is praising W.H. for virtues he does not possess, in the fond hope that he will be shamed into living up to the praise.
In the next four sonnets (LXXI–LXXIV) the poet anticipates his own death, urging his friend not to grieve –

> No longer mourn for me when I am dead
> Than you shall hear the surly sullen bell
> Give warning to the world that I am fled
> From this vile world with vildest worms to dwell

– lest he should be laughed at for choosing a friend from a lower social class, and (if the Poet is to be identified with Shakespeare himself) with a player, a rogue and a vagabond.[58] The same thought is continued in LXXII:

> My name be buried where my body is
> And live no more to shame nor me nor you.

In LXXIII the Poet writes of the late autumn of his life, ascribing the apparent increase of W.H.'s love to his realisation that the Poet has not long to live.[59] In the next sonnet (LXXIV) the Poet claims that his spirit – his 'better part' in Horatian phrase – will survive in his poems. One curious line –

> The coward conquest of a wretch's knife

– may be, as several editors believe, an allusion to the death of Marlowe, stabbed to death in a tavern brawl, for 'a great reckoning in a little room', though some critics have argued that the wretch is Death, the 'churl Death' of XXXII, and that 'the destruction of the body by death and its subsequent corruption is a squalid tragedy'.[60]

Although LXXV, as critics have pointed out,[61] shares rhymes with LII, and although its opening words, 'So are you', parallel 'So am I' in that sonnet, it also has links with LXXIV ('away', 'life'). Moreover, the line

> Doubting the filching age will steal his treasure

looks back to XLVIII, where the same fear is expressed:

> Art left the prey of every vulgar thief. . . .
> And even thence thou wilt be stol'n, I fear. . . .

It is possible, perhaps, that LXXV had been written earlier and moved to its present position to lead on to the sonnets about the rival poets. But the links between LXXV and LII could be explained more plausibly by supposing that Shakespeare either remembered, or consulted, earlier pages of his manuscript.

As we have seen, the sonnets on Time have given place to others concerned with the approaching death of the poet, human mortality being the most personal and disastrous effect of Time. Yet it is characteristic of Shakespeare that he should contemplate his own death, not from the point of view of his own extinction, but from the point of view of the survivor.

(f) LXXVI–XCVI

In the next sonnet the Poet defends his avoidance of the style that was becoming fashionable – 'new found methods' and 'compounds strange'. As he confesses, he continues to write in his own way in a 'noted weed', so that his lines are immediately recognisable as 'Shakespearian'. He explains this by the fact that his subject is always the same. The next sonnet (LXXVII) accompanied the present of a note-book in which W.H. was encouraged to jot down quotations from his reading. The Poet, by mingling advice in his love and praise, was doing what was regarded as the justification of a friendship between a man and a boy.[62] In LXXVIII he continues the line of thought begun in LXXVI: as his subject and style remained the same, it was inevitable that other poets should imitate him in both respects –

> every *Alien* pen hath got my use
> And under thee their poesy disperse.

Leslie Hotson ingeniously explained the italicising of 'alien' by arguing
that it referred to Thomas Watson, who was apparently born in France.
Ironically enough, there is evidence that Shakespeare was influenced by
Hecatompathia, and none that *The Tears of Fancie* owed anything to
Shakespeare's sonnets. Watson's sonnets, moreover, were addressed not
to a patron but to a disdainful mistress and he is therefore unlikely to
be the alien pen. Shakespeare suggests that W.H. should be prouder of
inspiring his 'rude ignorance' to write as well as more learned poets
than of merely adding 'feathers to the learned's wing' and thus adding
an extra grace to their style.

In the next sonnet (LXXIX) the Poet moves from the general to the
particular – from alien pens to a single rival,' a worthier pen', 'thy poet'.
Once again it has been argued that the reference to the young man's
virtue –

> He lends thee virtue, and he stole that word
> From thy behaviour

– is absurdly incompatible with the condemnation of his vices in earlier
sonnets, which must therefore have been written to someone else, or at
some later time; but such contradictions and fluctuating moods are
characteristic of the whole sequence – not least, as we shall see, of the
sonnets relating to the Dark Lady. We should remember, too, once more,
that we should not read the Sonnets as an autobiography of William
Shakespeare.

The rival is acknowledged (LXXX) as 'a better spirit' as a 'proud
sail', a 'tall' ship, compared with the Poet's 'saucy bark'. Although there
is no overt irony, there may have been a suggestion, in the years following
the destruction of the Spanish Armada, that saucy barks sometimes defeat
great galleons.

The next sonnet (LXXXI) is another promise to immortalise W.H.
– the tenth in the series, and not one of the best, but a reminder to the
recipient that the Poet, unlike his rivals, was able to carry out his
promise. Then the rival poet is criticised more directly (LXXXII). W.H.
is quite entitled to seek

> Some fresher stamp of the time-bettering days

but the rivals are guilty of the 'strained touches' of rhetoric, whereas
Shakespeare aims only at plainness and sincerity:

> Thou truly fair wert truly sympathiz'd
> In true plain words by thy true-telling friend;
>   And their gross painting might be better us'd. . . .

In his heart, one suspects, Shakespeare must have been conscious of the superiority of his own verse. This is apparent at the end of LXXXI and also in his scorn of the volubility of his rivals, which is so different from his own reticence (LXXXIII):

> For I impair not beauty, being mute.
> When others would give life and bring a tomb

– the exaggerations and unreality of a monumental inscription.[63] He turns in the next sonnet (LXXXIV) to reprove what he regards as the bad taste of his friend, declaring that to be so avid for praise is a fault:

> You to your beauteous blessings add a curse,
> Being fond on praise, which makes your praises worse.

The 'beauteous blessings' are the blessings of his beauty, which he enjoys himself and which are blessings also to the beholder. His encouragement of the rival poet –

> When your countenance fill'd up his line

had enfeebled Shakespeare's own verse. It is in this sonnet, which takes up the image of the ship from LXXX, that the Poet hints that his chief rival was not writing for love of W.H., but (as Sir Sidney Lee accused Shakespeare, though he did not regard it as an accusation) for the material rewards of patronage. He had not been abashed by his rival's claim to be supernaturally inspired, either by spirits or by

> that affable familiar ghost
> Which nightly gulls him with intelligence. . . .

In spite of this satirical portrait, which neatly mocks at his rival's pretensions – solemn, bombastic and deluded – the Poet apparently concedes defeat and says farewell to his friend, 'too dear for my possessing', as he ruefully confesses (LXXXVII). He then proposes to prove that W.H. is virtuous, although forsworn, by setting down a list of his own faults (LXXXVIII), though he is never very specific:

> With mine own weakness being best acquainted,
> Upon thy part I can set down a story
> Of faults conceal'd wherein I am attainted. . . .

He declares that, if he has been abandoned for some offence, he will deliberately disgrace himself to prove his friend justified:

> Speak of my lameness, and I straight will halt. . . . (LXXXIX)

He then urges W.H., if he is going to break off their friendship, to do it at once and 'join with the spite of fortune' – some blow, either professional or personal, presumably unconnected with the story of the Sonnets – and not postpone his desertion until later, and

> Come in the rearward of a conquer'd woe. (XC)

But the friend's love, precarious as it now seems, is still 'better than high birth', 'Richer than wealth' (XCI),

> Wretched in this alone, that thou mayst take
> All this away and me most wretched make.

He comforts himself with the thought that he is not dependent on W.H.'s humour; for he will either be happy in his continued friendship or die if he loses it (XCII). At the end of this sonnet, and throughout the next, the Poet surmises that W.H. may be false without his knowing it:

> So shall I live, supposing thou art true
> Like a deceived husband. . . .

The friend's beauty would then be like Eve's apple, and this would raise in an acute form what proved to be Shakespeare's obsessive concern, the contrast between virtue and show, between appearance and reality.

The next sonnet (XCIV), as many critics have recognised,[64] appears at first sight to be a warm testimonial to a self-controlled man, one who is not

> a pipe for Fortune's finger
> To sound what stop she please.

But the character described in the sonnet – and from the parallel with LXIX mentioned above one is driven to suppose he is W.H. – is observed with irony, and even with a trace of repulsion. It is by no means admirable to move others – to arouse their love or enmity – and to remain as stone. To 'husband Nature's richest from expense' is to be like the miser condemned in the procreation sonnets, living and dying to himself, or like the servant in the parable who buries his talent. To be 'the lords and owners of their faces' implies a ludicrous self-sufficiency; and the warning about base infection and festering lilies reads almost as a prophecy. Indeed, in the next two sonnets (XCV, XCVI) the flower has met with base infection. Now the Poet speaks frankly of his friend's shame, of his sins and vices, warning him that his beauty will not permanently cover up every blot (XCV.11). The nature of his vices is apparent from the way people gossip,

> Making lascivious comments on thy sport. . . .

But, as the Poet makes plain, the contrast between W.H.'s beauty and the ugliness of his behaviour is a danger in itself, for it makes the vices acceptable:

> How many lambs might the stern wolf betray,
> If like a lamb he could his looks translate!
> How many gazers mightst thou lead away
> If thou wouldst use the strength of all thy state!

As Alden suggested, the character sketched in these two sonnets is similar to that of the anti-hero of 'A Lover's Complaint'.[65]

> Thus merely with the garment of a grace
> The naked and concealed fiend he cover'd,
> That th' unexperient gave the tempter place,
> Which, like a cherubin, above them hover'd.

> O, that infected moisture of his eye,
> O, that false fire which in his cheek so glowed,
> O, that forc'd thunder from his heart did fly,
> O, that sad breath his spongy lungs bestowed. . . .

It should be mentioned, however, that the seducer of the poem does not seem to be 'as stone', but he appears to his victims to be passionately in love.

(g) XCVII–CVIII

At this point there is a break in the sequence: some months appear to have elapsed. The Poet has been absent in the summer and autumn (XCVII) –

> this time remov'd was summer's time
> The teeming autumn, big with rich increase

– and also in April (XCVIII), but this was probably on some previous occasion:

> From you have I been absent in the spring
> When proud-pied April, dress'd in all his trim,
> Hath put a spirit of youth in everything. . . .

There are no longer any criticisms of W.H.; instead, the Poet thinks of their separation as a winter, and he is full of apologies because of the drying up of his verse-tributes to his friend. His Muse has played truant (CI) and he asks:

> Where art thou Muse that thou forget'st so long
> To speak of that which gives thee all thy might? (C)

He claims that, despite appearances, his love is stronger than ever (CII).

Sandwiched between these sonnets is a fifteen-line poem (XCIX), a sonnet preceded by a kind of stage-direction – 'The forward violet thus did I chide' – and including comparisons of W.H.'s qualities with other flowers. It is one of the most trivial poems in the whole sequence, but it is closely linked to XCVIII by references to the odour and hue of different flowers, including lilies and roses. But, whereas the flowers in that sonnet 'were but sweet, but figures of delight drawn after' W.H., the more precise comparisons in XCIX are much more artificial. It may be worth pointing out that XCVIII has rhyme-links with C ('delight'/'light'; 'play'/'decay'), and it is possible that the intervening sonnet was inserted between them as an afterthought. In CIII, in which the Poet complains of the poverty of his Muse, blaming it unreasonably on his friend's face

> That overgoes my blunt invention quite,
> Dulling my lines,

we may, perhaps, detect a realisation that the straining for effect in XCIX was a danger sign.

The normal deduction to make from CIV is that the Poet had become acquainted with W.H. some three years earlier:

> Three winters cold
> Have from the forests shook three summers' pride,
> Three beauteous springs to yellow autumn turn'd.

Sir Sidney Lee, however, anxious to prove that Shakespeare's inspiration was literary rather than personal, pointed out that Ronsard, Desportes and Daniel all spoke of a three-year period. It is not a question of either/or. What matters rather is that the scents, sounds and colours of the four seasons are beautifully conveyed in the first two quatrains – marred only by the jarring juxtaposition in line 2 of 'eye I eyed'. In the final couplet, there is an interesting switch from 'thou' to 'you':

> hear this, thou age unbred,
> Ere you were born was beauty's summer dead.

This was presumably to distinguish between the age and the people living in it, and not, as some have suggested,[66] to avoid an excess of sibilants, since 'thou wert', substituted for 'you were', would not substantially add to them.

It has been suggested by a number of critics[67] that a line in the next sonnet (CV) –

> To one, of one, still such, and ever so

– is linked with one in LXII –

> And all my soul, and all my every part

– and hence with the motto of the Southampton family, 'Ung par tout, et tout par ung'. (Hotson is equally plausible when he uses the sonnet in support of his case that William Hatcliffe was the recipient.) Although Baldwin supported the Southampton theory, the long and learned chapter in which he argues for it does not necessarily lead to this conclusion. He quotes from many Elizabethan writers – Sir John Davies, Drayton, Kyd, Sylvester, Marston – to show that Shakespeare's contemporaries were familiar with the belief that the soul was 'all in all, and all in every part'. The idea is to be found in Plotinus and St Thomas Aquinas, and it had become a commonplace by the sixteenth century. Pistol, who was more at home in the playhouse than among philosophers, quotes it in *2 Henry IV* (Act V, sc. v, ll. 25 *ff.*) and by this time it had become assimilated with *semper idem* and with the idea of constancy. This is the burden of Shakespeare's 'songs and praises':

> Kind is my love today, tomorrow kind,
> Still constant in a wondrous excellence;
> Therefore my verse, to constancy confin'd,
> One thing expressing, leaves out difference.

In the next sonnet (CVI), which is analogous to LIII, the Poet suggests that in old descriptions of 'ladies dead and lovely knights'

> I see their antique pen would have express'd
> Even such a beauty as you master now.

There follows a sonnet (CVII) which has attracted a vast commentary because it appears to refer to some historical event – a belief which is supported, as Hotson pointed out, by its relationship with Psalm 107, a psalm of deliverance.[68] Rollins details the various dates which have been advanced for this sonnet – from 1579, when Shakespeare was fifteen years of age, to 1609, when peace was signed between Spain and the United Provinces. In that thirty-year period, the least improbable dates would appear to be 1588 – in which case the mortal (or deadly) moon would refer to the crescent formation of the Armada in the English Channel; 1596, when Elizabeth I – the mortal moon as opposed to the immortal Diana – survived her grand climacteric; and 1603, when Elizabeth was succeeded peacefully by James I – in which case 'endured' must mean 'suffered'. Some have supposed that there was an allusion to an actual, rather than a metaphorical, eclipse; but as there were twenty-one eclipses between 1592 and 1609 this does not help us to date the sonnet.

It is by no means certain, however, that there are allusions to actual events. Baldwin suggested that the sonnet originated in the prophecies of CVI – the praises of old writers being prophecies of W.H. – and in the fears of mortality expressed in CIV.[69] The first quatrain is an answer to the question posed in LXV:

> How with this rage shall beauty hold a plea,
> Whose action is no stronger than a flower?

The Poet answers that the lease of his true love cannot be controlled. Baldwin believed that the lines

> Incertainties now crown themselves assur'd,
> And peace proclaims Olives of endless age

do not refer to the end of a war or the signing of a peace treaty but simply to the certainties in the poet's heart that his love is not subject to time, and that he and his friend will live in his 'poor rhyme'. This is ingenious, but most readers will continue to believe that Shakespeare was alluding to actual events in the world of affairs. Whatever the historical events, whether real or imaginary, the Poet declares that his love is not controlled by fears of the future, or even by the death that awaits us all; but he is encouraged by some unexpected good news to reaffirm his confidence that both his love, and his expression of it in his poetry, would endure:

> Now with the drops of this most balmy time
> My love looks fresh, and Death to me subscribes,
> Since, spite of him, I'll live in this poor rhyme,
> While he insults o'er dull and speechless tribes.
>   And thou in his shalt find thy monument,
>   When tyrants' crests and tombs of brass are spent.

In this sonnet the Poet's love looks fresh: in the next he writes of 'eternal love in love's fresh case', comparing the repetitions inevitable in a sonnet sequence with the ritual of divine prayers. He had asked earlier (CV):

> Let not my love be called idolatry. . . .

In the present sonnet he comes near to idolatry in his echo of the Lord's Prayer:

> Even as when first I hallow'd thy fair name.

(h) C I X – C X X V I

In many of the last group of sonnets addressed to the friend the Poet is defending himself against the accusation that he has been unfaithful. Travel is now merely a metaphor. His friend's breast is his 'home of love' (CIX):

> If I have rang'd,
> Like him that travels I return again,
> Just to the time, not with the time exchang'd. . . .

He protests that his nature could never

> so preposterously be stain'd
> To leave for nothing all thy sum of good. . . .

But in the next sonnet he admits:

> I have gone here and there
> And made myself a motley to the view,
> Gor'd mine own thoughts, sold cheap what is most dear,
> Made old offences of affections new.

The theatrical image does not imply that he was referring to his job as an actor, or that he had made use of his friendship for dramatic copy. As L. C. Knights observes, 'the reference seems to be to the way in which a sensitive intelligence has displayed its wares of wit and observation in common intercourse'.[70] It is not unlike Jonson's remark, '*sufflaminandus erat*', though this probably referred to Shakespeare's writings, as it was part of a retort to Hemming and Condell's boast that there were hardly any blots or erasures in his manuscripts. Although, as Ingram and Redpath note, 'gored' was a term used both in dressmaking and heraldry, the primary meaning here is 'wounded'. Both Achilles and Hamlet are perturbed by the way their fame, or name, has been gored. The Poet's new friendships are offences against his old friendship with W.H. both because they are inferior and because they have a smack of infidelity; and he excuses himself by saying that experiences with others proved that W.H. was his 'best of love'.

In CXI, however, he does blame his profession, explaining that public means breed public manners, either because an actor is tempted to go on performing in his social life, or because, as the following lines suggest, he is compelled to give the public what it wants:

> And almost thence my nature is subdu'd
> To what it works in, like the dyer's hand.

He rejects some charges as 'vulgar scandal' and declares that his ears are stopped both to critics and flatterers and that he cares only for what his friend thinks (CXII). A few sonnets later (CXVIII) he admits again that he has neglected W.H., that he has 'frequent been with unknown minds', and that he has busied himself with less important things than his friendship; then he tries to excuse himself – it is palpably an excuse rather than a defence – by saying that he had done those things to test 'the constancy and virtue' of W.H.'s love. The last of his defences (CXXI) is a variation on the theme of 'judge not that you be not judged':

> No: I am that I am, and they that level
> At my abuses reckon up their own;
> I may be straight though they themselves be bevel;
> By their rank thoughts my deeds must not be shown

– unless his traducers admit that all men, including themselves, are equally corrupt, that they believe in the doctrine of man's total depravity.

Amongst this group of apologetic sonnets are others in which the Poet protests that he loves his friend more than ever, notably in CXV:

> Those lines that I before have writ do lie,
> Even those that said I could not love you dearer.

The next sonnet, as Ingram and Redpath say, is 'a meditative attempt to define perfect love', with no direct reference to W.H. Nevertheless, as Landry points out, the sonnet does have links with those adjacent to it, in which it appears that the Poet himself has been guilty of 'alteration' (CXV.8), and in which, as we have seen, he has expressed sorrow for his behaviour and tried to excuse it. So the couplet in CXVII –

> Since my appeal says I did strive to prove
> The constancy and virtue of your love

– could be regarded as an allusion to:

> If this be error and upon me prov'd,
> I never writ, nor no man ever lov'd.

Landry therefore concludes that

> if anyone is to allow impediments to the marriage of faithful, con-
> stant minds, it must be the friend addressed, not the unfaithful poet.
> The remover in question is the speaker, the one who has recently
> changed allegiance, and the one who is guilty of alteration. It is the
> friend's love for him which must not alter in the face of alteration or
> be inclined to seek a new object.[71]

This is part of Landry's reply to Winters's misinterpretation of the
sonnet, but it relies too much on the immediate context and too little on
the general context of the sequence as a whole, which is more concerned
with W.H.'s coldness, self-sufficiency, betrayal and inconstancy than with
the Poet's temporary alienation. It is obvious, too, that the reference to
'rosy lips and cheeks' are much more appropriate to the master-mistress
of the Poet's passion than to the Poet himself – if, indeed, they should
be applied to either. True love, Shakespeare is saying, does not depend
on reciprocity or constancy in the beloved, and it survives the loss of
external beauty,

> Outliving beauty's outward, with a mind
> That doth renew swifter than blood decays.[72]

It is not subject to Time. This is the Poet's credo, irrespective of the
immediate experience to which it is related.[73]

In CXVIII the Poet compares his newer friends with 'bitter sauces',
'eager compounds' and medicines, because he was 'sick of welfare' in
W.H.'s love, but in the next sonnet he claims

> That better is by evil still made better,
> And ruin'd love when it is built anew
> Grows fairer than at first, more strong, far greater.

He appeals to the fact that W.H. was once unkind to him, 'how once
I suffer'd in your crime', and urges him, with another allusion to the
Lord's Prayer, to forgive his trespass as he had once forgiven his friend's.
Then he renews his vow to be true (CXXIII), despite Time's scythe,
referring again to the declaration of CXVI that Love was not Time's
fool.

In CXXIV the Poet contrasts the permanence and security of love with the impermanence and insecurity of public life – as he had done in XXV before the various threats to his feeling of security – and now calls to witness

> the fools of time
> Which die for goodness, who have liv'd for crime.

It has been implausibly suggested that Shakespeare was referring to the Catholic martyrs of Elizabeth I's reign. It is difficult to believe that he would regard the missionary priests as living for crime, or that he would think that the Babington conspirators or Guy Fawkes had died for goodness – whatever his own religious beliefs. Perhaps he is merely referring to people who foolishly imagine that a death-bed repentance ensures their salvation. There may be topical references – as with CVII and CXXIII – but the main argument of the sonnet is straightforward. It contrasts the short-sighted policy, which is subject to changes of fortune, to accident, and to disaffection ('thralled discontent'), with the true policy of love, which is not Time's fool – the one policy which is not heretical and is not affected by the dangers previously outlined. The next sonnet continues the same idea. The Poet is denying once more that he is one of the fools of Time, one of the heretics against the true doctrine of love, those who pursue an ultimately self-frustrating policy of self-interest. He is not interested, as he accused his rivals of being, in any material rewards he may obtain from a patron.

> No, let me be obsequious in thy heart,
> And take thou my oblation, poor but free,
> Which is not mix'd with seconds, knows no art,
> But mutual render only me for thee.
> 　　Hence, thou suborn'd informer, a true soul,
> 　　When most impeach'd, stands least in thy control.

The accusation was that the Poet had borne, or wanted to bear, the canopy; but it is not known whether this should be taken literally or metaphorically.

The last poem in the sequence (CXXVI) consists of six couplets in which the Poet frankly admits that his friend will lose his good looks, get old, and eventually die. Whatever the power of poetry may be in preserving for posterity the appearance of the friend as he once was, the lovely boy will cease to be a boy and lose his beauty. It sounds almost as a threat, only partially mitigated by the remembrance that true love is not affected by these effects of Time.

(*i*) CXXVII–CLIV

The remaining sonnets are concerned with the Poet's relations with a woman – some addressed to her (CXXVIII, CXXXI–CXXXVI, CXXXIX–CXLIII, CXLIX–CLII), some about her (CXXVII, CXXX), some discussing the effects of the relationship on him (CXXIX), and some seven or eight dealing with the triangular affair covered in the main sequence, notably those containing quibbles on the various meanings of 'will' and CXLIV in which he writes of his two loves of comfort and despair – the 'man right fair' and the 'woman coloured ill'. Brents Stirling's ingenious rearrangement of the Dark Lady sonnets makes a more coherent story, although still with a number of loose ends: CXXVII, CXXX; CXLIV, CXLIII, CXXXV–CXXXVI, CXXXI–CXXXIV; CXXXVIII–CXL; CXXXVII, CXLI–CXLII, CXLVII–CLII; CXXIX, CXLVI; CLIII–CLIV; CXXVIII? CXLV?[74] John Dover Wilson found the new order greatly superior to that of the Quarto: in it the bitterer sonnets, in which the Poet attacks his own infatuation as well as the woman's morals, are arranged so as to follow the seduction of the friend. Nevertheless, I have become convinced that the harsh juxtapositions of the original text ought not to be smoothed away. There are, as we have seen, similar shocks in the main sequence. It may well be that the order in which the Sonnets were printed differs from that of their composition, but the former may conform to Shakespeare's wishes. In what follows I am indebted to a stimulating chapter in *Shakespeare and the Confines of Art* by Philip Edwards and to an article by Michael J. B. Allen in *Shakespeare Survey*.[75] Professor Edwards argued that Stirling's rearrangement was less true to human experience than the violent oscillations of mood implied in the original order:

Another poet than Shakespeare might have made the lust-sonnet (129) and the mortification-sonnet (146) the culmination of his sequence; at the end of the affair the poet-lover is made to recognize the madness of desire and to turn his back on all earthly things. In his very ingenious and persuasive study, Brents Stirling writes that his hypothesis 'accounts for seemingly random displacement – the appearance of a grim sonnet on lust (129) between the dainty, affected 128 and 130, and the sequential absurdity of a pretty sonnet like 145 followed by the *de profundis* note of 146'. I have tried to show that 129 and 146 have a quite special importance in irrupting into the narrative just where they do in 1609, and in not coming at the end. Shakespeare is dealing with great complexities of the mind and the heart, on to which is added the driving need of the poet to use his art, with all *its* complexities, to make sense of his condition. The course of knowledge will not be a symmetrical graph.

The first sonnet (CXXVII) is a light-hearted defence of the Poet's
unfashionable taste in falling in love with a brunette:

> Therefore my mistress' eyes are raven black,
> Her eyes so suited, and they mourners seem,
> At such who not born fair no beauty lack,
> Sland'ring creation with a false esteem;
> Yet so they mourn becoming of their woe,
> That every tongue says beauty should look so.

It resembles in tone Berowne's defiant defence of his love for Rosaline,
except that the Poet of the Sonnets says nothing here in criticism of his
mistress's morals, whereas Berowne slanders the apparently chaste
Rosaline by calling her 'A whitely wanton with a velvet brow' and saying
that she is promiscuous, 'one that will do the deed'. There is nothing
in the rest of the play to suggest that there was any justification for this
attack: 'black is the badge of hell', but appearances are deceptive.

The next sonnet is a tender playful compliment to the Dark Lady's
skill as a musician; and Sonnet CXXX is at once a parody of bad
sonneteering conventions – similar to the Poet's complaints about the
hyperboles of some of his rivals – and an amusing compliment to the
lady whom he cannot praise in hyperbolic terms, but whom he believes
to be

> as rare
> As any she belied with false compare.

But sandwiched between these complimentary sonnets is one in which
the lady is not mentioned, but which is a violent exposure of the sin of
lust:

> Th'expense of spirit in a waste of shame

– the spending of sperm in a shameful waist, as well as the waste of
one's spiritual qualities in an unspiritual activity. This comes with double
force because of the innocuous nature of the surrounding poems.

'My mistress' eyes are nothing like the sun' is followed by a sonnet
which explicitly states that the mistress is black only in her deeds – a
remark which makes it unnecessary to assume that she was literally
dark, and nearly impossible to believe that she was a negress. The pity
of her eyes is next contrasted with the cruelty of her heart (CXXXII),
almost as though she were the chaste beauty of the sonneteering convention, and almost (we are tempted to think) as though the Poet had been
foiled in his attempts to share her bed. Even in CXXXIII, where the
Poet's friend is mentioned for the first time, it is not made clear that he

has been seduced, or whether he has been disappointed in his hopes. He, like the Poet, has been given a 'deep wound', he is 'slave to slavery', possibly, but not certainly, enslaved to lust. He is at least equally enamoured of the lady. From CXXXIV it has been surmised that the Poet had asked his friend to visit the lady – possibly to convey a message – and she had seized the opportunity of obtaining such an attractive (and affluent) young man as her lover. This interpretation, however, is by no means certain: 'He learn'd but surety-like to write for me' can have an innocent meaning (i.e. he was merely acting for me), but it is more likely to mean that he had taken the place of the Poet as the lady's lover, especially when we remember the quibbles on 'pen' in the last scene of *The Merchant of Venice*.[76] At least the Poet assumes, or fears, that he has lost both friend and mistress:

> For thou art covetous, and he is kind;
> He learn'd but surety-like to write for me
> Under that bond that him as fast doth bind.
> The statute of thy beauty thou wilt take,
> Thou usurer, that putt'st forth all to use,
> And sue a friend came debtor for my sake;
> So him I lose through my unkind abuse.

Booth points out a number of probable bawdy quibbles in this sonnet – e.g. the phrase 'putt'st forth all to use' can mean 'allow your body to be sexually used'.[77] In this sonnet the Poet admits that he is mortgaged to the woman's will; and in the next two he plays wittily, bawdily and cheerfully on the numerous meanings of 'Will': Will Shakespeare, Will H., possibly Will (the husband of the lady), Will meaning lust, Will meaning both the male and female sexual organs. The Poet pleads that since the lady already has several wills she should accept him, too, as her lover.

> Among a number one is reckon'd none:
> Then in the number let me pass untold

– as merely one, hardly noticeable, among her various Wills.

Then in CXXXVII the tone changes again. Since it is not addressed to the woman, the Poet can eschew both jests and euphemisms. His eyes have been corrupted 'by over-partial looks' and this seems to mean that the lady had given him 'strange oeillades and most speaking looks' to encourage him. His eyes are now 'anchor'd in the bay where all men ride'. He pretends to himself that the woman's favours – at least her extramarital favours – are granted to him alone, but he knows in his heart of hearts that he is one of many. As he savagely puts it, she is 'the wide world's

common place'. The epithet 'wide' reminds us of Thersites' reference to
Cressida being 'secretly open' when she is overly anxious for the consummation of her 'love' for Diomed, and 'common place' recalls the description of Doll Tearsheet as 'some road . . . as common as the way between
Saint Albans and London'.[78]

The bitterness of this sonnet is continued in the next (CXXXVIII) –
one of the poems which had been printed in *The Passionate Pilgrim*.
The poet again contrasts the pretence that he believes his mistress's
protestations of fidelity with his inner convictions that she is lying. For
her to tell such patent lies means that she is treating him as 'some
untutor'd youth', which is another falsehood, since she knows he is 'past
the best' of his age. But the Poet blames himself for pretending to be
hoodwinked, and he allows the lies and pretences because 'love's best
habit is in seeming trust' or, as Eliot was to put it, 'Human kind cannot
bear very much reality'. The sonnet ends with a characteristic quibble:

> Therefore I lie with her, and she with me,
> And in our faults by lies we flattered be.

In CXXXIX there is another change of tone. Now the Poet pleads
with the lady to be honest and confess that she loves elsewhere:

> but in my sight,
> Dear heart, forbear to glance thine eye aside –
> What need'st thou wound with cunning, when thy might
> Is more than my o'erpress'd defence can bide?

This is plainly not an address to a known wanton, but to a woman the
Poet thinks may still love him. Then in CXL he changes again. Now he
begs her, if she does not love him, at least to tell him that she still does,

> As testy sick men, when their deaths be near,
> No news but health from their physicians know.

The Poet is reduced in spirit to the abjectness of Molière's Alceste:

> Efforcez-vous ici de paraître fidèle,
> Et je m'efforcerai, moi, de vous croire telle.

In the next sonnet (CXLI) he describes how all his five senses dis-
approve of his infatuation. They do not

> desire to be invited
> To any sensual feast with thee alone.

Neither his five wits nor his five senses can deter him from loving her; but he derives some consolation from the pain she inflicts, since he can regard it as a punishment for his sin: 'she that makes me sin awards me pain'.

Some of the pain she awards is revealed in CXLII. She professes to hate him:

> Hate of my sin, grounded on sinful loving.

He protests that her lips

> have profan'd their scarlet ornaments
> And seal'd false bonds of love as oft as mine,
> Robb'd others' beds' revenues of their rents.

He knows that her real reason for repulsing him is that she is pursuing other lovers. One such pursuit is playfully described in the next sonnet, in terms of a housewife, a feathered creature, and the woman's baby. The Poet, in the rather absurd rôle of her baby, apparently acquiesces in her promiscuity, if he is allowed to share her favours. The idea goes back to CXXXV and CXXXVI, but is here developed more feebly:

> So will I pray that thou mayst have thy Will

– the other William and her sexual satisfaction –

> If thou turn back and my loud crying still.

Here the sin is forgotten, but it is remembered again with additional force in CXLIV, when the Poet makes his most explicit statement of his two loves, of comfort and despair, of his uncertainty, apparently during his absence, whether W.H. had fallen a victim to the woman's attempts to seduce him. He will not know for certain until 'my bad angel fire my good one out' – until, that is, she infects his friend with a venereal disease. It is a brutal way of implying that she is a common whore, rather than a medical diagnosis or an acknowledgement that he himself had become infected. The contrast between the good and evil angels, between saint and devil, between purity and 'foul pride', and between hell and heaven is a general contrast not so much between two people – for W.H. is more lascivious than saintly – as between two kinds of love: selfless adoration, the marriage of true minds, the spiritual love celebrated by Ficino and Castiglione on the one hand, and the expense of spirit in a waste of shame on the other. This contrast is one which is crucial to the Poet of the Sonnets, but not necessarily to Shakespeare himself.

The next sonnet, in octosyllabics, is trivial and gay. It may even be Shakespeare's earliest extant poem written to Anne Hathaway before Shakespeare's marriage.[79] At least we are worlds away from the soul-searching of his previous sonnet. Then in CXLVI we move from the most trivial of all Shakespeare's poems to the only sonnet directly concerned with salvation, an address to the soul, urging it to lay up for itself treasure in heaven. This is one of the dramatic meditations discussed by Melchiori, and we shall have occasion to return to his interpretation.[80] Here it need only be said that tidy minds would like this to be the last sonnet in the sequence – a farewell to love, like the two sonnets that earlier editors tacked on to the *Astrophil and Stella* sequence. But, as Dowden rightly argued, CXLVII is linked with the previous one. The feeding metaphor –

> Within be fed, without be rich no more;
> So shalt thou feed on Death, that feeds on men

– is carried over into the sickness image of CXLVII:

> Feeding on that which doth preserve the ill,
> Th' uncertain sickly appetite to please.

Reason, the Poet's physician, who had warned him that desire was death, had now left him for not following his prescription. As a result,

> Past cure I am now reason is past care. . . .

He is 'frantic mad' and 'At random from the truth':

> For I have sworn thee fair, and thought thee bright,
> Who art as black as hell, as dark as night.

The idea of this couplet is developed in CXLVIII where the Poet admits his blindness and lack of judgement. Blindness is also the culmination of CXLIX:

> But, Love, hate on; for now I know thy mind:
> Those that can see thou lov'st, and I am blind.

These four sonnets are linked by common rhymes as well as by continuity of theme: 'lease' (CXLVI)/'please' (CXLVII); 'bright' (CXLVII)/'sight' (CXLVIII); 'blind' (CXLVIII)/'blind' (CXLIX). It may be added that CL echoes 'sight' from CXLVIII, 'sway' from CXLVI, 'ill' from CXLVII, 'more' from CXLVI. Both CXLIX and CL are appeals for pity because the Poet has given the lie to his true sight and worshipped even the defects of his mistress. The penultimate line of CL –

> If thy worthiness raised love in me

– leads on to the bawdiness of CLI where the raising of love becomes avowedly sexual, and where 'rise and fall' are used in the sense of tumescence and detumescence. Earlier in this sonnet, the Poet plays on the two meanings of conscience and writes of his erotic experiences with the lady with some relish and no overt sense of sin. This sense returns, however, in the next sonnet, with a full consciousness of his own adultery and that of his mistress, and of her infidelity to him, and also of his blindness – one of the recurrent themes of this second sequence :

> In loving thee thou know'st I am forsworn,
> But thou art twice forsworn, to me love swearing;
> In act thy bed-vow broke, and new faith torn
> In vowing new hate after new love bearing.
> But why of two oaths' breach do I accuse thee,
> When I break twenty? I am perjur'd most;
> For all my vows are oaths but to misuse thee,
> And all my honest faith in thee is lost;
> For I have sworn deep oaths of thy deep kindness,
> Oaths of thy love, thy truth, thy constancy;
> And, to enlighten thee, gave eyes to blindness,
> Or made them swear against the thing they see;
>   For I have sworn thee fair – more perjur'd I,
>   To swear against the truth so foul a lie!

The last two sonnets, alternate versions of a variation by a Latin poet of a poem in the Greek Anthology, seem to have little connection with the rest of the sequence. Stirling, however, links them with the group of sonnets which mention the lady's eyes. They both refer to the failure of the waters to cure the Poet of his infatuation and therefore echo the 'past cure' of CXLVIII. The sequence ends, therefore, on a quiet indeterminate note after all the drama, the self-laceration, the obscene wit and the shame.

CHAPTER 5

Style

(a) STRUCTURE

We have been concerned in the last chapter with what Hubler calls 'the sense of Shakespeare's sonnets', and we have touched on questions of style only when it was necessary for the exposition of that concern. But, of course, it is the style that lifts the Sonnets far above those of Shakespeare's contemporaries and justifies his confidence in the survival of his powerful rhyme.

One characteristic of his style has already been mentioned[1] – the impression he gives of complete naturalness, however 'poetic' the diction, however elaborate the imagery, however complex the phonetic patterns,[2] and however many types of ambiguity he has up his sleeve. This naturalness is due partly to his tact and restraint, partly to his consciousness, aroused perhaps by Sidney, of the poetic cliches of the time and his avoidance of those which had not been proved upon his pulses, but mostly to the instinct of a practising dramatist not to stray too far from colloquial speech. Often he does stray, but always to return again: even with his singing robes about him, he is a man speaking to men. This was a lesson that Shakespeare learnt painfully as he gradually abandoned the stilts of his predecessors and began to walk on his own feet.

In this chapter the first thing that needs to be stressed is the variety of structure in the sequence. The Shakespearian form – of three quatrains followed by a couplet – is often contrasted with the Italian form divided into octave and sestet. It may be mentioned that some Italian poets deliberately avoided a break at the end of the eighth line; but it is true that the differing structures influence the organisation of material. The sestet in the Italian form is often a particular application of a general statement enunciated in the octave, and sometimes a reply to it; whereas the three quatrains of the Shakespearian sonnet, whether parallel statements or a continuous argument, are often clinched or contradicted by the epigrammatic couplet. But as soon as one makes a generalisation of this kind, one realises that there are so many exceptions that its validity is called in question. Shakespeare, in fact, wrote so many different kinds of sonnet that any definition fits only a proportion of the whole. This may be illustrated from T. W. Baldwin's book, which is packed with information valuable to any serious reader of the Sonnets. Having shown that Erasmus in a text-book for grammar school consumption, bases his most perfect *argumentatio* upon *Ad Herennium* and *Cicero* as follows (1) *propositio,* (2) *ratio,* (3) *propositionis assumptio,* (4) *assumptionis ratio,* (5) *complexio,* Brinsley phrases this framework for a theme as (1) *exordium,* (2) *narratio,* (3) *confirmatio,* (4) *confutatio,* (5) *conclusio.*

Baldwin goes on to argue that Shakespeare used these basic forms:

> In the sonnets, the first quatrain is always *propositio,* the couplet is always intended to be some form of *complexio* or *conclusio.* The second quatrain is regularly some form of *ratio.* The third quatrain then has its choice from the numerous possibilities of the other two sections

(i.e. Erasmus' 3 and 4, Brinsley's 3 and 4, *rationis confirmatio* and *exornatio.*)[3]

We may take III as an example:

1st quatrain: 'Now is the time that face should form another. . . .' (*Propositio*) You ought to marry.

2nd quatrain: 'Where is she . . . Disdains the tillage of thy husbandry?' (*Ratio*) Any woman would be glad to bear your children.

3rd quatrain: 'Thou art thy mother's glass . . . So thou . . . shalt see . . . this thy golden time.' (*Confirmatio*) You could see yourself in your children.

Couplet: 'Die single and thine image dies with thee.' (*Conclusio*) If you don't marry, your image will not be perpetuated.

There are a number of other sonnets which fit neatly into Baldwin's scheme, but one has to search for them. To the great majority it appears to be quite inappropriate. The scheme was a valuable means of training pupils to set out their arguments or themes in an orderly way – one could wish that some persons in our public life had undergone as rigorous a training – but it was less useful for poetic composition. Some of the sonnets have an argument to advance and could properly use the techniques the poet learnt at school; but even here Shakespeare characteristically used what he had been taught merely as guide-lines: his practice varied according to the material with which he was wrestling.

One structural device used by Shakespeare is to make the couplet act as a kind of QED to the argument advanced in the quatrains. Then the thirteenth line begins with such words as 'Thus', 'Therefore', 'Then' and 'So', and these appear to clinch the argument:

> So thou, thyself outgoing in thy noon,
> Unlook'd on diest unless thou get a son. (VII)

> Then happy I that love and am beloved
> Where I may not remove, nor be removed. (XXV)

> Thus have I had thee as a dream doth flatter
> In sleep a King, but waking no such matter. (LXXXVII)

Sometimes the couplet offers a reason to confirm what has gone before:

> For thy sweet love rememb'red such wealth brings,
> That then I scorn to change my state with kings. (XXIX)

> For I am sham'd by that which I bring forth,
> And so should you, to love things nothing worth. (LXXII)

More common, however, is the use of the couplet to contradict or modify the quatrains. This is signalled by 'But' and 'Yet' in some thirty sonnets; and there are others beginning with 'Oh' and 'Or else' which have the same effect.

> But flowers distill'd, though they with winter meet,
> Leese but their show, their substance still lives sweet. (V)

> But if the while I think on thee (dear friend)
> All losses are restor'd, and sorrows end. (XXX)

> And yet to times in hope my verse shall stand
> Praising thy worth, despite his cruel hand. (LX)

> But what's so blessed fair that fears no blot;
> Thou maist be false, and yet I know it not. (XCII)

Other couplets merely carry on and complete the ideas expressed in the three quatrains; and often in such cases the thirteenth line begins with 'And':

> And all in war with Time for love of you,
> As he takes from you, I engraft you new. (XV)

> And even thence thou wilt be stol'n I fear,
> For truth proves thievish for a prize so dear. (XLVIII)

> And other strains of woe which now seem woe,
> Compar'd with loss of thee, will not seem so. (XC)

Some critics have regarded the Shakespearian form of the sonnet as unsatisfactory because a lyric should not end with an epigram; and Shakespeare's own couplets have been regarded as insincere or meretricious because they conflict with the genuine feeling of the previous twelve lines. A perfunctory compliment to W.H. fails to dissipate the sense of melancholy and tragedy which the Sonnets mainly express. Even Hubler and Barber complain of the feebleness of the couplets. The best defence is that of Rosalie Colie, who begins by quoting Harington's comparison of the sonnet and the epigram – sugar and salt – and Scaliger's division of epigrams into *mel* (honey), *fel* (gall), *acetum* (vinegar) and *sal* (salt). She notes the reputation of Shakespeare for his 'sugared sonnets' and suggests that

> in his friend and his mistress, Shakespeare animated lyric and epigrammatic styles, gave concentrated personality to *mel* and *sal*, worked out in human terms the implications of their separate decorums. Out of the styles, twinned and opposed, linked and contrasted, of epigram and amatory epigram, he constructed his triangle of active figures, with himself as poet responding to the demands of both friends, coming to terms with their requirements of him, and through their means coming to terms with love and with himself as lover. Both the banquet of *agape* and the sensual feast were heightened and refined, to this poet's taste anyway, by the pinch of salt.[4]

When we turn to the quatrains, we find an even greater variety. Sometimes, as we have mentioned, the three quatrains seem to be variations on a single theme, using different metaphors for parallel statements. Sonnet LXXIII is a splendid example. Each quatrain states that the Poet is getting old, but with a complexity of imagery which we shall examine later. Another example is LXV, in which each quatrain describes the ravages of Time, each ending with a question:

> Since brass, nor stone, nor earth, nor boundless sea,
> But sad mortality o'ersways their power,
> How with this rage shall beauty hold a plea,
> Whose action is no stronger than a flower?
> Oh how shall summer's honey breath hold out
> Against the wrackful siege of batt'ring days,
> When rocks unpregnable are not so stout,
> Nor gates of steel so strong but time decays?
> O fearful meditation! where, alack,
> Shall Time's best jewel from Time's chest lie hid?
> Or what strong hand can hold his swift foot back,
> Or who his spoil [of] beauty can forbid?

There are, however, comparatively few sonnets constructed in this way. More frequently the argument is developed throughout the three quatrains, without this kind of repetition. In one sonnet, LXVI, the single-line units make us forget that we are reading quatrains:

> And needy nothing trimm'd in jollity,
> And purest faith unhappily forsworn,
> And gilded honour shamefully misplac'd,
> And maiden virtue rudely strumpeted. . . .

In a few sonnets the first quatrain is followed by a second which qualifies it:

> What old December's bareness everywhere!
> And yet this time. . . .   (XCVII)

> That heavy Saturn laugh'd and leapt with him,
> Yet. . . .   (XCVIII)

A more usual turning-point of the argument is after the second quatrain, thus dividing the sonnet into an octave and sestet. As with the comparable couplets, the turn is signalled by 'but' and 'yet':

> And every fair from fair sometime declines,
> By chance, or Nature's changing course untrimm'd: (8)
> But thy eternal summer shall not fade. (XVIII)

> With what I most enjoy contented least. (8)
> Yet in these thoughts my self almost despising. . . . (XXIX)

> To me, fair friend, you never can be old
> For as you were when first your eye I eyed,
> Such seems your beauty still. . . .
> Since first I saw you fresh which yet are green.
> Ah! yet doth beauty like a dial hand. . . . (CIV)

Stephen Booth believes that in 96 of the 152 fourteen-line sonnets there 'is a perceptively distinct octave' and in the 56 others no distinct octave.[5] Some would transfer several of the latter category (e.g. XXXI, XXXVIII, LIII, LX), but this depends on how far we press the word 'distinct'. Booth's divisions are generally acceptable. But he is one of the critics who have shown the extraordinary variety of the structure of the Sonnets and the necessity of considering each one separately. He rightly points out that C. S. Lewis's pages on the Sonnets, which start from the remark that 'the rhetorical structure is often that of theme and variations', are most successful when Lewis gets down to individual and exceptional cases. Booth, Winifred Nowottny in two brilliant articles, and Giorgio Melchiori in his commentary on five sonnets have provided us with concrete examples of the value of detailed analysis of the structure of individual sonnets.[6]

A few examples may be given of diverse structural patterns. In XLIX each quatrain begins with the words 'Against that time'. The first, using an image of auditing, imagines W.H. frowning on the Poet's defects; the second supposes that love has been superseded by disapproval; the third declares that when that time comes the Poet will support the decision. In LXIII the three quatrains form a single sentence, with an actual enjambment between the fourth line of the first quatrain and the first line of the second:

> When his youthful morn
> Hath travell'd on to age's sleepy night. . . .

Sonnet XVIII has been described by C. S. Lewis:

> As often, the theme begins at line 9 . . . occupying four lines, and the application is in the couplet. Line 1 proposes a simile ('Shall I compare thee to a summer's day?'). Line 2 corrects it ('Thou art more lovely and more temperate'). Then we have two one-line *exempla* justifying the correction: then a two-line *exemplum* about the sun: then two more lines
> > (And every fair from fair sometime declines,
> > By chance or Nature's changing course untrimm'd)
> which do not, as we had expected, add a fourth *exemplum* but generalize. Equality of length in the two last variations is thus played off against difference of function.[7]

As a last example, we may recall that in XXIII the first two lines of the second quatrain refer to the simile of the first two lines of the first quatrain ('As an unperfect actor') and the remainder of the second quatrain refers to the simile of lines 3 and 4. So the Poet attributes his inability to express his love fully to fear and to excess of love. In the sestet the fear and love are joined to plead for recompense.

It is, of course, impossible to discuss structure in isolation since it becomes meaningful only in relation to phonetic and imagistic patterns.

(b) SOUND

It is difficult to discuss the phonetic patterns of the Sonnets without using phonetics; but, to judge from reactions to David Masson's pioneering articles in this field, phonetics are a discouragement to most readers of poetry, even if I were competent to use them as expertly as he. Most readers seem to prefer to appreciate Shakespeare's sound-effects without analysing them too scientifically. Any good reader can convey to a listener how a sonnet should sound more directly and economically than several pages of commentary. Moreover, Shakespeare never seems to have been as interested in making the sound suggest the sense as Tennyson was. A person with no knowledge of English might possibly guess the subject of the line

> And murmuring of innumerable bees

but no one without knowledge of the language could guess that

> The singing masons building roofs of gold

also referred to bees.[8] Tennyson was also much concerned, and very consciously aware, of the importance of vowel-music and of alliteration. Shakespeare would have learnt about alliteration, along with scores of other devices, from text-books of rhetoric; but his manipulation of vowels seems to have been instinctive.

It is easy to demonstrate the use of simple alliteration and cross-alliteration – of medial as well as of initial letters – the internal rhyme and assonance, and to show that these things please the ear; it is much more difficult to explain what function these devices have apart from the musical.

It will be necessary to discuss in some detail the different kinds of word-patterns used in the Sonnets: (1) the alliteration of initial letters where only two are involved; (2) the alliteration of three or more initial letters; (3) cross-alliteration; (4) the alliteration of other consonants; (5) the linking of lines and sometimes whole quatrains by alliteration; (6) various kinds of internal rhyming; (7) repetitions of words or phrases, some of which were mentioned earlier.

Two alliterated words may be adjacent ('bud buriest' – I.11) or separated –

> Mine eye hath play'd the painter and hath stell'd (XXIV.1)

> And being frank she lends to those are free (IV.4)

> So is it not with me as with that Muse (XXI.1)

In the last two examples the alliteration, as in Old English or medieval verse, binds the two halves of the line together, although in a different way

Often there are three or more alliterated words:

> When to the *s*essions of *s*weet *s*ilent thought (XXX.1)

> *B*eauty's effect with *b*eauty were *b*ereft (V.11)

In *h*im those *h*oly antique *h*ours are seen (LXVIII.9)

(in this line the word 'hours' is presumably not aspirated, though to the eye it seems alliterated)

No, neither he, nor his compeers by night (LXXXVI.9)

(where the alliteration hammers home the poet's scorn of his rival)

The coward conquest of a wretch's knife (LXXIV.11)

The next type is cross-alliteration, sometimes alternating, and sometimes in sandwich form.

As *Ph*ilomel in *s*ummer's *f*ront doth *s*ing (CII.7)

*M*ay *s*till *s*eem love to *m*e, though alter'd new (XCIII.3)

To the ear the repetition of consonants which are not initial letters can nevertheless be significant, especially when they are at the beginning of a syllable.

*W*hen forty *w*inters *s*hall be*s*eige thy *b*row (II.1)

Than you sha*ll* hear the *s*urly *s*u*ll*en be*ll* (LXXI.2)

The linking of lines by alliteration can be illustrated by the first quatrain of CXVIII:

> Like as to make our a*pp*etites more *k*een
> With eager *c*ompounds we our *p*alates urge,
> As to *p*revent our maladies u*n*see*n*,
> We *s*icke*n* to *s*hun *s*ick*n*ess whe*n* we *p*urge.

The internal rhyming is of various kinds. Sometimes the rhyme is in a single line:

The *clear* eye's moiety, and the *dear heart's part* (XLVI.12)

Lean *pe*nury within that *pe*n doth dwell (LXXXIV.5)

Stirr'd by a painted beauty to his *ver*se (XXI.2)

Sometimes the rhyme occurs on the following line:

> O benefit of *ill*! now I find true
> That better is by evil st*ill* made better. (CXIX.9–10)

> Or shall I *live* your epitaph to make,
> Or you *survive*. . . . (LXXXI.1–2)

Sometimes there is a rhyme separated by two lines, which is nevertheless closely linked in sense so that the reader will be conscious of the rhyme:

> Never *believe* . . .
> That it could so preposterously be stain'd
> To *leave* for nothing all thy sum of good. (CIX.9–12)

Occasionally there are whole chains of rhyming.

> And every f*air* with his fair doth rehearse,
> Making a couplement of proud *compare* . . .
> With April's first-born flowers and all things *rare*,
> That heaven's *air* in this huge rondure hems. . . .
> And then believe me, my love is as *fair*
> As any mother's child, though not so bright
> As those gold candles fix'd in heave'n's *air* (XXI)

In XLIII there are numerous repetitions and rhymes on 'bright' (4, 5): 'light' (7), 'night' (11), 'sightless' (12), 'nights' (13), 'night's bright' (14).

The repetition of actual words has already been illustrated under the last heading; but sometimes there is repetition without rhymes. In LXXVII, for example, 'glass' and 'show' appear in the first lines of the first two quatrains; 'memory' appears in lines 6 and 9, 'look' in lines 9 and 13.

It is important, when considering Shakespeare's use of alliteration and assonance, to bear three points in mind – first, that much of it will be missed if one considers only the initial letters of words; secondly, that one ought to consider larger units than the line; and, thirdly, that an alliteration of an initial letter of a stressed word is more significant than the alliteration of a letter in an unstressed word. These points can be illustrated from almost any of the sonnets, but it will be convenient to take the first, which has been discussed in detail by George Wyndham and Anton M. Pirkhofer.[9] The latter, who ignores the three points mentioned above, thinks there are only four lines in the first sonnet which exhibit certain 'horizontal' alliteration, but Wyndham is much less restrictive in his analysis:

> From fairest creatures we desire increase,
> That thereby beauty's Rose might never die,
> But as the riper should by Time decease,

His tender heir might bear his memory.
But thou contracted to thine own bright eyes
Feeds't thy light's flame with self-substantial fuel,
Making a famine where abundance lies,
Thyself thy foe, to thy sweet self too cruel.
Thou that are now the world's fresh ornament,
And only herald to the gaudy spring,
Within thine own bud buriest thy content,
And, tender churl, mak'st waste in niggarding.
    Pity the world, or else this glutton be,
    To eat the world's due by the grave and thee.

In line 1 the first syllable of 'creatures' is echoed in the second syllable of 'increase'. Lines 2 and 3 are linked by assonance ('Die'/'riper') and alliteration ('Die'/'decease'), and lines 3 and 4 by alliteration ('time'/ 'tender') and by assonance ('decease'/'His'). In line 4 'heir' rhymes with 'bear'. In line 5 there is alliteration ('*th*ou con*t*rac*t*ed *t*o *th*ine own brigh*t*') and assonance ('bright eyes'); in line 6 there is alliteration of the letters *s, f, t* and *l* – 'Feedst *th*y *l*ight's *f*lame with se*lf*-substan*t*ial *f*uel'. In the next line 'famine' echoes 'flame'. 'Thyself' in line 8 echoes 'lies' at the end of line 7; and 'foe' alliterates with 'famine'. In the same line, five words begin with *t* and there is assonance in the juxtaposition of 'too' and 'cruel'. In line 9 'thou' rhymes with 'now'. This line is linked by assonance with the next ('spring'/'Within'); and there is alliteration and assonance in the juxtaposed words 'bud buriest'. The last syllable of 'content' is echoed in 'tender' in line 12. In that line, too, there is more assonance ('mak'st waste') and the lines of the final couplet are linked by assonance ('be'/'eat'), by repetition ('world') and by alliteration ('glutton'/'grave'). Pirkhofer doubted whether line 7 contained alliteration; but this picks up the *f* and *l* of line 6 and passes them on to line 8. It should be added that in discussing later sonnets he mentioned the spreading of alliteration over successive lines.[10] It will be unnecessary to examine other sonnets for their sound-effects: it will be apparent from this one example that Shakespeare was fully aware of what he was doing; and, although some of the later sonnets are less highly wrought, the first is not untypical of the sequence.

(c) IMAGERY

The use of imagery in the Sonnets is extremely varied. At times the image is embodied in a single word (e.g. 'beauty's Rose'); at other times in a single line –

Now stand you on the top of happy hours (XVI.5)

And Art made tongue-tied by Authority (LXVI.9)

> And loathsome canker lives in sweetest bud (XXXV.4)

> Your monument shall be my gentle verse (LXXXI.9)

Some of the single-line images are proverbial:

> Lilies that fester smell far worse than weeds (XCIV.14)

> The hardest knife ill-us'd doth lose his edge (XCV.14)

More frequently the images are expressed in two lines:

> Like as to make our appetites more keen
> With eager compounds we our palate urge. (CXVIII.1–2)

> Ah! yet doth beauty like a dial hand
> Steal from his figure and no pace perceiv'd. . . . (CIV.9–10)

Often the image is extended over a quatrain, sometimes over two, and occasionally throughout a whole sonnet. Sonnet XXXIII, for example, is an extended comparison of the Poet's disappointment with W.H.'s conduct with the clouding over of a sunny morning:

> Full many a glorious morning have I seen
> Flatter the mountain-tops with sovereign eye,
> Kissing with golden face the meadows green,
> Gilding pale streams with heavenly alchemy;
> Anon permit the basest clouds to ride
> With ugly rack on his celestial face,
> And from the forlorn world his visage hide,
> Stealing unseen to west with this disgrace:
> Even so my sun one early morn did shine
> With all-triumphant splendour on my brow;
> But, out, alack! he was but one hour mine,
> The region cloud hath mask'd him from me now.
>   Yet him for this my love no whit disdaineth;
>   Suns of the world may stain when heaven's sun staineth.

The image, indeed, is continued in the first two quatrains of the next sonnet with the picture of a man who went out without his cloak and was overtaken by a storm.

When we turn to the fields from which the images are drawn, we are reminded that the prevalence of legal imagery is such that it has been surmised that Shakespeare's lost years were spent as a solicitor's clerk; but there is nothing to indicate that Shakespeare had acquired a specialist knowledge of the law. Some sonnets which use the phraseology of testaments are derived from the fear that W.H. will die without leaving an heir:

Why dost thou spend
Upon thy self thy beauty's legacy? . . .
What acceptable audit can'st thou leave?
Thy unus'd beauty must be tomb'd with thee,
Which used lives th'executor to be. (IV.1–2, 12–14)

To be Death's conquest and make worms thine heir. (VI.14)

Others are concerned with common legal terminology:

When to the sessions of sweet silent thought
I summon up remembrance of things past. . . . (XXX.1–2)

Thy adverse party is thy advocate. . . . (XXXV.10)

The charter of thy worth gives thee releasing:
My bonds in thee are all determinate. (LXXXVII.3–4)

More significant, perhaps, are the images taken from warfare, some expressing inner conflict –

Thyself thy foe (I.8)

Mine eye and heart are at a mortal war (XLVI.1)

– but most with mankind's conflict with Time:

And all in war with Time for love of you. . . . (XV.13)

But wherefore do not you a mightier way
Make war upon this bloody tyrant, Time? (XVI.1–2)

When forty winters shall besiege thy brow
And dig deep trenches in thy beauty's field. . . . (II.1–2)

These images are connected with those derived from the four seasons, which were associated commonly (e.g. by Ovid and Palingenius) with man's four ages. Spring symbolises youth and beauty, as in the exquisite phrase 'the lovely April of her prime'. Winter symbolises old age and the approach of death, so that it represents a threat to youth and beauty, an ally of Time the tyrant.

For never-resting Time leads summer on
To hideous winter. . . . (V.5–6)

Then let not winter's ragged hand deface
In thee thy summer. . . . (VI.1–2)

Linked with the imagery drawn from the seasons are the still more
numerous flower images:

> And many maiden gardens yet unset,
> With virtuous wish would bear your living flowers. . . . (XVI.6–7)

> Great Princes' favourites their fair leaves spread
> But as the marigold at the sun's eye. . . . (XXV.5–6)

> The rose looks fair, but fairer we it deem
> For that sweet odour which doth in it live:
> The canker blooms have full as deep a dye
> As the perfumed tincture of the roses,
> Hang on such thorns, and play as wantonly
> When summer's breath their masked buds discloses;
> But for their virtue only is their show,
> They live unwoo'd, and unrespected fade,
> Die to themselves. Sweet roses do not so:
> Of their sweet deaths are sweetest odours made:
> And so of you. . . . (LIV.3–13)

> How sweet and lovely dost thou make the shame,
> Which like a canker in the fragrant rose
> Doth spot the beauty of thy budding name! (XCV)

It will give a fuller idea of the use of imagery in the Sonnets if we
examine two complete poems. The first of these, XC, is not one of the
supreme masterpieces, but it will illustrate the evolving nature of the
imagery:

> Then hate me when thou wilt, if ever, now,
> Now while the world is bent my deeds to cross,
> Join with the spite of fortune, make me bow,
> And do not drop in for an after-loss.
> Ah do not, when my heart hath 'scaped this sorrow,
> Come in the rearward of a conquer'd woe;
> Give not a windy night a rainy morrow,
> To linger out a purpos'd overthrow.
> If thou wilt leave me, do not leave me last,
> When other petty griefs have done their spite,
> But in the onset come; so shall I taste
> At first the very worst of fortune's might.
> > And other strains of woe, which now seem woe,
> > Compar'd with loss of thee will not seem so.

After the first line, which is without a figure of speech, the remainder
of the sonnet is expressed entirely in imagistic terms. Two lines speak

of Fortune's spite and might, and 'spite' is repeated in line 9 in relation
to 'other petty griefs'. Several lines contain variant images for the effect
of W.H.'s feared desertion after the Poet has recovered from some other
sorrow: 'an after-loss', 'the rearward of a conquer'd woe', 'Give not a
windy night a rainy morrow', 'do not leave me last . . . But in the onset
come' (i.e., as Booth glosses, 'as one of the first wave of attackers').
Apart from these images, a number are taken from warfare – 'conquer'd
woe', 'purpos'd overthrow' and possibly 'scap'd' – and 'strains' (13) is a
quibble since it can mean both 'kinds' and 'stresses'.

Sonnet LXV is one of the sonnets on mutability:

65

Since brass, nor stone, nor earth, nor boundless sea,
But sad mortality o'ersways their power,
How with this rage shall beauty hold a plea,
Whose action is no stronger than a flower?
Oh how shall summer's honey breath hold out
Against the wrackful siege of batt'ring days,
When rocks impregnable are not so stout,
Nor gates of steel so strong but Time decays?
O fearful meditation; where, alack,
Shall Time's best jewel from Time's chest lie hid?
Or what strong hand can hold his swift foot back;
Or who his spoil [of] beauty can forbid?
   Oh none, unless this miracle have might
   That in black ink my love may still shine bright.

The sonnet is a continuation of LXIV, 'this rage' (3) referring to 'mortal
rage' of the previous sonnet. We may notice the list of apparently strong
and permanent things which are subject to mutability – brass, stone,
earth, sea, rocks, steel. The contrast to these apparently strong things is
the frail things which the Poet loves – beauty, flowers, summer's honey
breath, and the jewel which stands for W.H. There are legal images in
'hold a plea' and 'action'; war images in 'o'ersways their power',
'wrackful siege of batt'ring days' and 'spoil'; and summer and flowers
(as we have seen) are symbols of youth and beauty. The antithesis in the
last line between 'black' and 'bright' brings home the paradox that the
beauty of W.H. can be preserved, if at all, only by the miracle of words.

It may be useful to devote the rest of this chapter to a more detailed
discussion of half a dozen of the more complex sonnets. J. B. Leishman
in his *Themes and Variations in Shakespeare's Sonnets* has traced the
theme of the immortalising power of poetry from Horace, Ovid and
Propertius, through Petrarch, Tasso and Ronsard to Shakespeare's
English predecessors.[11] The theme was a commonplace, though
Shakespeare does not use it in a commonplace way. Propertius congratu-
lated Cynthia on having been celebrated in his poems – poems which

were so many monuments of her beauty outlasting the pyramids, the
temple of Jupiter at Elis or the tomb of Mausolus. Petrarch told Laura
that his poems, which had little effect on her, would inflame thousands.
Tasso boasted that his sonnets were more lasting than Memphis or
Babylon or Rome. Ronsard told Hélène that when she was old, long
after he himself was dead, she would read his immortal praise of her
beauty. Spenser, to give a last example, told Elizabeth Boyle:

> My verse your virtues rare shall eternize.

This sonnet of Shakespeare's is written in the same tradition, but, as
we have noted, he is less concerned than the other poets are with his
personal glory.

> Not marble nor the gilded monuments
> Of princes shall outlive this powerful rhyme;
> But you shall shine more bright in these contents
> Than unswept stone, besmear'd with sluttish time.
> When wasteful war shall statues overturn,
> And broils root out the work of masonry,
> Nor Mars his sword nor war's quick fire shall burn
> The living record of your memory.
> 'Gainst death and all-oblivious enmity
> Shall you pace forth; your praise shall still find room,
> Even in the eyes of all posterity
> That wear this world out to the ending doom.
>   So, till the judgement that yourself arise,
>   You live in this, and dwell in lovers' eyes.

We have seen how this sonnet was suggested by two famous passages
of Latin poetry, the end of the *Metamorphoses* and one of Horace's odes
(book III, ode 30), both of which Shakespeare would have read at school.
In the first quatrain he substitutes marble and gilded monuments for
Horace's bronze, as he was recalling ornate tombs in English churches.
He personifies Time as a sluttish charwoman who allows the monuments
to be besmeared with dust and grime.

The second quatrain, in which Shakespeare speaks of more dangerous
hazards than mere neglect – war and civil disturbances – is derived partly
from Ovid, and partly from Regius's note on the passage. He uses Ovid's
sword and fire, but he omits Jove's anger as being inappropriate to a
Christian setting.

In the third quatrain, Shakespeare deviates from his models. Whereas
Horace and Ovid had been concerned merely with the immortality of
their poetry, Shakespeare characteristically is concerned with the
immortality of his verse – which in CVII he calls 'this poor rhyme' –

only in so far as it was a means of immortalising his friend. He would
live until the Last Judgement in Shakespeare's poems, and he would
dwell in lovers' eyes because lovers, reading the Sonnets as an expression
of their own feelings for each other, would think of the object of
Shakespeare's affections.

Possibly, as Lever suggests, the word 'room' (10) was suggested by
Rome, since elsewhere Shakespeare quibbles on the two words.[12]

> As the sonnet sweeps to its conclusion, the great name of Rome is
> coupled to the Friend's eternalization. Wherever Roman power extends
> over the conquered lands, Ovid proclaimed . . . there he would live
> on throughout all the ages. . . . Thus the conquest of Time is also a
> conquest of space.

The immortalising power of poetry is a theme Shakespeare first
broaches in XV, and he returns to it again and again, sometimes doubt-
fully and sometimes confidently; but in this sonnet the theme is enunciated with the greatest power and confidence. As many critics have
recognised, the imagery of the sonnet is magnificently concrete, as the
words 'besmear'd' (4), 'root out' (6) and pace 'forth' (10) exemplify. It
is also superbly musical. The lines are knit together not merely by
alliterated initial letters – 'marble'/'monuments'; 'princes'/'powerful' –
but by a complex pattern of alliteration of other letters, as in the line:

> *T*han unswep*t s*tone, be*s*mear'd with *sl*u*tt*ish *t*ime.

Alliteration is supported by assonance, as when 'Mars' is echoed in the
same line by 'war's', and 'pace' by 'praise', or 'sword' (7) is echoed by
'record' in the next line.

In spite of the influence of the classics, the tone of Shakespeare's poem
differs from Horace's or Ovid's. This is partly because the immortality
conferred by poetry or art was the only kind in which those poets
believed; but Shakespeare juxtaposes it with the idea of the Last
Judgement, with the implication, as Sir Thomas Browne puts it, that
'the sufficiency of Christian Immortality frustrates all earthly glory, and
the quality of either state after death makes a folly of posthumous
memory'.

LXXIII

The imagery of this sonnet is divided according to the three quatrains.
In each an image is used to describe the age of the Poet – winter,
twilight and a dying fire. But in each quatrain the central image is
complicated by subsidiary ones.

That time of year thou may'st in me behold,
When yellow leaves, or none, or few, do hang
Upon those boughs which shake against the cold,
Bare ruin'd choirs, where late the sweet birds sang.
In me thou seest the twilight of such day,
As after sunset fadeth in the west,
Which by and by black night doth take away,
Death's second self that seals up all in rest.
In me thou seest the glowing of such fire,
That on the ashes of his youth does lie,
As the death-bed, whereon it must expire,
Consum'd with that which it was nourish'd by.
   This thou perceiv'st, which makes thy love more strong,
   To love that well, which thou must leave ere long.

We may note first that the boughs shivering with cold reinforce the comparison of the Poet with the wintry trees. In the fourth line the trees are compared with ruined churches or abbeys, open to the sky, and the singing which once filled the choirs is compared with the singing of birds in the trees. (We may be reminded, too, that a poet may be called a singer.) In the second quatrain the common idea is recalled that sleep is Death's second self, though here the phrase is applied to night. The words 'seals up all in rest' carry an undertone of meaning, of closing a coffin, and possibly, as Ingram and Redpath suggest, of the seeling of a hawk.[13] (Macbeth speaks of 'seeling night'.) We may doubt whether Booth is right when he suggests that in lines 7 and 8 there is 'a dimly perceptible metaphor of a child taken off to sleep . . . by a sinister nursery maid or wet nurse'.

In the third quatrain the funereal meaning implied in the second comes to the surface in the picture of the deathbed; but this is subsidiary to that of the dying fire. The vital forces of youth have now turned to ash which chokes the fire of life they once sustained.

The word 'leave' in the last line (which Booth fancifully takes to be an echo of the 'leaves' of line 2[14]) is usually glossed as 'forgo' and, if the text is accurate, this is presumably right. But there appear to be ambiguities inherent in the word – that the Poet substitutes 'leave' for 'lose' because of the often-expressed fear that W.H. will leave him, and also because he himself values life more because it is drawing to an end.

XCIV

Ever since William Empson's essay in *Some Versions of Pastoral* (1935) this sonnet has been a favourite subject for exegesis. Among recent critics who have contributed to the interpretation may be mentioned Hubler (1952), Hallett Smith (1952), Lever (1956), Landry (1963),

Booth (1969, 1977), Martin (1972) and Melchiori (1976). Empson subtitled his essay 'Twist of heroic-pastoral ideas into an ironical acceptance of aristocracy'. Ironical the sonnet certainly is, but not primarily about aristocracy, and implying rejection rather than acceptance. Hubler is surely right when, in his chapter on 'The economy of the closed heart', he declares that the man ostensibly praised in the octave is elsewhere in Shakespeare's works treated with abhorrence.

> They that have power to hurt and will do none,
> That do not do the things they most do show,
> Who, moving others, are themselves as stone,
> Unmoved, cold, and to temptation slow,
> They rightly do inherit heaven's graces
> And husband nature's riches from expense;
> They are the lords and owners of their faces,
> Others but stewards of their excellence.

As Booth points out, the first line is proverbial: 'To be able to do harm and to be unwilling to do it is noble.' It had been used by Sidney in *Arcadia*: 'the more power he hath to hurt, the more admirable in his praise that he will not hurt'. This is genuine praise of a good ruler. It is also admirable, as Booth insists, to be slow to temptation. But the total effect of the octave is to give a repellent picture of the man whose virtues are admitted:

It is preposterous on the face of things to proclaim as the inheritors of heaven's graces those who are 'as stone'. It can be other than ironical only to the cynic, for even the hard-hearted man thinks of himself as generous and cherishes an abstract admiration for warmth. In addition, it will be noticed that what Shakespeare says here contradicts everything that he has said elsewhere on the subject. The irony of the octave is Swiftian in both method and force. In specious terms the poet states as true that which he is well known to consider false: those men whose appearance does not square with reality, whose deeds do not fulfill their promise, who move others while remaining cold, are proclaimed the heirs to heaven's graces. They are the owners of themselves, whereas throughout Shakespeare's works self-possession in the sense of living without regard for others is intolerable.[15]

A number of critics have compared the portrait of the man so described with Angelo in *Measure for Measure*. He moves others, as one sees from Mariana's feelings for him, but he is as stone.

It is plain that the contrast between 'show' and 'do', however necessary to a 'scurvy politician', must destroy the mutuality necessary to the personal life; that to arouse affection without giving it is (to say the least)

unamiable; that to be as stone is inhuman – 'will you give him a stone?';
that to be slow to temptation, however admirable in itself, may be due
more to coldness than to virtue; and that to 'husband nature's riches
from expense' is to be like the man in the parable who buried his talent
in a napkin. As Vincentio told Angelo in lines quoted by Hubler:

> Thyself and thy belongings
> Are not thine own so proper, as to waste
> Thyself upon thy virtues, they on thee.

Moreover, the self-sufficiency described, and ironically praised, in the
sonnet is the very sin deplored by the Poet in the procreation sonnets,
and the sign of Richard of Gloucester's damnation when he boasts: 'I
am myself alone.'

At first sight the third quatrain gives a more favourable impression
of the man, or type, described: the beautiful flower is justified simply
by existing. Critics remind us of the lilies of the field; but we cannot
help being reminded of the earlier flower imagery and of the contrast
between the roses which are turned into perfume and the canker-blooms
which

> have as deep a dye
> As the perfumed tincture of the roses
> Hang on such thorns, and play as wantonly,
> When summer's breath their masked buds discloses. (LIV)

Moreover, if the flower meets with infection, the basest weed becomes
its superior – as the humble citizen, even if corrupt, is superior to the
corrupt aristocrat. We are again reminded of the repressed Angelo, the
festering lily, who is led into worse sin than the Claudios and Lucios he
despises. As he puts it himself, he corrupts with virtuous season.

How, then, do we take the words 'rightly do inherit heaven's graces'?
There is perhaps a quibble on two meanings of 'rightly' – 'by right' and
'appropriately' – though, as Melchiori points out, Shakespeare never
elsewhere uses the adverb to mean 'rightfully', 'justly', 'legitimately' or
'of right'.[16] There may also be a faint echo of the beatitude 'Blessed are
the meek, for they shall inherit the earth'; and this would be savagely
ironical since the 'they' of the sonnet are the very opposite of meek.
'Heaven's graces' seem not to be those normally understood by the
term, but rather the beauty and polish which belong to those born with
silver spoons in their mouths: they are not morally or spiritual qualities.

Melchiori treats the sonnet as one of Shakespeare's 'dramatic meditations' and points out that it is not addressed to an invidual and does not
use either 'I' or 'thou'. He therefore argues that it should be considered
in isolation rather than in the context of the other sonnets. Despite the

subtle, and generally convincing, interpretation he provides, I believe nevertheless that we should not ignore the position of the sonnet in the sequence. We have already seen that the last line of XCIII –

> If thy sweet virtue answer not thy show

– is picked up by the theme of hypocrisy in XCIV, as well as by the rhyme-word; and XCV speaks of the beautiful mansion in which W.H.'s vices are housed. In LXIX, moreover, there is the same contrast between lilies and weeds as in XCIV, between show and inner reality, and also some of the same rhymes ('deeds', 'weeds', 'show'). Although, therefore, XCIV is not addressed to W.H. and may not have been intended for his eyes, it is nevertheless about him, or about what he is likely to be in a few years' time.

CXVI AND CXXIX

These two sonnets may conveniently be discussed together as definitions of love and lust. One is concerned with the marriage of true minds, the other with the coupling of untrue bodies; one with constancy even when the partner is inconstant, the other with a momentary act; one an inspiration to the lover, the other a temptation and an obsession which the victim bitterly regrets; one eternal, the other ephemeral; one life-enhancing, the other life-degrading; one a sacrament, the other a deadly sin.

Both sonnets, unlike the rest of the sequence, have the opening statements overflowing into the second line, giving to both an impetuous energy which is carried on to the end:

> Let me not to the marriage of true minds
> Admit impediments. . . .

> Th'expense of spirit in a waste of shame
> Is lust in action. . . .

The first statement echoes the priest's charge to the couple who have come to be married:

> I require and charge you (as you will answer at the dreadful day of judgment, when the secrets of all hearts shall be disclosed) that if either of you do know any impediment why ye may not be lawfully joined together in matrimony, that ye confess it.

Perhaps the memory of these words coloured the reference to the Last Judgement in line 12. But the Poet is concerned with the marriage of minds, with any sexual element excluded. The other sonnet appears to exclude everything except the sexual. The initial statement depends on three quibbles: the expense of spirit can mean the squandering of higher qualities or simply the 'spending' of semen; and 'waste' puns on 'waist' (which Hamlet took to mean 'secret parts'.)

In CXVI the first quatrain expresses the Poet's credo in the most direct way possible. The other two quatrains support the statement by metaphoric elaboration, true love being an ever-fixed sea-mark which guides man on life's voyage, or the star by which he can navigate, even though it is too far above him to estimate its worth – and the epithet 'wandering' may indicate that without the star of love we should go astray. (In *Romeo and Juliet* the hero compares the poison he is about to take with a desperate pilot running on the rocks his weary bark.) In the third quatrain there is a contrast between the love that is subject to time, depending as it does on physical attractions (rosy lips and cheeks), and the ideal love that lasts till Doomsday.

Booth is quite right to point out bawdy undertones in a number of the sonnets, but I doubt myself whether 'sexually suggestive elements in this poem are obvious', or that the words 'bark', 'fool', 'mark' and 'looks' in this context constitute sexual innuendo; and still more that Drayton's 'Since there's no help' has a 'coherent sexual undermeaning'.

In the couplet, 'error' is a legal term (e.g. a fault in a judgement); so that, as Ingram and Redpath say, 'The poet is asserting not merely that his definition of true love is right but also that true love exists, as proved by his own case'.

The companion sonnet on lust is very different in construction. It depends hardly at all on imagery, but almost entirely on its rhetorical structure and rhythmical power. The first twelve lines rush on as a single sentence, and there is an extraordinary accumulation of derogatory and forceful epithets, once compared by me with the hammering of nails into a coffin:

> . . . perjur'd, murd'rous, bloody, full of blame,
> Savage, extreme, rude, cruel, not to trust. . . .

There follow eight antithetical lines – the antitheses rammed home by alliteration – in which the anticipation of the act of lust is contrasted with its aftermath: 'Enjoy'd'/'despised', 'hunted'/'hated', 'bliss'/'woe', 'joy'/'dream'. The word 'extreme' is repeated later in the sonnet, and the poet stresses the irrationality of the pursuit and of the hatred that follows possession; and, indeed, one has the impression that it is a case of possession in the demoniac sense, as it is certainly madness. The swallowed bait

> On purpose laid to make the taker mad

reminds one of Claudio's words on lechery:

> Our natures do pursue
> Like rats that ravin down their proper bane,
> A thirsty evil; and when we drink we die.

Robert Graves and Laura Riding, justifiably incensed that *The Oxford Book of English Verse* printed Tottel's revisions of Wyatt when his own manuscript version was greatly superior, were on shakier ground when they objected to the generally accepted emendations in this sonnet – shakier because the 1609 text of the Sonnets has dozens of misprints and because the punctuation is unreliable throughout.[17] It is difficult to believe, for example, that we should retain the original text of lines 10 and 11:

> Had, hauing, and in quest, to haue extreame,
> A blisse in proofe and proud and very wo. . . .

The comma after 'quest' leaves us with the awkward phrase 'to haue extreame', for which no real parallel has been discovered; and although Graves and Riding did extract a meaning from the second of these lines – that lust was both bliss and woe before, during, and after the act – the usual emendation ('a' for 'and') makes better, if simpler, sense. All through the poem Shakespeare is relying on an antithetical structure –

> A bliss in proof, and prov'd a very woe

– as in the lines that precede and follow this pair. The only two points which have any real substance in the Graves–Riding argument are their plea for the retention of 'Made' (9), which quibbles on 'mad' in the previous line and reinforces 'make', and their objection to the insertion of a semi-colon in the middle of the penultimate line. It is not that there is anything sacrosanct in the punctuation of the careless compositors, but that the nice antithesis between 'well knows' and 'knows well' is plainer and more effective if the latter is not riveted to the line which follows. Line 13, as Graves and Riding argue, refers back to the analysis of lust in the previous twelve lines and forward to the epigrammatic summary in the line that follows.

Melchiori quotes one of Watson's *Hecatompathia* (XCVIII) which is an attack on love and points out of parallels between it and this sonnet.[18] Love, says Watson, is 'fierce by kind', 'a *Murd'ring Thiefe*', '*A Poysned Choaking Bayte*', 'in speach untrue', 'a *Toilsome webbe* of woe', 'a *lasting Lunacie*' and 'A Hellish Gaile'. But, despite the possible influence of Watson's poem on Shakespeare's, Melchiori argues that Shakespeare was not 'denouncing or renouncing "Desire" '; on the contrary, for him lust is murderous and treacherous as long as it remains 'lust', that is to say 'unsatisfied desire'. Lust, says Melchiori, 'is not the body-and-soul killing vice of the moralities or popular physiology, but, as sex, an essential element of the human personality.

Melchiori is a persuasive writer, but in this case he seems to have credited Shakespeare with views he would like him to hold. By treating this sonnet as a dramatic meditation, rather than as part of the sequence, he is able to ignore not merely the surroundings, but also the overall contrast between the two kinds of love, of comfort and despair, of friendship and passion. Perhaps Shakespeare was closer to the moralities than Melchiori allows, although for dramatic reasons he excluded lust from his conception of ideal love, and even if he did not altogether exclude love from his documentation of lust. This does not mean, of course, that in his other works or in his life he segregated love and lust. But here, surely, he (or his persona) is lamenting his slavery in almost Pauline terms.[19]

I am carnal, and sold unto sin, for what I would, that do I not; but what I hate, that do I . . . For I know that in me (that is in my flesh) dwelleth no good thing; for the good that I would I do not; but the evil which I would not, that I do. I delight in the law of God . . . but I see another Law in my members, warring against the law of my mind, and bringing me into captivity to the law of sin which is in my members. O wretched man that I am! Who shall deliver me from the body of this death?

CXLVI

The simple meaning of this sonnet is that the soul is poor and starved because the body is pampered; that the body after death will be eaten by worms; that the soul can be aided by the mortification of the body; and that by this means we are able to conquer death. The poem belongs to the *contemptus mundi* tradition. Booth quotes a poem from Davison's *Poetical Rhapsody*, 'Dialogue betweene the Soule and the Body', which the sonnet, at least superficially, remembles.[20] But B. C. Southam has argued that the sub-text gives a totally different impression:

It is Shakespeare the humanist speaking, pleading for the life of the body as against the rigorous asceticism which glorifies the life of the spirit at the expense of the vitality and richness of sensuous experience. Neither spiritual nor bodily life can be fulfilled at the other's cost, for the whole man, body and spirit indivisible, will suffer thereby. We can see how very much higher is the charity which motivates this sonnet than the type of Christianity which moves on the surface of the poem, and at which the irony is directed.

Melchiori quotes this passage with approval.[21] Then with some subtle use of linguistic analysis, and a number of diagrams to illustrate the structure of the sonnet, he argues that it is God who is implicitly criticised as the 'careless and avaricious landlord towards his poor but ambitious tenant, the Soul'; that in the question 'Is this the body's end?' 'end' may mean 'purpose'; that 'Shakespeare must see soul and body as merely antagonistic to each other with Man as the sufferer'; and that 'the real concern that emerges in the final couplet' is 'the wearisome condition of humanity'. Melchiori's arguments are ingenious, and more convincing than this summary can suggest. Moreover, the political and theological ideas with which he credits Shakespeare are ones that many of us would like him to have held. But whatever Shakespeare's personal beliefs – and they were not static – the present sonnet seems to be the expression of a much more orthodox position than Southam and Melchiori allow. The death of Death in the last line implies the immortality of the Soul; and few Christians, one suspects, even in Shakespeare's day, believed that the resurrection would resemble Stanley Spencer's painting of it. Nor is it necessary, or desirable, to assume that the eating imagery – with its suggestion of cannibalism – and the idea that both Soul and Body are vampires, absorbing life from the other's pining, should be taken to mean that the Poet was revolted by the whole process. Of course, the eating of his body by worms – to which he refers more than once in the Sonnets – is not a pleasant thought; but it is compensated by the conviction that by death and subsequent corruption the soul is set free.

We may, perhaps, regret the dualism of the Sonnets – a legacy of neo-Platonism and Christianity – a dualism which is apparent in the opposition between the Poet's two loves, as well as in the Soul's battle with the Body in this sonnet. But it is there, and we cannot explain it away by searching for elusive ironies and dubious sub-textual meanings.

CHAPTER 6

The Truest Poetry

In 1876, Robert Browning wrote a series of poems in which he gave vent to his long-suppressed irritation with his critics. These included 'Of Pacchiarotto, and How He Worked in Distemper' and the 'Epilogue' to the same volume; but three shorter poems are particularly concerned with the relation of a poet's work to his life. In 'At the "Mermaid" ', Browning takes Shakespeare as his persona, protesting that nothing can be deduced about his life and opinions from his plays:

> Here's my work: does work discover –
> What was rest from work – my life?
> Did I live man's hater, lover?
> Leave the world at peace, at strife?
> Call earth ugliness or beauty?
> See things there in large or small?
> Use to pay its Lord my duty?
> Use to own a lord at all? . . .
>
> Which of you did I enable
> Once to slip inside my breast,
> There to catalogue and label
> What I like least, what love best,
> Hope and fear, believe and doubt of,
> Seek and shun, respect – deride?
> Who has right to make a rout of
> Rarities he found inside?

In 'House', Browning refers specifically to Wordsworth's claim that Shakespeare unlocked his heart with the key of the Sonnets:

> Shall I sonnet-sing you about myself?
> Do I live in a house you would like to see?
> Is it scant of gear, has it store of pelf?
> 'Unlock my heart with a sonnet-key? . . .'
>
> Outside should suffice for evidence:
> And whoso desires to penetrate
> Deeper, must dive by the spirit-sense –
> No optics like yours, at any rate!

'Hoity toity! A street to explore,
  Your house the exception! *"With this same key*
Shakespeare unlocked his heart," once more!'
Did Shakespeare? If so, the less Shakespeare he!

A similar point is made in 'Shop'.

The conflicting views of Wordsworth and Browning on Shakespeare's Sonnets are not as irreconcilable as they seem at first sight. Browning rightly argues that they should not be taken as confessions, that they are poems which may be based ultimately on personal experience, but are an unreliable guide to the precise nature of that experience. Wordsworth, on the other hand, implies that the Sonnets were no mere poetic exercises and that, even if we cannot know if the story is true, the poet reveals his personal thoughts and feelings about love, time, fame, death, beauty and lust.

Browning nearly always expressed himself through characters apparently unlike himself, and was naturally anxious not to be credited with their opinions; but in his later years the gulf between man and poet became more and more apparent. Henry James could not understand how 'the rich proud genius one adored' could live, or have lived, in such a man as Browning had become; and he wrote 'The Private Life' as a kind of allegory on the complete divorce of the vulgar insensitive bourgeois from the writer of the poems.

A great poet of the present century, T. S. Eliot, continually emphasised that all poetry was dramatic; that emotions which the poet has never experienced 'will serve his turn as well as those familiar to him'; that 'Poetry is not a turning loose of emotion, but an escape from emotion; it is not the expression of personality but an escape from personality'; and that 'the more perfect the artist the more completely separate in him will be the man who suffers and the mind which creates'.[1] Perhaps Eliot protested too much. The more we learn about the composition of *The Waste Land*, the more we are brought to realise that it was greatly influenced by Eliot's psychological state at the time, even if in the poem, as cut by Ezra Pound, the personal feelings have been utilised for the purposes of art.

Tennyson shared Browning's views on curiosity about the private lives of poets. In verses supposed to have been prompted by the publication of Keats's letters to Fanny Brawne, he wrote bitterly:

For now the Poet cannot die,
  Nor leave his music as of old,
  But round him ere he scarce be cold
Begins the scandal and the cry:

'Proclaim the faults he would not show:
    Break lock and seal: betray the trust.
    Keep nothing sacred: 'tis but just
The many-headed beast should know.'²

In fact Browning wrote an introduction to some Shelly letters which proved to be forgeries; and one presumes that Tennyson would not have objected to the publication of Shakespeare's letters to the Dark Lady if they had turned up at the Public Record Office.³

Yet Browning and Tennyson were right to feel that curiosity concerning the private lives of poets leads to a misreading of their poems, either because the distance between personal experience and finished poem is minimised or ignored, or else because the poem is ransacked for clues instead of being regarded as an end in itself.

About the work of some poets we have enough information to compare the poem with its origins in experience. Three examples may be given from Wordsworth's poems. It is well known that 'Resolution and Independence' was based on an actual incident which took place on 3 October 1800 when Wordsworth and his sister met an old man on the road, who had been, but was no longer, a leech-gatherer.⁴ The poem was written between May and July 1802, and it was partly based on Dorothy's account. If we did not know the facts, we might well have assumed that the encounter took place as described in the poem, and that the poet's initial despondency belonged to 1800 rather than to 1802. 'The Solitary Reaper' owes more to a passage in Thomas Wilkinson's *Tour in the Highlands* than to an actual incident in the Wordsworths' tour undertaken two years previously.⁵ A third Wordsworthian example is even more revealing.⁶ It is well known that *The Prelude* does not give a true account of many incidents in the poet's life, where independent evidence exists. As the poem was meant not as an autobiography but as an account of the growth of a poet's mind, Wordsworth was entitled to alter the facts as a means of revealing the essential truth, and of creating a better poem. Even with an avowedly autobiographical poem, there are bound to be elements of artifice. Now, if Wordsworth, the notorious example of the egotistical sublime, who, as Shelley said (with some obvious exaggeration)

                never could
        Fancy another situation
    From which to dart his contemplation,
        Than that wherein he stood,⁷

if Wordsworth was led to tamper with the literal truth for the sake of imaginative truth, we should expect a poet who possessed what Keats called negative capability to use the facts merely as a diving-board from which to plunge into the waters of creation. In one of his marginalia Keats compares the passions with hogsheads of wine in a vast cellar: the poet does not have to get drunk in order to know what the wine tastes like.[8] We all accept this when we are talking of plays. No one supposes that Shakespeare had to murder his wife before writing *Othello*, or that he had to attempt to murder King James before writing *Macbeth*.

John Keats, on whom we have detailed biographical information, believed that 'Shakespeare led a life of allegory: his works are the comments on it'. Many critics have sought to track down the genesis of his own poems, and to relate them directly to his life. We know that Isabella Jones suggested the subject of *The Eve of St Agnes*, but we cannot deduce from the climax of the poem that Keats was celebrating his success with Mrs Jones.[9] The biographical hypothesis does not affect our interpretation of the poem. Much more is known about the genesis of his first great sonnet – 'On First Looking into Chapman's Homer'. We know that it was written within a few hours of the event described, when he was introduced by Cowden Clark to the translation. We know that the imagery of the poem was based on John Evelyn's verses on Creech's translation of Lucretius, on Robertson's *History of America* and on Bonnycastle's *Introduction to Astronomy*. It is possible that the poet was remembering his first sight of the sea at Margate, and that the new planet was a kind of symbol for his feelings about the Moon. But the sonnet can be fully understood without knowledge of any of these facts and hypotheses – which may, indeed, be obstacles to our appreciation of it.[10]

We have detailed knowledge of Milton's life, partly from his own autobiographical digressions; but the dangers of using his poems as straightforward autobiography are obvious. If one considers, for example, the numerous passages in his works, both prose and verse, in which he writes of his blindness, one is struck by the fact that they vary, not according to his personal feelings, but according to the kind of literature he was writing at the time. When he was replying to the charge that he was stricken blind as a punishment for defending the regicides, he wrote as a patriotic supporter of the English revolution, anxious that the defence should not be weakened by attacks on his own character. It was necessary in these circumstances to provide clinical details, so as to show that his blindness was a natural, rather than a supernatural, visitation. When he writes the invocation to Light at the beginning of the third book of *Paradise Lost*, he adopts the persona of the blind bard who has acquired additional powers through his deprivation. When he writes *Samson Agonistes*, he identifies with a man who has recently been blinded – not because the play was written soon after the tragedy struck him, but because this treatment was dramatically appropriate. The various sonnets in which he treats of his blindness, expressing patience, grief on the death of his wife, and pride in his fame as the defender of the revolution, are all different in tone and different equally from the epic and dramatic treatments of blindness. For the biographer it is necessary to decide whether the poet's 'late espoused saint' was the second Mrs Milton or the first; but it matters to the critic only in so far as it affects the interpretation of one or two phrases in the sonnet.

From the time that Milton wrote 'On the Morning of Christ's Nativity', a poem which neatly illustrates the union of tradition and the individual talent, of personal dedication and the demands of a complex and original poetic structure, Milton sought, and nearly always found, an appropriate form. His poems are the channelling of emotion for the precise purposes of an art which Milton believed to be divinely inspired, 'not to be obtained by the invocation of Dame Memory and her Siren daughters'.[11]

From these examples we can see that the relationship between the poet and his work varies from case to case. At one extreme, a poem may describe an actual experience as accurately as possible; at the other extreme, a poem may be pure fiction; but it is doubtful whether any poetry of real excellence belongs to either extreme. The choice of subject may be determined by external pressures or by personal motivation (e.g. falling in love, divorce, repressed homosexuality, growing old, a publisher's advance). The treatment may be determined by the requirements of the genre, by the ability of the poet, by the models in fashion, and (with plays) by the talents of the available actors.

Now, it is obvious that in a narrative poem, or in a play, the poet cannot be simply identified with his characters, not even with a tragic hero or with a supposedly 'choric' character – Kent, Ulysses or Thersites. Milton had to speak through Adam, Eve and Satan, as well as through the blind Bard, his persona, through God and through archangels, as Shakespeare was able to speak through a wide range of characters. It has been argued, indeed, that the greater the dramatist, the wider the range of characters through whose eyes he can look, through whose mouths he can speak.[12] But his ability to identify with murderers and psychopaths, with rapists and their victims, with princes and pimps, with Cleopatra as well as Isabella tells us nothing about the poet's character, except the breadth of his sympathies and the power of his imagination. A lyrical poem written in the first person may seem to be the direct expression of the poet's personal feelings, but even here there is always a process of selection, of modification, of dramatisation, and it is therefore unsafe to rely on them for biographical facts. Autobiographies, in prose as well as in verse, are usually designed to give a self-portrait from which the warts have been surgically removed, or at least artistically rearranged. A love-poem may be written as an aid to seduction – such as Marvell's 'To His Coy Mistress' – but the main aim of the poet is to write good poetry. Indeed, the quality of that poem would not be affected if it could be proved that the coy mistress was an invention, either not coy, or not the poet's mistress, or not anyone.

We have been considering a number of poets, many of them temperamentally unlike Shakespeare, who was not given to the egotistical sublime. Several of them wrote formal criticism or discussed poetry in their letters. Shakespeare, so far as is known, did not write any criticism; and, although there are remarks on the subject of poetry scattered through the plays, and several characters who are designated as poets, the remarks are appropriate to their contexts and to the speakers, and the poets (one hopes and believes) are not self-portraits.[13] When Theseus compares the poet with the lunatic and the lover because they 'are of imagination all compact', his remarks are intended primarily to disparage the credibility of the lovers in the play; and when he goes on to speak of the poet's fine frenzy he is echoing Sidney or Plato. Shakespeare himself in *A Midsummer Night's Dream* was giving 'to airy nothing A local habitation and a name'; but he is unlikely to have shared Theseus' opinions, especially as Hippolyta immediately refutes them as applied to the adventures of the lovers in the forest.

Timon's poet describes the composition of poetry not so much as the spontaneous overflow of powerful feelings as an involuntary secretion –

> a gum which oozes
> From whence tis nourish'd

– and as a gentle flame which provokes itself.

The poet depends on patronage, deserts Timon when he loses his fortune, and returns to him when he is reported rich. In his defence it can be said that his projected allegory of Fortune is a warning to Timon about his fair-weather friends, and that the only fragment which oozes from him could be regarded as self-criticism:

> When we for recompense have prais'd the vile,
> It stains the glory of that happy verse
> Which aptly sings the good.

Shakespeare, as always, gives the devil his due, but we cannot be certain that his views on poetry coincided with those of his character. It may be mentioned that Keats in one of his aphorisms says that if poetry 'comes not as naturally as the leaves to a tree, it had better not come at all'.[14] Timon's poet, if not Shakespeare, would have agreed.

With regard to Touchstone's remark that provides the title to this chapter, one has to remember on the one hand that his aim was to bemuse Audrey, and on the other that he is distorting only slightly Sidney's argument that the poet never lies because he never affirms.[15]

Not labouring to tell you what is or is not, but what should or should
not be. And therefore, though he recount things not true, yet because
he telleth them not for true, he lieth not.

As so often, Shakespeare's personal views are concealed from us, not
merely by his pervasive irony but by the fact that the views never seem
out of place on the lips of his characters. With Marlowe, on the other
hand, there are moments when he seems to allow his characters to
express his own ideas. Tamburlaine is an obvious example. A lover of
beauty may be inordinately ambitious and savagely cruel, but when
Tamburlaine meditates on the difficulties of poetic creation one cannot
help feeling that Marlowe is using his hero as a mouthpiece.[16]

> If all the pens that ever poets held,
> Had fed the feeling of their maisters thoughts,
> And every sweetnes that inspir'd their harts,
> Their minds, and muses on admyred theames:
> If all the heavenly Quintessence they still
> From their immortall flowers of Poesy,
> Wherein as in a myrrour we perceive
> The highest reaches of a humaine wit.
> If these had made one Poems period
> And all combin'd in Beauties worthinesse,
> Yet should ther hover in their restlesse heads,
> One thought, one grace, one woonder at the least,
> Which into words no vertue can digest. . . .

With this preamble, we are in a position to consider how far the Sonnets
are autobiographically, as well as imaginatively, true. It is a problem
which has exercised the critics for two centuries – some believing that
the Sonnets give a faithful record of Shakespeare's life, and others
believing that the autobiographical element is minimal or even non-
existent. Hyder Edward Rollins provided a masterly summary of the
various opinions, to which the following pages are largely indebted,
particularly for the versions of German criticism.[17]

A. W. von Schlegel (1796) said that the Sonnets were 'valuable
because they seem to be inspired by a real love and friendship, and
because, otherwise, we should know little or nothing about the poet's
life'.[18] The second reason given is not always so frankly admitted. A
few years later (1808) Schlegel reiterated that the Sonnets 'paint
unequivocally the actual situation and sentiments of the poet; they make
us acquainted with the passions of the man; they even contain remarkable
confessions of his youthful errors'.[19]

James Boswell the younger replied (1821) that he was 'satisfied that
these compositions had neither the poet himself nor any individual in

view; but were merely the effusions of his fancy, written upon various topicks for the amusement of a private circle'.[20]

Tieck echoed Schlegel, saying that the Sonnets were the 'confessions of a man about whom we know so little'.[21] Thomas Campbell (1838) was clearly reluctant to believe that Shakespeare wrote affectionate sonnets to a man or was guilty of the passion described in the Dark Lady sonnets:

Shakespeare's sonnets give us no access to his personal history . . . they paint his friendship hyperbolically, and mixed with jealousies that belong not to manly friendship. Nor though some twenty of his sonnets are addressed to a female, with whom he feigns himself in love, is it certain that his erotic language, even in these, was not tinged with phantasy. . . . I have a suspicion, moreover, that if the love affair had been real, he would have said less about it.[22]

The motive of shielding Shakespeare's moral character is equally apparent in Dyce's belief (1832) that the Sonnets were 'written under an assumed character',[23] in another critic's claim[24] that they expressed 'the feelings of imaginary characters in imaginary situations' and in Coleridge's strange remark in 1833 that 'the sonnets could only have come from a man deeply in love, and in love with a woman'.[25] Apparently he thought that even the sonnets addressed to a man were inspired by heterosexual feelings.

The opposing point of view was put by Heine (1838), who declared that the Sonnets are 'authentic records of the circumstances of Shakespeare's life'.[26] Charles Armitage Brown called his book *Shakespeare's Autobiographical Poems* (1838): he may well have discussed the subject with Keats, whose belief that Shakespeare's middle years were clouded over was derived largely from the Sonnets.[27] Carlyle declared (1840) that the Sonnets 'testify expressly in what deep waters' Shakespeare 'had waded, and swum struggling for his life'.[28]

The argument continued all through the nineteenth century. Delius (1851) argued that the Sonnets were essentially dramatic.[29] R. G. White (1854) agreed, adding that Shakespeare wrote them as a professional for other people to use.[30] Robert Bell (1855) admitted that all poetry is, in a sense, autobiographical: 'But the particle of actual life out of which verse is wrought may be, and almost always is, wholly incommensurate to the emotion depicted, and remote from the forms into which it is ultimately shaped'.[31] Masson (1856) erroneously thought that there was general agreement that the Sonnets are 'autobiographic – distinctly, intensely, painfully autobiographic'.[32] Furnivall (1877) thought that only fools could think otherwise.[33] Swinburne (1880) and Dowden (1881) concurred.[34] Charles Mackay (1884), a minor poet, argued that the

Sonnets were dramatic.[35] Sidney Lee in 1897 produced two contra-
dictory views.[36] In the English edition of *The Dictionary of National
Biography* he came down on the side of autobiography; in the American
edition he declared that the Sonnets were 'to a large extent undertaken
as literary exercises'. But, although in his many later writings on the
subject he continued to stress the conventional nature of the Sonnets,
he admitted on occasion that there might be some slight basis of personal
experience. The polemical tone of Lee's contributions and his *ex cathedra*
pronouncements aroused opposition from critics who overlooked his
concessions. Sir Walter Raleigh absurdly declared that to deny that the
Sonnets expressed Shakespeare's 'own feelings in his own person' was
to accuse him of insincerity.[37] Beeching (1904) and A. C. Bradley (1909)
both argued that the missing links in the sonnet story and its obscurities
make it certain that the story is essentially true.[38] John Middleton Murry
(1921) believed that the Sonnets 'contain the record of the poet's own
disaster in love'.

Kittredge (1916) made an obvious, but overlooked, point when he
showed that a good sonnet inevitably sounds like autobiography: 'There
is no escape; a good sonnet appears to be a confession. These are terms
from which not even the supreme genius can be exempt'.[39] In the same
year M. J. Wolff tried to show that the sonnets to W.H. slavishly follow
the model set by Italian sonneteers – addressing a mistress in masculine
terms (e.g. Michelangelo), a one-sided relationship with a patron, the
poet submitting to the other's insults, extenuating his faults, admitting
his own unworthiness, in everything the opposite of his patron, old instead
of young, ugly instead of beautiful, of low birth instead of aristocratic,
friendless instead of popular, and apologetic about the feebleness of his
verse.[40] To this one can only say that there is no evidence that
Shakespeare was aware of these conventions, no evidence that he had
read Sannazaro or Giovanni della Casa, and that Wolff's description of
Shakespeare's attitude is difficult to substantiate. The poet, as we have
seen, is highly critical of W.H.'s faults, and he is confident that his
powerful rhyme will outlast the gilded monuments of princes.

There is no need to follow the controversy during the last half-century
since it continues along the same lines. Biographers generally rely on the
Sonnets to add flesh to the skeleton of fact. Quennell, Rowse and Burgess
all assume that the Sonnets tell a true story. Most editors, who accept
the necessity of attaching names to the main characters of the story,
naturally believe that the Sonnets are near enough to the facts to make
this a profitable exercise. Ingram and Redpath, and recently Stephen
Booth, with rare restraint, refuse to follow the example of other editors.
John Dover Wilson, who backs Herbert; Rowse, who backs Southampton;
and Hotson, who backs Hatcliffe – to take three examples – all concur
in the belief that Shakespeare was unpacking his heart with words.[41]

On the face of it, we should expect the Sonnets to have some basis in fact; but whatever the facts were we should expect them to be of less significance than Shakespeare's continuing concern with mutability and mortality, with the conflict between Agape and Eros, and with the desire to create immortal verse. The early sonnets, urging W.H. to marry, since they are unlike any other English sonnets, may well be based on an actual situation, and (as critics have suggested[42]) have been commissioned by the young man's parents. The poet's admiration of beauty and the added glamour of W.H.'s rank and wealth would have led inevitably to love, enforced as it would be by neo-Platonic theory.[43] Either this happened, or Shakespeare imagined it happening; and that his love was reciprocated, at least in part, seems to be a reasonable assumption. The tension normally provided by the inaccessibility of a cruel mistress – in love with, or married to, someone else or determined not to marry the poet – was in Shakespeare's case provided by the sexual inaccessibility of his beloved because he was a man, and by the difficulties and mis-understandings likely to arise from a difference of class.

The resulting complications may result partly from Shakespeare's dramatic sense and partly from actual events, rearranged so as to give the maximum effect but still preserving the discontinuities of actual life. If W.H. was Shakespeare's patron, as he appears to be the patron of the Poet of the Sonnets, there would be other poets seeking his patronage and arousing Shakespeare's disquiet. It would soon become apparent that the idealisation of the young man was something that he could hardly live up to, and inevitable disappointment would set going something that haunted Shakespeare for the rest of his life – the contrast between appearance and reality, between external beauty and inner ugliness.[44] But this contrast cuts across the major contrast of the Sonnets between the pure, selfless and avowedly sexless love for W.H. and the sexual infatua-tion for a woman.

Shakespeare, of course, may have been drawing on previous experience, unconnected with the sonnet story. As Baudelaire said of his mistress, Nature had used her, a vile animal, to mould a genius.[45] The woman was not necessarily dark. In one sonnet, indeed, it is stated:

In nothing art thou black save in thy deeds. . . . (CXXXI)

But to provide a suitable contrast to the fair W.H. she had to be dark, and her character had to conform to Berowne's unjust description of Rosaline. It is impossible to tell whether the seduction of W.H. by the Dark Lady really took place. It could be a figment of Shakespeare's incorrigibly dramatic imagination, based on hypotheses. Supposing the Dark Lady met W.H. and invited him to share her bed, would he, out of friendship or loyalty, repulse the lady's advances? Knowing the lascivious comments made on W.H.'s activities, Shakespeare knew the answer. If he were to be betrayed in this way, would the poet be jealous? Would he break with his friend or forgive him? He knew that W.H.'s friendship was more valuable to him than his love for the Dark Lady.

I am not maintaining that Shakespeare's mistress – if he had one – did not seduce his friend, but merely that we do not and cannot know. Of course the account given in the Sonnets is very circumstantial, and while we read we accept it as true. But we have to remember that there are countless invented scenes in the plays which give the impression that Shakespeare was there – yet Hamlet's conversation with Rosencrantz and Guildenstern or with the grave-digger, Lady Macbeth's temptation of her husband, and Isabella's painful interview with Claudio are scenes which are not even based on source material.

In the Sonnets the Poet's attitude both to W.H. and to the Dark Lady – and even to his own feelings – is wildly inconsistent, and could be used to support the view that W.H. is an amalgam of more than one man. W.H. is sometimes depicted as a man whose character is as praiseworthy as his beauty, sometimes as a rake, sometimes as selfish and cold-hearted, if slow to temptation. The Dark Lady is sometimes cruel (which in the jargon of the sonneteers meant chaste), sometimes deceitful and promiscuous. The Poet himself vows eternal fidelity to W.H., but on occasion partially admits he has neglected him for newer friends; and with the Dark Lady he alternates remorse and delight. Nor do these changes come in a logical order. The warmest praise of W.H.'s character comes after he has been severely criticised for moral failings; the description of the tortures of lust is followed by a description of sexual enjoyment without any overt consciousness of guilt.

Some critics would have preferred a tidier story – that W.H. should be treated as faultless only before his faults were exposed, that the Poet's relationship with his mistress should change from attraction to lust, from lust to repentance. But, it may be argued, it is the very untidiness which helps to give the illusion of truth to life. It has not been admitted by all critics that in the most obscene sonnets Shakespeare takes as much delight as John Donne in the confidence of his power, and in the exercise of his sometimes outrageous wit. The Dark Lady, if she existed, would have shared his delight; so, indeed, would Rosalind, another creature of his imagination. 'Th'expense of spirit in a waste of shame', though ostensibly, and even genuinely, a stern condemnation of lust, is also triumphant; and we can hardly doubt that the sense of triumph is due to the Poet's consciousness of his own genius in being able to express absolutely and intensely what was in his mind. Shelley lamented that the mind in creation was like a fading coal – but this sonnet is incandescent.[46]

CHAPTER 7

Links With Other Works

We shall be concerned in this chapter with the use made by Shakespeare in his other works, both narrative and dramatic, of the themes and images of the Sonnets. As there is still uncertainty about the relative dates of plays and sonnets,[1] we cannot say that in the plays Shakespeare was converting private experiences and feelings for public consumption, goring his own thoughts; nor can we imply that the Sonnets are reliable autobiography. As we have seen in the previous chapter, the matter is complicated by the element of dramatisation in even the most apparently confessional poems. Moreover, as the Sonnets were probably not printed in the order of their composition, we can seldom be certain of the direction of the influence – whether plays echoed sonnets or the other way round. Even close parallels cannot be taken to prove proximity of date since a situation in a play may recall, after a lapse of many years, a situation or an idea treated in one of the Sonnets. Nor is it only situations which trigger associations, as we know from the image clusters which persisted in play after play in totally different contexts, the clusters growing in successive years.[2] A simple example from another poet's work may serve to warn us of the dangers. When Thomas Hardy published 'In the Time of "the Breaking of Nations" ' during the First World War, no one would have suspected that the poem had been conceived more than forty years earlier during the Franco-Prussian War, though they might have suspected from the line 'When dynasties pass' that the poem had been coloured by Hardy's epic drama on the Napoleonic wars, written in the early years of the twentieth century.[3] One final caveat: although there are more parallels between the early plays of Shakespeare and the Sonnets than with those written after 1600, this may be due to similarity of content rather than to proximity of composition.[4]

Let us begin, then, by considering two examples of borrowings, though in neither case do we know which passage was written first. In *Edward III* the King tries unsuccessfully to seduce the Countess of Salisbury, using her father as a reluctant go-between. The father's speech to the Countess is on the King's sinfulness, the more reprehensible because of his power and position. It is a speech which has often been attributed to Shakespeare:[5]

> The freshest summer's day doth soonest taint
> The loathed carrion that it seems to kiss;
> That sin doth ten times aggravate itself
> That is committed in a holy place;
> An evil deed done by authority
> Is sin and subornation; deck an ape
> In tissue, and the beauty of the robe
> Adds but the greater scorn unto the beast.
> A spacious field of reasons could I urge
> Between his glory, daughter, and thy shame:
> That poison shows worst in a golden cup;
> Dark night seems darker by the lightning flash;
> Lilies that fester smell far worse than weeds.

The last line of this passage appears also at the end of Sonnet XCIV. In an earlier scene Lodowick describes the King blushing in the line

> His cheeks put on their scarlet ornaments.

In Sonnet CXLII the same phrase, 'scarlet ornaments', is used to describe the Dark Lady's lips:

> not from those lips of thine,
> That have profan'd their scarlet ornaments,
> And seal'd false bonds of love. . . .

Here the red lips suggested, by a characteristic Shakespearian twist, red sealing-wax.

Several explanations are possible. If Shakespeare did not write the scenes in question:

(1)   He may have echoed a line or a phrase from a play he had read, or seen.
(2)   The anonymous author had read two of Shakespeare's sonnets which had been circulating in manuscript.

If, on the other hand, Shakespeare wrote the two scenes in *Edward III*:

(3)   He could have used phrases from his yet unpublished sonnets;
(4)   Or he could have used in the Sonnets phrases from the scenes he had contributed to *Edward III*. One line beginning 'lilies that fester', is equally appropriate in both contexts; and critics are divided on whether 'scarlet ornaments' is more appropriate to blush or lips (on the whole, if the implication is that the lady used cosmetics, the latter seems more natural). But this does not help us to determine which was written first.

The other example is from *The Merchant of Venice*. Bassanio, confronted with the caskets, meditates on the danger of judging by appearances and so decides not to choose the golden casket. One of his examples of misleading appearances is the use of dead persons' hair to make blonde wigs:

> Look on beauty
> And you shall see 'tis purchas'd by the weight,
> Which therein works a miracle in nature,
> Making them lightest that wear most of it;
> So are those crisped snaky golden locks
> Which make such wanton gambols with the wind
> Upon supposed fairness often known
> To be the dowry of a second head –
> The skull that bred them in the sepulchre.

In LXVIII Shakespeare refers to 'these bastard signs of fair':

> Before the golden tresses of the dead,
> The right of sepulchres, were shorn away,
> To live a second life on second head,
> Ere beauty's dead fleece made another gay.

There seems to be no way of telling which of these passages was written first, and certainly no proof that they were written about the same time.[6]

With these cautions in mind, we can proceed to consider some of the links between plays, narrative poems and sonnets. The first seventeen sonnets, urging the friend to marry, contain some of the same arguments used by the goddess in *Venus and Adonis*. The arguments, as we have seen, were familiar to Elizabethan readers from Sidney's *Arcadia*, Erasmus's model letters and colloquies, and Marlowe's *Hero and Leander*, though that poem was not published until later. Venus urges Adonis:

> Make use of time, let not advantage slip;
> Beauty within itself should not be wasted.
> Fair flowers that are not gather'd in their prime
> Rot and consume themselves in little time. (ll. 129 *ff.*)

> Is thine own heart to thine own face affected?
> Can thy right hand seize love upon thy left?
> Then woo thyself, be of thyself rejected;
> Steal thine own freedom, and complain on theft.
> Narcissus so himself himself forsook,
> And died to kiss his shadow in the brook. (ll. 157 *ff.*)

Although he is not mentioned by name in the Sonnets, there are clear allusions to the fate of Narcissus.

> Torches are made to light, jewels to wear,
> Dainties to taste, fresh beauty for the use.
> Herbs for their smell, and sappy plants to bear:
> Things growing to themselves are growth's abuse.
>   Seeds spring from seeds, and beauty breedeth beauty;
>   Thou wast begot – to get it is thy duty.
>
> Upon the earth's increase why shouldst thou feed
> Unless the earth with thy increase be fed?
> By law of nature thou art bound to breed,
> That thine may live when thou thyself art dead;
>   And so in spite of death thou dost survive,
>   In that thy likeness still is left alive. (ll. 163 *ff.*)

Clearly Venus and the Poet of the Sonnets have different motives. Venus wants Adonis as her lover, and her talk about breed is sophistry; the Poet, more disinterestedly, wants his friend to take a wife.

The links between the Sonnets and *Lucrece* are less obvious; but the heroine's long lament after the rape parallels those sonnets which are concerned with Time's threat to beauty and love. Only procreation and poetry can offer any defence against Time's scythe, the Poet of the Sonnets declared. Time is a devourer and a cruel tyrant.

> Time doth transfix the flourish set on youth
> And delves the parallels in beauty's brow.

Time's hand is injurious and fell, and rosy lips and cheeks come within the compass of his sickle. Even Nature, we are told in the envoy, 'sovereign mistress over wrack' though she is, will eventually have to surrender W.H., her minion, to Time.[7] So Lucrece, after inveighing against guilty opportunity, attacks Time for allowing his servant to ruin her; but, unlike the Poet of the Sonnets, she recognises, as Renaissance iconographers invariably did, that Truth was Time's daughter, and that Time was a revealer of truth as well as a destroyer:

> Mis-shapen Time, copesmate of ugly Night.
> Swift subtle post, carrier of grisly care,
> Eater of youth, false slave to false delight,
> Base watch of woes, sin's packhorse, virtue's snare;
> Thou nursest all, and murd'rest all that are.
>   O hear me then, injurious, shifting Time!
>   Be guilty of my death, since of my crime.

Why hath thy servant Opportunity
Betray'd the hours thou gav'st me to repose?
Cancell'd my fortunes and enchained me
To endless date of never-ending woes?
Time's office is to fine the hate of foes,
   To eat up errors by opinion bred,
   Not spend the dowry of a lawful bed.

Time's glory is to calm contending kings,
To unmask falsehood, and bring truth to light,
To stamp the seal of time in aged things,
To wake the morn, and sentinel the night,
To wrong the wronger till he render right;
   To ruinate proud buildings with thy hours
   And smear with dust their glitt'ring golden tow'rs.

To fill with worm-holes stately monuments,
To feed oblivion with decay of things,
To blot old books and alter their contents,
To pluck the quills from ancient ravens' wings,
To dry the old oak's sap, and cherish springs,
   To spoil antiquities of hammer'd steel,
   And turn the giddy round of Fortune's wheel;

To show the beldam daughters of her daughter,
To make the child a man, the man a child,
To slay the tiger that doth live by slaughter,
To tame the unicorn and lion wild,
To mock the subtle in themselves beguil'd,
   To cheer the ploughman with increaseful crops,
   And waste huge stones with little water-drops.

Why work'st thou mischief in thy pilgrimage,
Unless thou couldst return to make amends?
One poor retiring minute in an age
Would purchase thee a thousand thousand friends,
Lending him wit that to bad debtors lends:
   O, this dread night, wouldst thou one hour come back
   I could prevent this storm, and shun thy wrack!

Thou ceaseless lackey to Eternity. . . .[8]

When we turn to some of Shakespeare's early plays we are confronted
with situations which seem to belong to the world of the sonneteers.
Since many of them were concerned with love, the similarity of atmos-
phere is not surprising; but even into the Plautine comedy of mistaken
identity, the *Menaechmi*, Shakespeare inserted a romantic scene, quite
alien to the tone of the original; and the rhymed quatrains in which

Antipholus of Syracuse and Luciana converse would not have seemed out of place in any of the minor sonnet sequences:

> *Luciana.* Bear a fair presence, though your heart be tainted;
> Teach sin the carriage of a holy saint;
> Be secret-false. What need she be acquainted?
> What simple thief brags of his own attaint?
> 'Tis double wrong to truant with your bed
> And let her read it in thy looks at board;
> Shame hath a bastard fame, well managed;
> Ill deeds is doubled with an evil word. . . .

> *Antipholus.* Teach me, dear creature, how to think and speak;
> Lay open to my earthy-gross conceit
> Smoth'red in errors, feeble, shallow, weak
> The folded meaning of your words' deceit.
> Against my soul's pure truth why labour you
> To make it wander in an unknown field?
> Are you a god? Would you create me new?
> Transform me, then, and to your pow'r I'll yield. . . .
> O, train me not, sweet mermaid, with thy note,
> To drown me in thy sister's flood of tears.
> Sing, siren, for thyself and I will dote;
> Spread o'er the silver waves thy golden hairs,
> And as a bed I'll take them, and there lie;
> And in that glorious supposition think
> He gains by death that hath such means to die.

These speeches are not typical of *The Comedy of Errors*. *The Two Gentlemen of Verona*, on the other hand, is startlingly close to the Sonnets in certain respects. The close friendship of the two gentlemen, expressed by their affectionate epithets – 'loving Proteus', 'sweet Valentine', 'sweet Proteus' – resembles the friendship celebrated in the Sonnets, save only that they belong to the same social class and are not threatened by class differences. The conflict between love and friendship, at first in the mind of Proteus (who sacrifices friendship to love) and then in the mind of Valentine (who sacrifices love to friendship), likewise resembles the climatic situation in the sonnet story where the friend is guilty of a betrayal of friendship by allowing himself to be seduced by the Poet's mistress. But here again there are significant differences. Silvia does nothing to encourage Proteus' treachery and attempted rape; and Valentine, forgiving his perfunctorily penitent friend, offers to relinquish the girl who loves him to the interrupted rapist. The Poet forgives W.H., who is apparently much less guilty than either the Dark Lady or Proteus. In the play Shakespeare is apparently demonstrating the absurdity of preferring the claims of friendship in such a way as to guarantee the maximum of misery to the greatest number of people. The sixteen lines which reveal Valentine's absurdity are the following. The wishes of both ladies in the case are ignored.[9]

> Proteus,
> I am sorry I must never trust thee more,
> But count the world a stranger for thy sake.
> The private wound is deepest. O time most accurst!
> 'Mongst all foes that a friend should be the worst!
>
> *Proteus.* My shame and guilt confounds me.
> Forgive me, Valentine; if hearty sorrow
> Be a sufficient ransom for offence,
> I tender here; I do as truly suffer
> As e'er I did commit.
>
> *Valentine.* Then I am paid;
> And once again I do receive thee honest.
> Who by repentance is not satisfied
> Is nor of heaven nor of earth, for these are pleas'd;
> By penitence th'Eternal's wrath's appeas'd.
> And, that my love may appear plain and free,
> All that was mine in Silvia I give thee.

The halting lines, the feeble phrasing, and the smug couplets make one uneasy. One cannot be sure that they were meant to be absurd, but as the play is otherwise competent one is driven to speculate that something could have happened to the prompt-copy between 1590 and 1623. One cannot help being struck by the contrast between the power of the relevant sonnets – 'Take all my loves, my love, yea, take them all', 'Those pretty wrongs that liberty commits' and 'That thou hast her, it is not all my grief' – and the feebleness of this scene.

If, however, one examines the remainder of the play, it is clear that it is not a straightforward romance. From the very first scene there is a satire of the love to which both gentlemen fall victim. Valentine tells Proteus (Act I, sc. i, ll. 45 *ff.*):

> And writers say, as the most forward bud
> Is eaten by the canker ere it blow,
> Even so by love the young and tender wit
> Is turn'd to folly, blasting in the bud,
> Losing his verdure even in the prime,
> And all the fair effects of future hopes.

The miserable state of lovers described by Valentine is a parody of the sonneteering convention (Act I, sc. i, ll. 29 *ff.*):

To be in love – where scorn is bought with groans,
Coy looks with heart-sore sighs, one fading moment's mirth
With twenty watchful, weary, tedious nights;
If haply won, perhaps a hapless gain;
If lost, why then a grievous labour won;
However, but a folly bought with wit,
Or else a wit by folly vanquished.

The same point is made by Speed at the beginning of Act II after he has handed Valentine Silvia's glove (Act II, sc. i, ll. 15–28):

Marry, by these special marks: first, you have learn'd, like Sir Proteus, to wreath your arms like a malcontent; to relish a love-song, like a robin redbreast; to walk alone, like one that had the pestilence; to sigh, like a school-boy that had lost his ABC; to weep, like a young wench that had buried her grandam; to fast, like one that takes diet; to watch, like one that fears robbing; to speak puling, like a beggar at Hallowmas. You were wont, when you laughed, to crow like a cock; when you walk'd to walk like one of the lions; when you fasted, it was presently after dinner; when you look'd sadly, it was for want of money. And now you are metamorphis'd with a mistress, that, when I look on you, I can hardly think you my master.

When the Duke pretends to consult Valentine about his coy mistress, Valentine advises him not to be deterred by initial repulses (Act III, sc. i, ll. 93 *ff.*):

A woman sometime scorns what best contents her.
Send her another; never give her o'er,
For scorn at first makes after-love the more.
If she do frown, 'tis not in hate of you,
But rather to beget more love in you;
If she do chide, 'tis not to have you gone,
For why the fools are mad if left alone.
Take no repulse, whatever she doth say;
For 'Get you gone' she doth not mean 'Away!'
Flatter and praise, commend, extol their graces;
Though ne'er so black, say they have angels' faces.

The poem Valentine writes for Silvia is a sonnet with the first quatrain omitted. Later Proteus advises Thurio how to woo Silvia:

You must lay lime to tangle her desires
By wailful sonnets, whose composed rhymes
Should be full-fraught with serviceable vows.

'Ay,' says the Duke. 'Much is the force of heaven-bred poesy.' Proteus continues:

> Say that upon the altar of her beauty
> You sacrifice your tears, your sighs, your heart;
> Write till your ink be dry, and with your tears
> Moist it again, and frame some feeling line
> That may discover such integrity;
> For Orpheus' lute was strung with poets' sinews,
> Whose golden touch could soften steel and stones,
> Make tigers tame, and huge leviathans
> Forsake unsounded deeps to dance on sands.

This passage neatly satirises not romantic love but the sonneteering craze which, Shakespeare implies, does not exhibit much integrity and certainly is not heaven-bred.[10]

In *Romeo and Juliet* the conventional love of the hero for the unresponsive Rosaline repeats the situation of countless followers of Petrarch, and the language employed by Romeo in the first scene, exclamatory and antithetical, would not be out of place in the sequence of minor sonneteers:

> Why then, O brawling love! O loving hate!
> O anything, of nothing first create!
> O heavy lightness! serious vanity!
> Mis-shapen chaos of well-seeming forms!
> Feather of lead, bright smoke, cold fire, sick health!
> Still-waking sleep, that is not what it is!
> This love feel I, that feel no love in this. . . .
> Love is a smoke rais'd with the fume of sighs;
> Being purg'd, a fire sparkling in lovers' eyes;
> Being vex'd, a sea nourish'd with loving tears.
> What is it else? A madness most discreet,
> A choking gall, and a preserving sweet.

Rosaline, in accordance with the conventional heroine of the sonneteers, will

> not be hit
> With Cupid's arrow. She hath Dian's wit,
> And in strong proof of chastity well arm'd,
> From Love's weak childish bow she lives unharm'd.

Later in the play, Mercutio, who does not know that Romeo is now in love with Juliet, hails his approach:

Now is he for the numbers that Petrarch flow'd in; Laura, to his lady, was a kitchen-wench – marry she had a better love to berhyme

her; Dido, a dowdy; Cleopatra, a gipsy; Helen and Hero, hildings
and harlots; Thisbe, a gray eye or so, but not to the purpose.

Mercutio's satire and his frequent obscenities provide a healthy counter-
blast to Romeo's fashionable sentimentalities, so as to prepare the way
for his love for Juliet, the family feud being substituted for the
unresponsiveness of the lady as an obstacle in the path of true love. But,
despite satire on sonneteer's love, it has often been noted that Romeo and
Juliet share a sonnet on their first encounter and kiss on the final couplet
– a point which the original audience, including no doubt a number of
sonneteers and more admirers of sonnets, would be in a position to
appreciate.

Love's Labour's Lost contains three sonnets composed by the aristocratic suitors. In addition there are extended passages of rhymed verse
from which several sonnets could be extracted.[11] Berowne's farewell to
rhetoric, for example, is couched in the form of a regular sonnet:

> O, never will I trust to speeches penn'd,
> Nor to the motion of a school-boy's tongue,
> Nor never come in vizard to my friend,
> Nor woo in rhyme, like a blind harper's song.
> Taffeta phrases, silken terms precise,
> Three-pil'd hyperboles, spruce affectation,
> Figures pedantical – these summer-flies
> Have blown me full of maggot ostentation.
> I do forswear them; and I here protest,
> By this white glove – how white the hand, God knows! –
> Henceforth my wooing mind shall be express'd
> In russet yeas, and honest kersey noes.
>   And, to begin, wench – so God help me, law! –
>   My love to thee is sound, sans crack or flaw.

The portrait of the dark-haired Rosaline resembles that of the Dark
Lady, as depicted in some of the Sonnets; but we are not meant to
accept Berowne's unflattering sketch of her character as true:

> And, among three, to love the worst of all,
> A whitely wanton with a velvet brow,
> With two pitch balls stuck in her face for eyes;
> Ay, and, by heaven, one that will do the deed,
> Though Argus were her eunuch and her guard.

Although his fellows deplore Berowne's taste in falling in love with an
unfashionable brunette, telling him that black is the badge of hell,
neither they nor the Princess regard her as anything but virtuous. The
blackness which is a symbol of evil may be merely an appearance

concealing a totally different reality. The bawdy exchanges between the ladies and Boyet do not, of course, imply bawdy conduct.

The most interesting parallel between *Love's Labour's Lost* and the Sonnets is the feeling of distaste for the hyperboles of poets. It is apparent in Berowne's vow to forswear rhetorical artifice; it is apparent in the absurdity of Armado's epistolary style; it is apparent in Berowne's earlier disclaimer:

> Fie painted rhetoric! O she needs it not!
> To things of sale a seller's praise belongs.

And also in the Princess's dignified rebuke to Boyet:

> Good Lord Boyet, my beauty, though but mean,
> Needs not the painted flourish of your praise.
> Beauty is bought by judgement of the eye,
> Not utter'd by base sale of chapmen's tongues;
> I am less proud to hear you tell my worth
> Than you much willing to be counted wise
> In spending your wit in the praise of mine.

Several of the sonnets concerned with the Rival Poet echo the same sentiments.[12] In XXI, there is the same reference to the praise of sellers:

> O let me true in love but truly write,
> And then believe me, my love is as fair,
> As any mother's child, though not so bright
> As those gold candles fixed in heaven's air:
>> Let them say more that like of hearsay well,
>> I will not praise that purpose not to sell.

In LXXXII the strained touches of rhetoric are contrasted with the 'true plain words, by thy true-telling friend'. In LXXXIII the Poet declares:

> I never saw that you did painting need,
> And therefore to your fair no painting set. . . .
>> There lives more life in one of your fair eyes,
>> Than both your poets can in praise devise.

Similar ideas are expressed in Sonnets LXXXIV and LXXXV.

On the other hand, Berowne's long apologia for his fellow-victims, his claim that love is the best teacher, finds an echo in the neo-Platonism of some of the Sonnets:

> From women's eyes this doctrine I derive:
> They sparkle still the right Promethean fire;

> They are the books, the arts, the academes,
> That show, contain and nourish all the world,
> Else none at all in aught proves excellent.

The first of these lines is closely paralleled in the Sonnets, and the fact that it is there addressed not to a woman but to W.H. does not seriously affect the underlying meaning.

Several critics have supposed[13] that the relationship between Prince Hal and Falstaff is a dramatisation of that between W.H. and the Poet of the Sonnets. In both relationships there is a marked difference of social status – Prince and Knight, Aristocrat and Player – a difference in age, and a doubt by the older man whether his affection is fully reciprocated. Falstaff's death, soon after his rejection, may be linked with the Poet's belief that he would die if he were to be rejected. Both Falstaff and the Poet are, if on different levels, entertainers. Falstaff retains his hold on the Prince by his wit, his gaiety, by being the Prince's Fool as well as his tempter. The Poet of the Sonnets admitted that (metaphorically) he had made himself a motley to the view. The strongest evidence that there was a link in Shakespeare's mind is provided by Hal's first soliloquy which has strikingly similar imagery to XXXIII. Hal has just agreed to take part in a robbery in order to play a trick on Falstaff, and left alone on the stage he tells the audience that he will

> imitate the sun,
> Who doth permit the base contagious clouds
> To smother up his beauty from the world,
> That, when he please again to be himself,
> Being wanted, he may be more wonder'd at
> By breaking through the foul and ugly mists
> Of vapours that did seem to strangle him.

Here the clouds are the Prince's 'friends' (so to call them), and his rejection of them is symbolised by the sun emerging from amidst the clouds. In the sonnet the same situation is viewed from the standpoint of the rejected friend:

> Full many a glorious morning I have seen
> Flatter the mountain-tops with sovereign eye . . .
> Anon permit the basest clouds to ride
> With ugly rack on his celestial face . . .
> Even so my sun one early morn did shine
> With all triumphant splendour on my brow;
> But out, alack, he was but one hour mine,
> The region cloud hath mask'd him from me now.
>   Yet him for this my love no whit disdaineth;
>   Suns of the world may stain when heaven's sun staineth.

Beeching called attention to other parallels between the Sonnets and the two parts of *Henry IV*.[14] The King speaks of his politically rare appearances in public:

> My presence, like a robe pontifical,
> Ne'er seen but wonder'd at, and so my state,
> Seldom but sumptuous, show'd like a feast
> And won by rareness such solemnity.

In Sonnet LII five of the key words of this speech appear:

> Therefore are feasts so solemn and so rare,
> Since seldom coming in the long year set. . . .
> So is the time that keeps you as my chest,
> Or as the wardrobe which the robe doth hide.

The epithet 'sullen' is applied to a bell in Sonnet LXXI and *2 Henry IV*; and the King, echoing Ovid, like the Poet of the Sonnets speaks on the revolution of the times which

> Make mountains level, and the continent,
> Weary of solid firmness, melt itself
> Into the sea; and other times to see
> The beachy girdle of the ocean
> Too wide for Neptune's hips.

Troilus and Cressida is another play in which the obsession with Time is apparent. Lucrece's tirade is juxtaposed with the description of a painting of the siege of Troy, and this may partly account for the repetition of the Time theme in the play.[15] But a story about a woman's infidelity was inevitably concerned with the destructive power of Time. Moreover, Troilus's love for Cressida, according to the definition given in the sonnet (CXVI), is not true love since it alters when it alteration finds. He had tried to believe that love was not Time's fool

> though rosy lips and cheeks
> Within his bending sickle's compass come . . .

that his love for Cressida would outlive 'beauty's outward'; but it did not outlive the sight of her seduction by Diomed. Before this, when the lovers are separated, Troilus inveighs against 'injurious Time' comparing it with a robber, very much in the spirit of the Sonnets. The audience is already aware that Cressida is to be sent to her father in the Greek camp; and, before the decision is conveyed to the lovers, Ulysses has delivered a long harangue to Achilles on the destructive effects of Time, in which he argues that

                                        beauty, wit,
                    High birth, vigour of bone, desert in service,
                    Love, friendship, charity, are subjects all
                    To envious and calumniating Time.

This is a denial of the hardly won belief in love's permanence expressed
in the Sonnets but perfectly appropriate to the speaker in the play. It
is not always recognised that the fox, Ulysses, may not be the spokesman
for the poet, and hardly recognised at all that his premises are false.
The deeds of Achilles are not forgotten: on the contrary, that is why
the Greeks want him back. Ajax is not really worshipped, as Ulysses
pretends: he is ridiculed, and only becomes selected because the ballot
has been rigged. Ulysses' speech, effective as a piece of rhetoric, and
relevant to the theme of the play, is based on a lie and on an elaborate
charade. It does not even succeed in its aim, for Achilles returns to the
battle only because of the death of Patroclus.

It has been suggested that the man described in XCIV, 'unmoved,
cold, and to temptation slow', resembles Angelo, the festering lily of
Measure for Measure. Perhaps the resemblances have been exaggerated.
Despite the Duke's enthusiastic testimonial in the first scene, he can
hardly be described as an inheritor of heaven's graces; and he does not
possess, as the man in the Sonnets clearly does, the ability to inspire
love, except in the deserted Mariana; and, however virtuous he may
seem at the beginning, he has a mean streak which would prevent him
from being described as sweet. Nevertheless, he does illustrate the
potential corruption which overtakes the virtue which results from a
coldness of temperament.

All's Well that Ends Well at first sight seems to have no connection
with the Sonnets, though the resemblances between Parolles and Falstaff
could be taken to mean that the Bertram–Parolles friendship duplicates
the Hal–Falstaff friendship discussed above. More suggestive is the
painful class difference between Helena and Bertram, where the social
inferiority in the heroine is united with a moral superiority to the man
she loves.[16] There seems to be a similar situation in the Sonnets, though
neither the Poet nor Helena frankly admits that W.H. or Bertram is a
cad.

A year or two before the publication of the Sonnets, Shakespeare had
used some of the real or imagined experience of the Dark Lady in his
portrait of Cleopatra. It is, of course, based on the account given by
Plutarch. The Roman view of her character – the view of Antony himself
when he is ashamed of his infatuation, furious with her suspected
treachery, or jealous – is that she is a lustful gipsy, a threat to order and
dignity, a 'triple-turn'd whore', 'a boggler ever':

But when we in our viciousness grow hard –
O misery on't! – the wise gods, seel our eyes,
And in our own filth drop our clear judgments, make us
Adore our errors, laugh at's while we strut
To our confusion. . . .
I found you as a morsel cold upon
Dead Caesar's trencher. Nay, you were a fragment
Of Cneius Pompey's, besides what hotter hours,
Unregist'red in vulgar fame, you have
Luxuriously pick'd out. . . .

This resembles the bitterer Dark Lady sonnets, as Berowne's remarks about Rosaline resemble the lighter sonnets of the sequence. Yet the total impression we get of the relationship between Antony and Cleopatra is not simply 'Th'expense of spirit in a waste of shame'. Antony's suicide believing Cleopatra is dead, her suicide knowing Antony is dead, and even the epitaph spoken by Caesar all show that a sub-title 'All for Lust' would be a gross distortion of the play.

It will have become apparent in the discussion of the links between the Sonnets and Shakespeare's other works that he did not merely return again and again to several obsessive themes, but that he was using the same poetic powers in whichever genre he was writing in – as a sonneteer, as a narrative poet and as a dramatist. Those powers were essentially dramatic. One can go farther and say that phrases from the Sonnets used in other works, whether before or after, are always appropriate to the situation and to the characters who speak them; and what is true of lines and phrases is equally true of larger parallels.

One of Orlando's feeble poems is on precisely the same theme as, and is verbally close to, one of the finest of the Sonnets.[17]

Teaching all that read to know
   The quintessence of every sprite
Heaven would in little show.
   Therefore heaven Nature charg'd
That one body should be fill'd
   With all graces wide-enlarg'd.
Nature presently distill'd
   Helen's cheek, but not her heart,
Cleopatra's majesty,
   Atalanta's better part,
Sad Lucretia's modesty.
   Thus Rosalind of many parts
By heavenly synod was devis'd,
   Of many faces, eyes, and hearts,
To have the touches dearest priz'd.

This is Sonnet LIII:

> What is your substance, whereof are you made,
> That millions of strange shadows on you tend?
> Since every one hath, every one, one shade,
> And you, but one, can every shadow lend.
> Describe Adonis, and the counterfeit
> Is poorly imitated after you;
> On Helen's cheek all art of beauty set,
> And you in Grecian tires are painted new.
> Speak of the spring and foison of the year,
> The one doth shadow of your beauty show,
> The other as your bounty doth appear,
> And you in every blessed shape we know.

We should not deduce from this that Shakespeare was able to write superbly when he was expressing his own private feelings, but that he could not always transpose these successfully into the public world of the plays; for Orlando's poem is deliberately feeble. We can tell from Hal's prosaic wooing of Katherine, from Hotspur's attack on poets, from Benedick's inability to compose a poem for Beatrice, and from Hamlet's quatrain which is all that survives of his love-poetry, that dramatic heroes are the subject of poetry, not poets themselves. On the other hand, we should not suppose that the power of the best sonnets, compared with that of corresponding passages in plays, is that they express more directly the poet's own feelings. Even if T. S. Eliot was wrong to complain that *Hamlet* was unsuccessful because of the intrusion of the poet's personal feelings,[18] it may well be true that the closer the Sonnets approximated to autobiography the greater was the risk of failure.

CHAPTER 8

Critical History

(1)

The first recorded comment on Shakespeare's Sonnets was made by Francis Meres in 1598, when he remarked that 'the sweete wittie soule of *Ovid* lives in mellifluous & hony-tongued Shakespeare, witnes his *Venus and Adonis*, his Lucrece, his sugred Sonnets among his private friends, &c.'[1] It has been pointed out, however, that the sonnets Meres mentions may not be the ones published in 1609.

The only other comment made in Shakespeare's lifetime was by Leonard Digges on the fly-leaf of a copy of Lope de Vega's *Rimas* (1613): 'this book of sonnets, which with Spaniards here is accounted of their Lope de Vega as in England we should of our Will Shakespeare'.[2] Digges was the stepson of Shakespeare's overseer and he contributed commendatory verses to the First Folio.[3]

When John Benson brought out his edition of the poems in 1640, he said that they were 'excellent and sweetely composed poems'; but he omitted some, altered the 1609 order, and changed the sex of the person to whom most of the sonnets were addressed. By this time love-sonnets were out of fashion and they remained so for a century and a half. In 1709 Gildon complained that 'Petrarch had a little infected' Shakespeare's way of thinking,[4] and nearly all eighteenth-century critics, if they mentioned the Sonnets, found little to admire in them. Capell, however, said they had one thing to recommend them: 'that a single thought, vary'd and put in language poetical, is the subject of each sonnet; a thing essential to these compositions, and yet but rarely observ'd by either ancient or modern dealers in them'.[5]

Dr Johnson, following the example of his predecessors, did not include the Sonnets in his edition of Shakespeare. A writer in *The Gentleman's Magazine* takes one's breath away when he remarks:

A very trifling compliment is paid to Mrs Smith when it is observed how much her sonnets exceed those of *Shakespeare* and *Milton*. She has undoubtedly conferred honour on a species of poetry which most of her predecessors in this country have disgraced.[6]

One of Charlotte Smith's best sonnets, which secured an undeserved place in *The Oxford Book of Eighteenth Century Verse*, will exhibit the

peculiarity of gentlemanly taste at the end of the century. It is entitled
'Written at the Close of Spring':

> The garlands fade that Spring so lately wove,
>   Each simple flower, which she had nurs'd in dew,
> Anemonies that spangled every grove,
>   The primrose wan, and hare-bell, mildly blue.
> No more shall violets linger in the dell,
>   Or purple orchis variegate the plain,
> Till spring again shall call forth every bell,
>   And dress with humid hands her wreaths again.
> Ah! poor humanity! so frail, so fair,
>   Are the fond visions of thy early day
> Till tyrant passion, and corrosive care,
>   Bid all thy fairy colours fade away!
> Another May new buds and flowers shall bring;
> Ah! why has happiness – no second spring?

In 1793, George Steevens notoriously explained why he had not
reprinted the Sonnets and the other non-dramatic poems of Shakespeare:

> because the strongest act of Parliament that could be framed would
> fail to compel readers into their service. . . . Had Shakespeare produced
> no other works than these his name would have reached us with as little
> celebrity as time has conferred on that of Thomas Watson, an older
> and much more elegant sonneteer.[7]

A few years later, in 1790, Anna Seward complained of the 'stiff
infelicity of expression' in the Sonnets.[8]

By this time, however, there was a revival of the sonnet by a number
of minor poets – Warton, Russell, Bowles, Charlotte Smith – so that the
continued dislike of Shakespeare's cannot be attributed to disapproval of
the genre. When the eulogies of the plays (in the early years of
'Shakespeare idolatry') are contrasted with the unpopularity of the
Sonnets, one is led to suspect that the plays were enjoyed for character-
isation, plot and action, and for what were called 'beauties', while in the
Sonnets, if the reader is bored by poetry, he is lost.

The Romantic poets were very much divided on the merits of the
Sonnets. Byron and Landor, who had neo-classical tastes, disliked the
genre.[9] Keats, Shelley and Coleridge admired them.[10] The most curious
case is that of Wordsworth. Initially he had some harsh things to say
about the Dark Lady sonnets, which he described as 'abominably harsh,
obscure and worthless'. He admitted that the others had 'very fine' lines
and passages, but complained that 'their chief faults – and heavy ones
they are – are sameness, tediousness, quaintness, and elaborate

obscurity'.[11] To which remarks Coleridge retorted: 'I see no elaborate obscurity and very little quaintness – nor do I know any sonnets that will bear such frequent reperusal: so rich in metre, so full of thought and *exquisitest* diction.'[12] When, soon after this exchange, Wordsworth began to cultivate the sonnet, it was Milton he chose as his model; but when he wrote his 1815 essay he had apparently been converted to Coleridge's view. Attacking Steevens for being insensible to the beauties of the Sonnets, he declared that 'in no part of the writings of this Poet is found, in an equal compass, a greater number of exquisite feelings felicitously expressed'.[13] Seven years later Wordsworth wrote to Landor to confess that he might have been better employed than composing sonnets; and as late as 1831 he complained that Shakespearian sonnets 'are merely quatrains with a couplet tacked to the end; and if they depended much upon the versification they would unavoidably be heavy'.[14]

Landor's own comments on the Sonnets make sad reading. In one of his *Imaginary Conversations* (1823) Porson remarks that in the Sonnets

> there sometimes is a singular strength and intensity of thought, with little of that imagination which was afterwards to raise him highest in the universe of poetry. Even the interest we take in the private life of this miraculous man cannot keep the volume in our hands long together. We acknowledge great power, but we experience great weariness.[15]

That Landor would have repudiated his spokesman's opinion is unlikely, for in a later conversation with Southey (1846) he gives an even more unfavourable opinion of the Sonnets: 'not a single one is very admirable, and few sink very low. They are hot and pothery: there is much condensation, little delicacy; like raspberry jam without cream, without crust, without bread, to break its viscidity'.[16] Even Hazlitt, a more reliable critic than Landor, is lukewarm about the Sonnets;[17] and Thomas Campbell damns with the faint praise that the Sonnets 'form altogether, the best of our sonnet poetry anterior to that of Drummond'.[18]

Much of the criticism of the Sonnets in the nineteenth century (as we saw in Chapter 6[19]) was concerned with the debate on Wordsworth's claim that they were essentially autobiographical – 'with this key/ Shakespeare unlocked his heart'.[20] The other main topic, related to it, was the attempt to link the Sonnets with the known facts of Shakespeare's life. Shakespeare had two known patrons, Southampton and Pembroke; but anecdotes about the former's munificence (probably based on the dedication to *Lucrece*) and about the latter's favour (based on the dedication of the First Folio to him and his brother) cannot exclude other possibilities. If the critics signally failed to arrive at a consensus with regard to the identity of W.H., they were equally at loggerheads with regard to the identities of the Rival Poet and the Dark Lady. The five appendixes in which Rollins sardonically summarised opinion on these topics, from those of serious scholars to those of the lunatic fringe, are an impressive monument to misplaced ingenuity and the folly of the intelligent.

Apart from the concentration on biographical topics, many nineteenth-century critics discussed the relative value of the sonnets of Milton, Wordsworth and Shakespeare, and whether it was possible to write good sonnets of any kind. Edward FitzGerald confessed to Frederick Tennyson (1841),[21] 'I certainly don't like sonnets,' although nine years earlier he had declared after reading Shakespeare's: 'I had but half an idea of him, Demigod as he seemed before, till I read them carefully . . . they seem all stuck about my heart'.[22] Samuel Rogers allowed 'no merit to Shakespeare's sonnets' (1838 and 1846).[23] Mark Pattison, editing Milton's sonnets (1883), said that Shakespeare's were not sonnets at all.[24] Henry Hallam, in his *Introduction to the Literature of Europe* (1839), regretted that Shakespeare had written the Sonnets, but here his literary objections are probably sparked off by other considerations:

> There is a weakness and folly in all excessive and mis-placed affection, which is not redeemed by the touches of nobler sentiments that abound. . . . But there are also faults of a merely critical nature. The obscurity is often such as only conjecture can penetrate; the strain of tenderness and adoration would be too monotonous, were it less unpleasing; and so many frigid conceits are scattered around, that we might almost fancy the poet to have written without genuine emotion, did not such a host of other passages attest the contrary.[25]

Tennyson, who had been very much influenced by the Sonnets while he was writing *In Memoriam*, disagreed with his dead friend's father.[26]

Eulogy and detraction continued throughout the century, although with Shakespeare's canonisation detraction became muted. D. G. Rossetti, who himself wrote many sonnets in the Italian form, nevertheless declared that 'a Shakespearian sonnet is better than the most perfect in form because Shakespeare wrote it'.[27] Palgrave, always inclined to echo Tennyson's views, spoke of Shakespeare's 'unrivalled mastery over all the tones of love'.[28] George Saintsbury, in his chapter in *The Cambridge History of English Literature*, declared that 'in the *Sonnets* the absolute high water mark of poetry is touched'.[29] Less hyperbolically C. S. Lewis wrote, in *The Oxford History of English Literature*, that 'from extreme particularity there is a road to the highest universality. . . . In certain senses of the word "love", Shakespeare is not so much our best as our only love poet.'[30]

On the other hand, Courthope and Beeching deplored the moral tone of the Sonnets,[31] and John Davidson argued that the sonnet form used by Shakespeare crippled his imagination: 'The feebleness of the tag which concludes, is in sad contrast with the splendid energy which opens, almost every sonnet.'[32]

American critics generally took their cue from English ones and they were divided in much the same way. Emerson was an enthusiastic champion of the Sonnets. 'In their way', he said,[33] they were 'as wonderful as the plays'; and Whitman declared[34] that he knew 'nothing in all literature to come up to these sonnets'. Yet his description of them casts some doubt on his praise. He said that the virility apparent in the plays was 'totally absent from the Sonnets' which he described as 'exquisite, sweet: lush: eleganted: refined and refined then again refined'. This is not how one would expect the highest poetry to be described.

There are hardly any recent critics who object to the Sonnets on moral grounds, and few who have doubts about their quality. Individual sonnets are criticised for obscurity and unsuccessful conceits; objections are taken to the couplets; but the only serious critic who thinks the Sonnets do not deserve their reputation is John Crowe Ransom in *The World's Body* (1938).[35]

(2)

So much has been written about the Sonnets during recent years that it may be useful to devote the remainder of this chapter to a brief survey of those editions, books and articles which appear to have contributed most to our understanding of them. This is a continuing process and, despite the danger of new critics reviving old misinterpretations, they do also learn from their predecessors. The Rollins Variorum edition (1944), which embodied the exegesis of three centuries, together with the sane conclusions of the editor, left many passages obscure; and there has probably been more useful comment in the last three decades than in the previous three centuries.

Four recent editions may be mentioned. Martin Seymour-Smith (1963) retains the Quarto spelling and emends as little as possible. He argues that Daniel was one of Shakespeare's models and devotes a good deal of space to the question of homosexuality. But his notes, though brief, are often very good; and his later essay on the first forty-two sonnets, in the Landry symposium, *New Essays on Shakespeare's Sonnets*, is a sensible, if unprovable, psychological interpretation.

W. G. Ingram and Theodore Redpath in the following year brought out what is perhaps the most reliable of modern editions. The text is modernised in spelling and punctuation, and Redpath defends this procedure in another article in the Landry symposium. The editors make a valiant effort to explain every doubtful phrase, sometimes by quotation from the plays, sometimes by judicious paraphrase. They include a useful glossary and a key to the word-play. Their interpretations are supported by considerable learning, and where they disagree with their predecessors they argue with considerable skill. They deliberately eschew any attempt to identify W.H., the Dark Lady and the Rival Poet, and this has the effect of concentrating their attention on literary interpretation.

John Dover Wilson's edition (1966) was in proof by the time Ingram and Redpath's appeared; and, because of his failing eyesight, he was unable to make use of it for his revised edition (1967). Despite the handicap under which he was working, he has a good, clean, modernised text, brief and pointed annotations, and a long and lively introduction. On the debit side it should be said that the brevity of his notes makes it impossible for him to argue against rival interpretations; he is too ready to believe that the 1609 order is wrong – in his second edition he gave a conjectural new order; and most of his introduction is spent on an attempt to identify W.H. as William Herbert. He has only four pages on strictly literary criticism, and two of these are taken up with quotations from Lever and C. S. Lewis.

Stephen Booth followed up *An Essay on Shakespeare's Sonnets* (1970) with a mammoth edition (1977) which includes a modernised text facing a facsimile of the Quarto, followed by 400 pages of commentary. He points out in his preface that he seeks to answer how the Sonnets 'achieve the clarity and simplicity most of them have from the unstable and randomly dynamic locutions they employ'.[36] Whether the locutions are random is a moot point, but Mr Booth says that one great problem

is that words, lines and clauses often give a multitude of meanings – of which none fits a single 'basic' statement to which the others can be called auxiliary. The problem is alleviated and at the same time conplicated (particularly for an editor) because even when the lines are vaguest and most ambiguous, they are usually *also* simple and obvious.

He gives as an example the third quatrain of XVI. He goes on to ask: 'In demonstrating their complexity, will an editor not be guilty of making problems where he should be solving them?'

Although much of Mr Booth's commentary is indeed illuminating, there are too many occasions when he chases random associations – particularly those of a sexual nature – of which the poet was unconscious. Take, for example LXXVIII:

> So oft have I invok'd thee for my Muse,
> And found such fair assistance in my verse,
> As every *Alien* pen hath got my use.

And under thee their poesy disperse.
Thine eyes, that taught the dumb on high to sing,
And heavy ignorance aloft to fly,
Have added feathers to the learned's wing,
And given grace a double Majesty.
Yet be most proud of that which I compile,
Whose influence is thine, and born of thee,
In others' works thou dost but mend the style,
And Arts with thy sweet graces graced be.
    But thou art all my art, and dost advance
    As high as learning my rude ignorance.

Mr Booth has some 2000 words of commentary on this sonnet, much of it illuminating. But one wonders if it is useful to link 'style' with *stilus*, 'pen' with *penna* (Latin 'feather'), and all four words with *penis*.[37] Mr Booth, indeed, admits:

> Such wordplay as this is so tenuous and its effect is so insubstantial, that even to call it wordplay is to exaggerate its weight. Such logically extravagant and substantially gratuitous webs of pertinence contribute to a poem in much the way rhyme, rhythm, and alliteration do. A reader who recognizes them must resist any temptation to read substance into them, and, however much he may insist on his sense of proportion, an editor who points them out can become a Satan tempting his readers to ingenuity and may himseelf be charged with ingenuity.

But this frank admission does not undo the damage that has been done – the introduction of ideas which can only be distracting. As Shakespeare puts it:

> Th'offender's sorrow lends but weak relief
> To him that bears the strong offence's cross.

Future editors will find the Booth edition a valuable quarry, even though they may well disagree with many of his interpretations.

(3)

Booth's method carries a stage farther the study of complexities of meaning initiated by Robert Graves and Laura Riding in their comparison of the 1609 text of CXXIX with that of *The Oxford Book of English Verse*.[38] They were quite justified in their complaints of the text of 'They flee from me' in that anthology since Wyatt's own manuscript proved it to be corrupt. But, as it is unlikely that the compositor of the first edition of the Sonnets could be relied upon to reproduce his copy exactly, and by no means certain that the copy which Thorpe secured was in the hand of the author, Graves and Riding defended readings which were indefensible, and attacked emendations which nearly everyone accepts. Nevertheless, their teasing out of ambiguities was the avowed model for William Empson's *Seven Types of Ambiguity* (1931) and for his later analysis of XCIV in *Some Versions of Pastoral*.[39] Here, too, we may disagree with some of his interpretations and suspect that some of the subtleties are in his own mind rather than in Shakespeare's – Empson's own admirable poems are not exactly pellucid – but he undoubtedly alerted readers to ironies, undertones and sub-texts, so that the reading of Shakespeare – not merely of the Sonnets – will never be the same.

Empson was followed by Molly M. Mahood, whose *Shakespeare's Wordplay* (1957) contains a notable chapter on the Sonnets. She concerned herself not with ambiguities as such but with the quibbles in which Shakespeare, sometimes consciously and sometimes unconsciously, indulged. She was able to demonstrate that 'the wordplay helps to fuse the metaphors into an imaginative whole'.[40] In LX, for example,[41] 'main' (5) refers back by means of a quibble to the waves of line 1; 'crooked eclipses' (7) prepare the way for the crooked scythe of Time in the third quatrain; 'parallels' (10), 'by recalling the lines of latitude on a celestial globe, harks back to the astrological image'; and 'flourish' (9) in the calligraphic sense prepares the reader for 'hand' (13).

Winifred M. T. Nowottny, the editor of the forthcoming Arden edition of the Sonnets, wrote a brilliant essay entitled 'Formal elements in Shakespeare's Sonnets', in which she argued, by an analysis of the first six, that although the imagery is of great importance it is not of exclusive or even of paramount importance.[42] Imagery, she demonstrates, 'is subordinated to the creation of the form of the whole and . . . imagery itself is at its most effective when it supports or is supported by the action of formal elements of a different kind'. In the first six sonnets Shakespeare 'has sacrificed the integration of the imagery of the individual sonnet to larger considerations of form'. Mrs Nowottny concludes:

A close study of the language of the *Sonnets* makes it clear that, great as was Shakespeare's ability to use imagery not only for its beauty but also for its integrating power, he possessed in even greater measure the power to make the formal elements of language express the nature of the experience with which the language deals.

Some of the most interesting work on the Sonnets in recent years, whether it is directly influenced by this essay or not, has paid due attention to questions of form, using often the terminology of structuralism. As her essay was published in 1952, Mrs Nowottny was lucky enough to avoid this temptation: she makes do with ordinary lucid English.

Booth, in particular, is much concerned with the formal elements in the Sonnets;[43] and Giorgio Melchiori refers to Mrs Nowottny, although he believes that recent structural critics have 'reached such a rigorous application of semiotic and structural instruments as to exclude all spurious matter', although he admits that 'the validity of such meta-critical analyses is in practice limited to the identification of possible interpretative parameters, which in fact they refrain from applying'. His own method starts from I. A. Richards's article, 'Jacobson's Shakespeare: the subliminal structures of a sonnet' (i.e. CXXIX).[44] He agrees that it is necessary 'to reassess the importance of the instruments used' and to recognise that 'none of them, taken alone, is *the* key to an interpretation of the sonnets'.

He chooses four sonnets which he describes as 'Shakespeare's dramatic meditations', arriving at this choice because they are exceptions to exceptions. In the first place Shakespeare's sonnets as a whole are exceptions to the general run of Elizabethan sonnets as represented by Sidney, Drayton, Daniel and Spenser, particularly with regard to the prevalence of personal pronominal forms and to the comparative frequency of certain connotative words. Secondly, the four chosen sonnets differ from Shakespeare's other 150 sonnets in having as a subject not love but the ethics of power (XCIV), social behaviour (CXXI), sex (CXXIX) and religion (CXLVI). He might have added CXVI, which like the other four is not addressed to an individual, though it is about love.

Melchiori's statistics are marginally affected by his use of the Donow concordance;[45] and it should be said that personal pronominal forms are bound to be affected by the social position (and perhaps by the sex) of the person addressed. Sidney and Spenser were writing sonnets to their equals; Daniel, Drayton and Shakespeare to their social superiors. But Melchiori marshals his arguments ingeniously and impressively, using social history and psychological theory as well as linguistic analysis supported by diagrams. We may suspect at times, as when he accepts Southam's view[46] that CXLVI is ironical at the expense of the overt Christianity contained in the poem, or when he thinks that lust is murderous only as long as it is unsatisfied and that lust 'is not the body-and-soul-killing vice of the moralities, but, as sex, an essential element of the human personality', that, although we may sympathise with his views, they are his views rather than Shakespeare's.

(4)

A number of critics have discussed the Sonnets in relation to their
sources and to other sonnet sequences. Of these the most elaborate and
learned is T. W. Baldwin's *The Literary Genetics of Shakespeare's Poems
and Sonnets* (1950),[47] which is packed with useful information, but
which is rather too dogmatic in its assertions about influences and too
rigid in its assumptions about Shakespeare's use of rhetoric. Some of its
conclusions were challenged by Claes Schaar,[48] who worked out a
plausible chronology of the Sonnets by a discussion of Shakespeare's
indebtedness to other sonneteers, and other sonneteers' indebtedness
to him. A book of a similar kind is Katharine M. Wilson's *Shakespeare's
Sugared Sonnets* (1974), but this is partly spoilt by her assumption,
if I understand her, that many of Shakespeare's sonnets were
deliberate parodies, and others written in direct imitation. She thinks
that CXXVII is based on Sidney's VII (about Stella's eyes 'In colour
black');[49] that CXXX has numerous analogues in Watson, Barnes,
Constable, Daniel and Spenser; and that CXXXIII and the following
sonnets echo Barnes II–IX.[50] But these Barnes sonnets (as far as one
can decipher them) do not refer to the seduction of the poet's friend
by his mistress as Miss Wilson believes. In any case, she appears to
misjudge the tone of Shakespeare's sonnets.

A more valuable book is J. W. Lever's *The Elizabethan Love Sonnet*
(1956). He devotes nearly half his space to Shakespeare, but his previous
chapters on Petrarch and sixteenth-century poets help us to distinguish
the method and quality of Shakespeare's sonnets from those of his
contemporaries. He is sounder than Lee on the question of convention:
'The danger is twofold; of naivety, in accepting any sonnet as literal
autobiography; or of false sophistication, in dismissing it off hand as mere
"literary exercise".'[51] He goes on to suggest a way of avoiding both
dangers – by considering the nature of the imitation in representative
sonnets. This is the method he himself adopts. It is notably successful
when applied to Sidney and Spenser. He compares, for example,
Astrophil and Stella, LXXI, with Petrarch's 'Chi vuol veder quantunque
pò natura', and shows that, although Sidney's opening lines are inspired
by those of Petrarch, there are some striking contrasts. 'In Sidney's poem
the heightened tone, the transcendental vision is lacking.' His 'major
concern is with virtue and beauty as aspects of character; with their
effects upon society; and lastly with his own subjective response'.[52] Lever
is equally successful in comparing *Amoretti*, XIII, with Tasso's
'Quell'alma ch'immortal, donna, traesti', and XXII, with Desportes'
'Solitaire et pensif, dans un bois écarté'. The imitation of Tasso is
merely 'a parallel approach to the same theme'.[53] When he comes to

Shakespeare, however, Lever is unable to make comparisons of his sonnets with those of his predecessors because (with one or two doubtful exceptions) he did not imitate earlier sonneteers. Instead Lever points out Shakespeare's use of Erasmus, of *Arcadia* and, above all, of the last book of Ovid's *Metamorphoses*.

Lever is also concerned with the links between one sonnet and another; he therefore argues that XCIV should not be divorced from its context. 'Properly considered [it] will be found to bear a close and detailed relationship to its group in the sequence.'[54] Lever was apparently the first to point out that Sidney's observation, which Shakespeare echoed in the first line of this sonnet – 'the more power he hath to hurt, the more admirable is his praise that he will not hurt' – was made in connection with a triangular affair between Prince Plangus, his father and a married woman.[55] This situation was sufficiently like the sonnet triangle for the Poet to recall the episode. Plangus, like the Poet, resigns his mistress to his rival.

Another good book, more limited in scope but surer perhaps in its literary judgements, was J. B. Leishman's *Themes and Variations in Shakespeare's Sonnets* (1961).[56] He was mainly concerned with the resemblances and differences between Shakespeare's sonnets and sonnets and other poems by his predecessors and contemporaries – in particular the theme of immortalisation by means of poetry and the theme of devouring Time, *Tempus edax*. Occasionally he suggested that Shakespeare had been influenced by Horace, Ovid or Ronsard; but his main purpose was to demonstrate the essential individuality of Shakespeare's treatment of these themes, even though he was writing within a convention. The book is, indeed, a model of how such questions should be discussed. He shows, for example, that, unlike Petrarch's sonnets, and like some of Horace's odes, Shakespeare's sonnets are filled with 'an almost overwhelming sadness at the fact of human transience'. He compares 'Diffugere nives' (book IV, ode 7) and the two following Horatian odes with four of Shakespeare's sonnets (LXIV, LXV, LXXIII and LXXIV) and shows (as others have done) that 'the better part of me' comes from Ovid's 'parte tamen meliore mei'. He shows that in Tasso, but not in Shakespeare, there is 'a certain condescension towards the object of his affection', and that in Ronsard 'there is no trace of that humble and religious adoration, that spirituality' we find in Shakespeare.

Leishman proceeds to discuss the immortalisation theme in some of Shakespeare's English predecessors – Spenser, Daniel and Drayton. The book, as we have suggested, is limited in scope; but it displays not merely a knowledge of poetry in six different languages but also a genuine appreciation of varieties of poetry and a power of subtle differentiation.

(5)

The Mutual Flame (1955) is a characteristic book by G. Wilson Knight, in which he applies to the interpretation of the Sonnets and 'The Phoenix and the Turtle' the methods he had used in his series of books on Shakespeare's dramatic work – *The Wheel of Fire, The Imperial Theme, The Crown of Life*, etc. He assumes that the Sonnets were based on fact, but he admits that 'whether or not [Shakespeare] has exactly recorded a section of his autobiography we can never precisely know; but he has certainly left us a poetic record of considerable interest'.

The central argument of the book is that Shakespeare was bisexual, that the creative consciousness must be bisexual and that, whereas the male lovers in the plays are presented critically, Shakespeare seems to speak from within the women. It is certainly true that Rosalind, Beatrice, Viola and Imogen are more interesting than Orlando, Benedick, Orsino and Posthumus Leonatus; but there may be other reasons for this. Millamant outshines Mirabel, but no one has suggested that Congreve was bisexual. Poets can depict women in love sympathically because they would like to be loved by such women in such a way. The greater the dramatist the wider the range of characters of both sexes with whom we can momentarily identify, through whom he can convincingly speak; and it may be said that Shakespeare speaks through Hamlet more than he does through Ophelia. Nevertheless, Richard II's meditation at Pomfret supports Knight's view of the creative process –

My brain I'll prove the female to my soul.

Even here, however, the union of soul and brain, necessary for the begetting of 'thoughts', is not the same thing as the mingling of masculine and feminine elements in a man's personality. Of course, it is a commonplace of modern psychology that every man has an admixture of feminine traits – as women have some masculine characteristics – and no doubt Knight is justified in believing that Shakespeare was particularly successful in depicting women in love because he found it easy to identify with them.

Knight takes little interest in the Dark Lady sonnets, and says very little about the sonnets in which the Poet urges W.H. to marry. He concentrates, indeed, on the later sonnets of the main sequence, and he has interesting comments on individual sonnets.

Edward Hubler, in *The Sense of Shakespeare's Sonnets* (1952), provides a notably balanced and disinterested discussion of the question of homosexuality both with regard to Sonnet XX and in an appendix. The best chapter, however, is entitled 'The economy of the closed heart' – a discussion of XCIV in relation to Shakespeare's views as revealed elsewhere in his works. Here Hubler is mainly concerned with content; and he produces quotations from the Sonnets to suggest that Shakespeare himself would have agreed with this emphasis. One is less happy when Hubler comes to discuss the art of the Sonnets. He is so anxious to avoid idolatry that he seems to overemphasise Shakespeare's weaknesses. He seems almost to share the eighteenth-century dislike of quibbles. He complains of obscurity and frigidity. He prefers what he calls Shakespeare's 'homeliness' to his more elaborate metaphorical and rhetorical effects. He praises an admirable sonnet (LXXIV) for its bareness, though this is partly as effective as it is because it is a sequel to the complex metaphorical structure of the previous sonnet. Like other critics, he thinks that the couplets are usually inferior to the poems they conclude. He thinks that Shakespeare is guilty of excessive alliteration in such a line as

> And with old woes new wail my dear time's waste

and, indeed, he declares that 'most of the sonnets are not first-rate poetry'. This may be true if the Sonnets are considered one by one, as we have acknowledged in Chapter 4, but Hubler plays down the narrative or dramatic qualities of the sequence – oddly claiming that Spenser's *Amoretti* has more narrative interest.[57] Yet when Hubler is talking about the subject of his title – the meaning of individual sonnets – his perceptiveness and common sense have put all readers in his debt.

Other recent books on the Sonnets include Hilton Landry's *Interpretations in Shakespeare's Sonnets* (1963) and a volume edited by him, *New Essays on Shakespeare's Sonnets* (1976), Philip Martin's *Shakespeare's Sonnets: Self, Love and Art* (1972), J. Winny's *The Master-Mistress* (1968), and Murray Krieger's *A Window to Criticism* (1964).[58] The reader of these and of the other editions and critical works mentioned in this chapter will have a much greater chance than his father or grandfather did of understanding the meaning of the Sonnets, of appreciating the subtleties of structure, imagery and wordplay, and of avoiding the absurdity of supposing that the Sonnets must either be confessions or else insincere.

Appendixes

The argument of this book is that, even though there were probably events in Shakespeare's life which resembled in some respects those treated in the Sonnets, we cannot assume that any of the poems records an actual event. Even if some future Hotson were to discover a number of affectionate letters written by Shakespeare to a noble lord, or a diary kept by his mistress, we should not be much nearer to establishing the literal, as opposed to the imaginative, truth of the Sonnets, though we might be able to add some pages to Shakespeare's documentary life.

With this preamble, it will be convenient in the first three appendixes to summarise the main theories about the identity of the three main characters – the *dramatis personae* – of the Sonnets.

(A) MR W.H.

The Sonnets are dedicated, by the publisher and not by the author, to to Mr (or Master) W.H.

> TO. THE. ONLIE. BEGETTER. OF.
> THESE. INSUING. SONNETS.
> MR. W. H. ALL. HAPPINESSE.
> AND. THAT. ETERNITIE.
> PROMISED.
> BY.
> OUR. EVER-LIVING. POET.
> WISHETH.
> THE. WELL-WISHING.
> ADVENTURER. IN.
> SETTING.
> FORTH.
> T. T.

There are many unsolved problems connected with this dedication. Why is each word followed by a full stop? Is Mr W.H. the man who procured the copy for the printer or is he the man to whom the first 126 sonnets were addressed? Is T.T. referring to himself as the well-wishing adventurer (i.e. in publishing the book) or was W.H. going on a voyage? Is there any significance in the way the dedication is set out?

Apart from some candidates too absurd to merit discussion – William Himself, Willie Hughes (suggested by the italicised *'Hews'* in XX) – there are four main contenders: William Harvey, William Hatcliffe, William Herbert and (by reversing the initials) Henry Wriothesley, Earl of Southampton.

Sir William Harvey, the third husband of the Dowager Countess of Southampton, could presumably have obtained a copy of the Sonnets if they had been addressed to his stepson. Whether he would wish to reveal in print that man's youthful character or his association with a common player is rather doubtful. Moreover, it seems unlikely that Thorpe, however affected his phraseology, would use 'begetter' to mean 'procurer'; and still unlikely that he should wish the immortality promised by the Poet to anyone except the man of whom, and to whom, the Poet wrote.[1]

William Hatcliffe is Hotson's choice.[2] He was elected 'Prince of the Purpoole' at the Gray's Inn Revels in January 1587/8. Hotson was able to explain the peculiar setting of the dedication by showing that successive lines revealed the name of the dedicatee (in lines 3 Mr W.H.; 4 Hat; 7 Liv) and that the name is likewise hidden in a number of the sonnets themselves. Hotson notes eleven lines in which the two syllables of Hatcliffe are concealed, e.g.

IV.12 WHAT acceptable *Audit* can'st thou LEAVE?

IX.2 THAT thou consum'st thy selfe in single LIFE?

IX.6 THAT thou no forme of thee hast LEFT behind,[3]

Not everyone was convinced by Hotson's arguments. So many lines in the Sonnets necessarily use 'that', 'what' and 'hath' that it would be surprising if in the same or adjacent lines Shakespeare did not also use 'leave', 'liv', 'lef' or 'life'. Hotson's analysis of the dedication, however, has the merit of giving a plausible explanation of the stops.

Henry Wriothesley, Earl of Southampton, is one of the two favourite candidates. Shakespeare dedicated two of his narrative poems to the young Earl, and the *Lucrece* dedication appears to show a greater intimacy than that to *Venus and Adonis* in the previous year:

The loue I dedicate to your Lordship is without end: whereof this Pamphlet without beginning is but a superfluous Moity.... What I haue done is yours, what I haue to doe is yours, being part in all I haue, deuoted yours. Were my worth greater, my duety would shew greater, meane time, as it is, it is bound to your Lordship; To whom I wish long life still lengthned with all happinesse.

Whether by accident or design, Thorpe echoed the last two words in his dedication of the Sonnets sixteen years later.

Southampton was just twenty when *Venus and Adonis* was dedicated to him. He was, indeed, the recipient of many dedications (from Gabriel Harvey, Gervase Markham, George Peele and John Florio among others), and clearly the poet of the Sonnets had several rivals. It has further been suggested that '*Rose*' in the second line of the first sonnet is capitalised and italicised to call attention to a quibble on Rosely, which, it is alleged, was how Wriothesley was pronounced.[4] Assuming Southampton was the man, the first seventeen sonnets, urging him to marry, would have been written before September 1595 when he was anxious to marry Elizabeth Vernon. The various topical allusions in the Sonnets can be fitted in with events in Southampton's life, if not always convincingly.

The obscure poem *Willobie his Avisa* (1594) has been used in support of the Southampton case.[5] Henry Willoughby, the author of the poem, had an elder brother who married the sister of Mrs Russell – the first wife of Thomas Russell, the overseer of Shakespeare's will.[6] Avisa, the heroine of the poem, is wooed by a succession of men, including an 'old player', W.S., 'who not long before had tried the courtesy of the like passion', and H.W., who consults W.S. about his wooing. The book was suppressed in 1596, and B. N. De Luna has argued that Avisa represents Queen Elizabeth, and that the poem deals with the various suitors for her hand, all rejected by her because she is wedded to England.[7] One is less convinced by the argument that H.W. stands clumsily for two suitors, Leicester and Essex; and De Luna admits, on the evidence of ampersands, that this section of the poem has been tampered with. It is, moreover, the only section introduced by prose, and H.W. is plainly Henrico Willobego, the author of the poem, mentioned in the heading of canto XLIII. In spite of some resemblance to the situation described in the Sonnets, it is obvious that H.W. cannot be Southampton, nor the chaste Avisa the unchaste Dark Lady. W.S., we are told,

> in vewing a far off the course of this loving comedy he determined to see whether it would sort to a happier end for this new actor [i.e. H.W.], than it did for the old player. But at length this comedy was like to have growen to a Tragedy, by the weake & feeble estate that H.W. was brought into, by a desperate vewe of an impossibility of obtaining his purpose.

Although the references to actor, player, comedy and tragedy may be merely metaphorical, the use of W.S. suggests that a reference to Shakespeare was intended. Possibly Henry Willoughby (or his friend, Hadrian Dorrell) jokingly imagined himself as one of Queen Elizabeth's suitors; but it seems much more probable that he asked Shakespeare's advice about the courtship, or seduction, of a girl, and that this episode was incongruously grafted on the poem relating to Elizabeth's suitors.[8]

One obvious objection to Southampton is that his initials have to be reversed and that 'Master' is an improbable way of addressing an earl. Another objection is that several of the Dark Lady sonnets contain elaborate word play on 'Will', and this is often taken to mean that the man who shared Shakespeare's mistress also shared his first name.

The First Folio is dedicated to 'the most noble and incomparable paire of brethren', William Herbert, Earl of Pembroke, and Philip, Earl of Montgomery, the sons of Sidney's sister, poet and patron. Heminge and Condell refer to the plays as 'trifles', and then continue:

> But since your L.L. haue beene pleas'd to thinke these trifles something, heeretofore; and haue prosequuted both them, and their Authour liuing, with so much fauour; we hope, that (they out-liuing him, and he not hauing the fate, common with some, to be exequutor to his owne writings) you will vse the like indulgence toward them, you haue done vnto their parent.

On the strength of these remarks, William Herbert emerges as the other favourite candidate. He has the right initials; he was known, on the testimony of Shakespeare's fellows, to have patronised Shakespeare; he was averse to marriage, and he had a notorious intrigue with Mary Fitton. (No one, since a portrait revealed her as fair-haired, now believes that she was the Dark Lady.)

Yet there are some obvious difficulties in the way of accepting Pembroke as W. H. Meres refers to Shakespeare's sonnets in the year when the young nobleman first arrived in London, and Jaggard published two of the Dark Lady sonnets about the same time. Could Shakespeare, the author of at least fifteen plays and two accomplished narrative poems, refer in 1598 or later to his 'pupil pen' (XVI)? Although, as we have seen, the dating of the Sonnets is still a matter of debate, most critics tend to think that many were written earlier. To which the Herbertites retort that the Sonnets are written in a more mature style than the plays written between 1592 and 1595. It should be added that topicalities in the Sonnets can be as plausibly related to Pembroke's case as to those of Hatcliffe and Southampton.

It is, of course, possible that the Sonnets were inspired by Shakespeare's relationship with more than one patron, as Spenser's sonnets, though presented to his wife, were originally written to more than one woman; but, if so, this would undercut the poet's vows of eternal fidelity. It is possible, too, that W.H. has not yet been identified; and it is possible that there is such a large admixture of fiction in the sonnet story that it is a waste of time to treat them as contributions to the biography of any of the four candidates.[9]

(B) THE DARK LADY

Hotson's choice is a certain Luce Morgan, an employee of the Queen between 1579 and 1581, when she was apparently in the royal favour.[10] She married a man named Parker before 1588. By 1594/5 she was known as Lucy Negro, *Abbess de Clerkenwell*, i.e. keeper of a bawdy-house. In 1596/7 she pleaded guilty to the charge of keeping a brothel and she was fined and imprisoned. Hotson assumes that Shakespeare became intimate with her after she married and before she became a bawd. The evidence consists of two kinds: a number of quibbles on Morgan and many references to eyes, blindness, brightness and disease. The quibbles do not appear very plausible (e.g. XL.2 'more than'; CXXXIV.2 'morgag'd'; CXXVII.13 'mourn'), but it may be significant that *Lucia* means 'bright' and that St Lucy, who plucked out her eyes because they aroused the sexual desires of her lover, was 'the special patroness of those who suffer from diseases of the eyes'.[11]

Hotson rightly disagrees with those who think that Lucy Negro was a negress. Shakespeare himself declares: 'In nothing art thou black save in thy deeds.'[12] The Dark Lady is both adulterous and promiscuous; but she is depicted as the Poet's mistress rather than as a prostitute. Luce Morgan would therefore be a suitable candidate only before 1594. The poet would not have agonised so much at her seduction of W.H. if she were already a brothel-keeper.

Dr A. L. Rowse's candidate is Emilia Lanier, although he has modified his case since he first put her name forward.[13] She was the daughter of a court musician, Baptista Bassano and she was born *c*.1570. She became Lord Hunsdon's mistress, and when she became pregnant by him she was married off to Alfonso Lanier, another musician. Simon Forman, the astrologer, whom she consulted in May 1597, recorded that 'she hath been favoured much of her Majesty and of many noblemen, hath had great gifts and been made much of'. By the time she consulted Forman about whether her husband would be knighted, she was comparatively poor. In September, Forman spent the night with her. She allowed him to kiss and fondle her but refused to have intercourse with him. A few days later, however, if Forman is to be believed, she consented.[14]

Fourteen years later, in 1611, an Emilia Lanier published a volume of poems. Dr Rowse at first denied that this was his Emilia but later accepted the identification, even declaring that they were the sort of poems we should expect the Dark Lady to write.

But are they? The book is entitled *Salve Deus Rex Judaeorum* and the title-poem is a meditation on Christ's Passion. The volume also contains a number of dedicatory poems, varying from copy to copy – to the Queen, to Princess Elizabeth and various noble ladies – and a topographical poem on Cookham, the seat of the Countess of Cumberland, who had befriended the authoress. Dr Rowse makes a lot of the few references to Emilia's consciousness of sin. She speaks of her sorrow and affliction since the death of Queen Elizabeth; she addresses the Dowager Countess of Kent as

> the mistress of my youth,
> The noble guide of my ungoverned days,
> For you possessed those gifts that grace the mind,
> Restraining Youth whom Error oft doth blind.

She tells Sidney's sister:

> though our sins in number pass the sand,
> They are all purged by his Divinity. . .

She praises the Countess of Cumberland, who gives no countenance to licentiousness

> But in thy modest veil dost sweetly cover
> The stains of other sins . . .
> That by this meanes thou mai'st in time recover
> Those weake lost sheepe that did so long transgresse.

I cannot see that these passages – appropriate enough in a meditation on the Passion of Christ – reveal any great sense of sin; and the last quotation seems rather to rule out licentiousness as her besetting sin. I am happy to agree with Dr Rowse on one point. Emilia does seem to express personal resentment when she complains of the way men behave abominably to women, though they pretend that women are an inferior sex. She blames evil-disposed men who 'forgetting they were born of women, nourished of women, and that if it were not by the means of women they would be quite extinguished out of the world, and a final end of them all – do, like vipers, deface the wombs wherein they were bred'. This attitude finds its expression again in a long digression in the poem on the Passion, written in defence of Eve. Eve, she declares, 'was simply good'. She gave 'to Adam what she held most deare'. She intended no harm. She was deceived by the cunning of the Serpent. Adam, on the other hand, cannot be excused, since he was not deceived by the Serpent. Eve's fault was too much love, and much less of a sin than Adam's. Emilia concludes her digression with a plea for equality:

> Then let vs have our Libertie againe,
> And challendge to your selues no Sou'raigntie;
> You came not in the world without our paine,

> Make that a barre against your crueltie;
> Your fault beeing greater, why should you disdaine
> Our beeing your equals, free from tyranny?
> If one weake woman simply did offend,
> This sinne of yours hath no excuse, nor end.

Apart from this spirited defence of her own sex, the authoress appears from her poems to have been deeply religious and to have had a comprehensive knowledge of the Bible. She seems unlike the tantalising creature who allowed Forman to feel all parts of her body and kiss her often without allowing him to go any further. We feel bound to wonder if Forman was altogether truthful. And yet, of course, a lot can happen in fourteen years. Some pillars of respectability were not always chaste, and there have been genuinely pious women who have deleted from the decalogue the inconvenient seventh Commandment.

As Dr Rowse believes that the majority of the Sonnets were addressed to Southampton,[15] he has to argue that Shakespeare's association with Emilia dated from 1593, the year of her marriage. But the evidence that she was Shakespeare's mistress is somewhat meagre. She came of a musician's family and could therefore suit CXXXVIII, but many Elizabethan women could do as much. She came of Italian parentage and may have been dark-haired. She had been Lord Hunsdon's mistress and he was (later) the patron of Shakespeare's company. She apparently committed adultery in 1597 and may have committed the same sin four years earlier, but so did many other Londoners. She had been favoured of many noblemen, one of whom may have been the Friend of the Sonnets. All this comes far short of proof, and Dr Rowse's case is not advanced by the fact that Mrs Mountjoy consulted Forman in 1597-8, for she was not then Shakespeare's landlady.[16] This said, we can admit that Emilia Lanier is as likely a candidate for the part of the Dark Lady as any that have been suggested – and that is not saying very much.

(C) THE RIVAL POETS

Sonnets LXXVIII–LXXXVI, as we have seen, are concerned with Shakespeare's imitator and rivals, and with one in particular, who had earned the favour and patronage of W.H. It appears that some of the rivals were more learned than Shakespeare (LXXVIII.7) – university graduates, perhaps – that he looked on one as a better poet than himself (LXXIX.6, LXXX.7) or, in another mood, as given to 'strained touches' of rhetoric (LXXXII.10) and rather ornate in his style (LXXXV.4). Whether 'the proud full sail of his great verse' is sincere admiration or a hint that it is bombastic is still debated. This sonnet (LXXXVI) is linked by rhyme and content to LXXX, in which the poet contrasts his own 'saucy bark' with the 'tall building, and of goodly pride', of his rival.

For those critics who give an early date to the Sonnets, Marlowe is the favourite candidate. But it seems inappropriate to speak of the great verse of his translation of Lucan's *Pharsalia* (as Hotson does).[17] and *Hero and Leander*, lovely as it is, does not have the qualities celebrated in the sonnet. Rowse thinks that Southampton is portrayed as Leander.[18] Hotson is one of those who believes that 'great verse' carries with it the implication of bombast, that Shakespeare is hinting at Marlowe's job as a government agent, and that the 'affable familiar ghost' is Robert Greene.[19] But Greene has many rude things to say about Marlowe, and there is no reason to believe that Greene gulled Marlowe with intelligence, or that he was ever in a position to do so.

Those who think the Sonnets were written after Marlowe's death generally suggest that George Chapman was the author referred to in LXXXVI. The enthusiasm for Chapman's Homer has been influenced no doubt by Keats's sonnet; but the first books of *The Iliad* did not appear until 1598, and even if they had been presented to a patron before that date there is nothing in the much later dedicatory sonnets to suggest that Chapman had warm feelings of friendship for Pembroke or Southampton or that he had been given special marks of favour.

Chapman did not write – or did not publish – any love-poetry. His one sonnet sequence is addressed not to a woman or a friend, but to his mistress Philosophy. It is true that there are some slight indications that Shakespeare and Chapman found each other uncongenial. When the Princess in *Love's Labour's Lost* reproves Boyet for flattery, she refers, possibly with a quibble, to 'chapmen's tongues';[20] and Chapman, for his part, complains of poet's who indulge in 'Idolatrous platts for riches' and of 'Muses that sing loues sensuall Emperie'[21] – remarks that could be construed to imply that a love-poet had written flatteringly of a patron for mercenary reasons. Moreover, it has been suggested that the unflattering portraits of the Greek heroes in *Troilus and Cressida* are Shakespeare's sardonic comment on Chapman's translation of *The Iliad*. All this adds up to a plausible case, but it depends on too many hypotheses.

A third candidate has been put forward by the splendid biographer of Keats, Robert Gittings. In *Shakespeare's Rival* (1960) he claimed that Shakespeare's rival was the second-rate poet, Gervase Markham.[22] The argument starts from a line, referring to Markham, in Everard Guilpin's *Skialethia*:

> And his Muse soars a Falcon's gallant pitch.[23]

Gittings identifies the Falcon with Shakespeare on the strength of the falcon in his father's coat of arms. From Markham's statement that he

had 'lived many years where I daily saw this Earle' (Southampton)
Gittings surmises that Markham was 'for some time a member of
Southampton's household'; he does not, however, directly suggest that
Southampton was the recipient of the Sonnets. He argues that
Shakespeare revised *Love's Labour's Lost* so that Armado, who had been
intended as a satire on Antonio Perez, was now aimed at Markham's
'Arcadian' style, though there seems no resemblance between Armado's
style and the *Arcadia,* and though Shakespeare was an admirer of
Sidney's prose and verse. Lastly, Gittings finds some correspondences
between the sonnets concerned with the rival poet and Markham's
Devoreux, 'probably the most egregious piece of advertisement of Essex
ever attempted'. In stanza 108, Markham writes:

> O thou, Almightie power which didst infuse
> Spirit into my spirit. . . .

– lines which Gittings compares with Shakespeare's LXXXVI:

> Was it his spirit, by spirits taught to write . . . .?

Perhaps the most interesting suggestion, however, is that a stanza
sandwiched by Markham between 237 and 238 inspired Shakespeare's
sarcastic comment in LXXXIII –

> When others would give life, and bring a tomb.

Markham's stanza is actually headed

THE TOMBE
> You which desire to ope this dead mans dore,
> Or you that passe by it without regard,
> Rest here your eyes, and filling them with gore,
> Behold this tombe of words, and lines prepard:
> On Marble, Iet, and Iasper, mayst thou po're
> Tyll thou poure out thy sight, yet be debard
>> To read the sacred heau'n-out-lyuing scroule,
>> Which hath the deeds of this almightie soule.

It is possible that Shakespeare was thinking of this tomb in the line
quoted; but he ascribes it to 'others', not necessarily to the chief of his
rivals.

Other proposed candidates include Daniel and Barnes; and Winifred
Nowottny, I am informed, is grooming Charles Fitzgeffrey. We must
await her edition of the Sonnets.[24]

(D) 'A LOVER'S COMPLAINT'

Many critics have believed that Shakespeare was not the author of 'A Lover's Complaint', printed in the same volume as the Sonnets. These include Hazlitt, Saintsbury, Kittredge and C. S. Lewis. Some, including J. W. Mackail and John Dover Wilson, suggested that it was written by the Rival Poet. A few critics – Butler, Swinburne and George Rylands – have accorded it warm praise. In an article reprinted in *Shakespeare the Professional* (1973) I attempted to defend Shakespeare's authorship; and in a pamphlet written independently of my article M. P. Jackson came to the same conclusion.[25] We differ slightly about dating: I suggested 'about the turn of the century', Mr Jackson 'in the seventeenth century'. The evidence is of several kinds. First, similarity of imagery with Shakespeare's known works; secondly, parallels with his unpublished works; thirdly, the appropriate incidence of words hitherto unused by Shakespeare (in accordance with Hart's vocabulary tests); and, fourthly, its presence at the end of a volume of sonnets, as other poems in a similar genre were printed with those of Lodge, Daniel and Barnfield. It should be added that Professor Fowler includes the poem in his numerological calculations about the Sonnets volume,[26] and that Thomas Thorpe heads the poem 'BY WILLIAM SHAKESPEARE'.

It is unnecessary to go over the arguments in this place, which have (I believe) been generally accepted. It is not easy to imagine Chapman writing such a poem and impossible to suppose that a rival poet would depict W.H. as the seducer of 'A Lover's Complaint' in order to curry favour with him.

(E) THE PASSIONATE PILGRIM

William Jaggard's miscellany, published in 1599 or before,[27] contains twenty poems. Of these only five are known to be Shakespeare's – two of the Dark Lady sonnets (CXXXVIII and CXLIV), with a number of variants from the 1609 text, and three poems from *Love's Labour's Lost*, with fifteen variants from the printed text of 1598. The first is Longaville's sonnet 'Did not the heavenly rhetoric of thine eye'; the second is Berowne's 'If love make me forsworn, how shall I swear to love'; third Dumain's 'On a day, alack the day' (Sir Sidney Lee mistakenly ascribes this to Berowne and Berowne's to Dumain). One or two of the variants are arguably better than those of the Quarto text, so it is possible that this was not the source of *The Passionate Pilgrim* versions.

Two poems of the collection are from Richard Barnfield's *Poems in divers humours* (1598) – 'If Musicke and sweet Poetrie agree' and 'As it fell upon a day', perhaps his most successful poem. Barnfield's volume had been published by Jaggard's brother; another poem, ascribed in *England's Helicon* to the same author, was doubtless Barnfield's too. The penultimate poem in Jaggard's volume is a version of Marlowe's 'Come live with me and be my love' in a poor text, together with one stanza of Ralegh's answer. The only other poem which can be confidently ascribed is a version of a sonnet on Venus and Adonis which had appeared, with a different sestet, in Griffin's *Fidessa*. As the other three Venus and Adonis sonnets have been ascribed to Griffin by Lee, it may be worth while to print all four

> Venus with Adonis sitting by her,
> Vnder a Mirtle shade began to wooe him,
> She told the youngling how god Mars did trie her,
> And as he fell to her, she fell to him.
> Euen thus (quoth she) the warlike god embrac't me:
> And then she clipt Adonis in her armes:
> Even thus (quoth she) the warlike god unlac't me,
> As if the boy should vse like louing charmes:
> Even thus (quoth she) he seized on my lippes,
> And with her lips on his did act the seizure:
> And as she fetched breath, away he skips,
> And would not take her meaning nor her pleasure.
>> Ah, that I had my Lady at this bay:
>> To kisse and clip me till I run away.

(The *Fidessa* text is obviously correct in not repeating the epithet 'warlike'.)

> Sweet Cythera, sitting by a Brooke,
> With young Adonis, louely, fresh and greene,
> Did court the Lad with many a lovely looke,
> Such lookes as none could looke but beauties queen.
> She told him stories to delight his eaers.
> She shew'd him fauors, to allure his eie;
> To win his hart, she toucht him here and there,
> Touches so soft still conquer chastitie.
> But whether vnripe yeares did want conceit,
> Or he refusde to take her figured proffer,
> The tender nibler would not touch the bait,
> But smile, and ieast, at every gentle offer:
>> Then fell she on her backe faire queen, and toward:
>> He rose and ran away, oh foole too froward.

> Scarce had the Sunne dride up the deawy morne,
> And scarse the heard gone to the hedge for shade,
> When Cytherea (all in Loue forlorne)

A longing tariance for Adonis made
Vnder an Osyer growing by a brooke,
A brooke, where Adon vsde to coole his spleene:
Hot was the day, she hotter that did looke
For his approch, that often there had beene.
Anon he comes, and throwes his Mantle by,
And stood starke naked on the brookes grene brim:
The Sunne look't on the world with glorious eie,
Yet not so wistly, as this Queene on him:
   He spying her, bounst in (whereas he stood)
   Oh *Ioue* (quoth she) why was not I a flood?

Faire was the morne, when the faire Queene of Ioue,
Paler for sorrow then her milk white Doue,
For Adonis sake, a youngster proud and wilde,
Her stand she takes vpon a steep vp hill.
Anon Adonis comes with horne and hounds,
She silly queene, with more than loues good will,
Forbad the boy he should not passe those grounds,
Once (quoth she) did I see a faire sweet youth
Here in these brakes, deepe wounded with a Boare,
Deepe in the thigh a spectacle of ruth,
See in my thigh (quoth she) here was the sore,
   She shewed hers, he saw more wounds than one
   And blushing fled, and left her all alone.

It will be observed that Griffin's sonnet differs from the other three not merely because he calls the goddess Venus, but also because of his own intrusion in the final couplet. It reads like an imitation of Shakespeare's *Venus and Adonis* (ll. 97 ff.) In the other three sonnets Cytherea is called queen and each incident is recounted from her point of view. In each of them Cytherea is frustrated in her amorous designs by Adonis' reluctance; and these sonnets share with Shakespeare's poem this conception of Adonis.

These facts suggest one of two explanations. Either Griffin and the author of the other three sonnets were imitating the highly successful *Venus and Adonis*, or Griffin, who also imitated some of Shakespeare s sonnets, was here imitating and vulgarising the central situation of the poem, and the other three sonnets were written before *Venus and Adonis*, presumably by Shakespeare himself. In other words, Shakespeare may have intended before 1593 to tell the story of Venus and Adonis in the form of a sonnet sequence and found, perhaps, that this consisted of a series of individual incidents rather than a true narrative.[28]

NOTES

CHAPTER 1   PRELIMINARIES

1 J. Leslie Hotson, *Mr W. H.* (1964), *passim.*
2 cf. A. Gurr, *EC*, vol. XXI (1971), p. 221, who suggested that the penultimate line contained a quibble on Hathaway.
3 J. Leslie Hotson, *Shakespeare's Sonnets Dated* (1949). Rival views are
  given in *A New Variorum Edition of Shakespeare. The Sonnets*, ed.
  Hyder E. Rollins (1944), vol. I, pp. 263*ff.*
4 Claes Schaar, *Elizabethan Sonnet Themes and the Dating of Shakespeare's
  Sonnets* (1962).
5 ibid.; cf. T. W. Baldwin, *On the Literary Genetics of Shakespeare's
  Poems and Sonnets* (1950), p. 282.
6 Schaar, *Elizabethan Sonnet Themes.*
7 ibid., p. 185.
8 *The Sonnets*, ed. J. Dover Wilson (1966), p. xc, citing Beeching's edition.
9 ibid., p. lix.
10 cf. Rollins, vol. II, pp. 166*ff.*
11 cf. ibid., p. 326.
12 cf. ibid., p. 10.
13 MacD. P. Jackson, *The Library*, vol. XXX (1975), pp. 1–24.
14 Brents Stirling, *The Shakespeare Sonnet Order* (1969).
15 Alastair Fowler, *Triumphal Forms* (1970), pp. 174–97.
16 A. Kent Hieatt, *Short Time's Endless Monument* (1960).
17 Hotson, *Mr W. H.*, pp. 269*ff.*
18 In a private letter to the author. He has since pointed out that Shakespeare
  may have used the Vulgate numbering.
19 cf. Kenneth Muir, *NQ* (1954), pp. 424–5; Henry Constable, *Poems*, ed.
  Joan Grundy (1960), p. 88. Stirling, *Shakespeare Sonnet Order*, modifies
  the theory.

CHAPTER 2   THE VOGUE OF THE SONNET

1 Patricia Thomson, *Sir Thomas Wyatt and His Background* (1964), and her
  notes in Sir Thomas Wyatt, *Collected Poems*, ed. Kenneth Muir and
  Patricia Thomson (1969).
2 There were a few translations from Petrarch: cf. 'Sonnets in the Hill
  Manuscript', *Proceedings of the Leeds Philosophical and Literary Society*
  (1950).
3 Patrick Cruttwell, *The Shakespearian Moment* (1954), has a detailed
  comparison; and Giorgio Melchiori, *Shakespeare's Dramatic Meditations*
  (1976), calls attention to resemblances between CXXIX and Watson's
  XCVIII:

> Harke wanton youthes, whom Beawtie maketh blinde,
> And learne of me, what kinde a thing is Loue;
> Loue is a Brainesicke Boy, and fierce by kinde;
> A willfull Thought, which Reason can not moue;
>   A Flattring Sycophant; a Murd'ring Thiefe;
>   A Poysned chaoking Bayte; a Tysing Griefe;

A Tyrant in his Lawes; in speach vntrue;
A Blindfold Guide; a Feather in the winde;
A right Chameleon for change of hewe;
A lamelimme Lust; a Tempest of the minde;
    A Breach of Chastitie; all vertues Foe;
    A Priuate warre; a Toilsome Webbe of Woe;

A Fearefull Iealosie; a Vaine Desire;
A Labyrinth; a Pleasing Miserie;
A Shipwracke of mans life; a smoaklesse fire;
A Sea of teares; a lasting Lunacie;
    A Heauie seruitude; a Dropsie Thurst;
    A Hellish Gaile, whose captiues are accurst.

In an earlier poem (XVIII), as Melchiori points out, Watson speaks of love as 'a bayte for fooles . . . A Labyrinth of doubts; and ydle lust;/A priuate hell; a very world of woe'.

4 Fulke Greville's *Caelica* (*c*.1585) included songs; Spenser's *Amoretti* contained the splendid 'Epithalamion' and some feeble anacreontics; Daniel's *Delia* was printed with a narrative poem; and in *Parthenophil and Parthenophe* Barnes included twenty-six madrigals, twenty-one elegies, twenty odes, three canzons and five sestines.

5 Ariosto, *Le opere minori. Rime*, 1915 edn. (*Sonnets*, VI).

6 Edmund Spenser, *Daphnaida and Other Poems*, ed. W. L. Renwick (1929), pp. 194–5.

7 An anagram of Marie Cufeld.

8 cf. F. A. Yates, *A Study of 'Love's Labour's Lost'* (1936), and *'Love's Labour's Lost*, ed. R. W. David (1951).

9 Jack Lindsay, *The Parlement of Pratlers* (1928), p. 108.

10 Cited in A. Esdaile's edition of Drayton's *Idea* and Daniel's *Delia* (1908).

11 The following verses, signed 'E.G.N.', are inscribed on the fly-leaf of a copy of Sir Sidney Lee's *Elizabethan Sonnets* (1904):

> Better by far to plagiarize,
>   And with poetic art
> To prettify a pack of lies
>   Than say what's in your heart.

> Better to play the sonneteer
>   And sponge upon an Earl
> Than to confess a love sincere
>   For Ganymede or girl.

> Sydney, whatever he might swear,
>   With love was unacquainted;
> So with relief we may declare
>   That Shakespeare was untainted.

12 John Keats, *Letters*, ed. Hyder E. Rollins (1958), 27 February 1818.

13 See above, p. 8.

14 Katharine Wilson, *Shakespeare's Sugared Sonnets* (1974).

15 J. B. Leishman, *Themes and Variations in Shakespeare's Sonnets* (1961).

16 Spenser's comedies are lost and presumably were not intended for the professional stage. Drayton's dramatic attempts are of little interest.

Greville's neo-Senecan plays were never performed; and Daniel's *Cleopatra* and *Philotas* were not performed by the adult companies.

17   e.g.:

>   Sweet Corrall lips, where Nature's treasure lies,
>   The balme of blisse, the soueraigne salue of sorrow,
>   The secret touch of loues heart-burning arrow,
>   Come quench my thirst or els poor Daphnis dies.   (VI)
>
>   Cherry-lipt *Adonis* in his snowie shape
>   Might not compare with his pure Ivorie white,
>   On whose faire front a Poets pen may write,
>   Whose rosiate red excels the crimson grape,
>   His love-enticing delicate soft limbs,
>   Are rarely fram'd t'intrap poor gazing eies:
>   His cheeks, the Lillie and Carnation dies,
>   With lovely tincture which *Apolloes* dims.
>   His lips ripe strawberries in Nectar wet,
>   His mouth a Hive, his tongue a honey-combe,
>   Where Muses (like Bees) make their mansion;
>   His teeth pure Pearle in blushing Correll set.   (XVII)

The penultimate line appears to be corrupt: the rhyme-scheme requires 'home'.

CHAPTER 3   TRADITION AND THE INDIVIDUAL TALENT

1   Rollins, vol. II, p. 144; S. Schoenbaum, *Shakespeare's Lives* (1970), p. 510.
2   Stephen Booth, *An Essay on Shakespeare's Sonnets* (1969), notes that CLIII has the same couplet-rhymes as CLII.
3   Lee (ed)., *Elizabethan Sonnets*, vol. I, p. cx.
4   Dover Wilson.
5   A. Davenport, *NQ* (1951), pp. 5–6.
6   Schaar, *Elizabethan Sonnet Themes*, pp. 105*ff*.
7   Melchiori, *Shakespeare's Dramatic Meditations*, p. 190.
8   E. Hubler, *The Sense of Shakespeare's Sonnets* (1962 edn.), p. 95.
9   See above, p. 21.
10 The earlier commentators are summarised by Rollins. Later ones include J. W. Lever, T. W. Baldwin, J. Dover Wilson and Stephen Booth.
11 'He does not die who leaves a living likeness of himself': Erasmus, *The Education of a Christian Prince*, trans. L. K. Born (1936), p. 142; *Opera*, vol. IV (1703), p. 562.
12 See below, p. 38.
13 cf. Kenneth Muir, 'Shakespeare among the commonplaces', *RES* (1959), pp. 283*ff*.; E. I. Fripp, *Shakespeare, Man and Artist* (1938), vol. I, p. 267.
14 Cited by G. L. Kittredge.
15 *MND*, Act I, sc. i, ll. 76*ff*.
16 Ovid, *Metamorphoses*, trans. Arthur Golding (1567), bk. XV, 11, 222*ff*.
17 Edmund Blunden, 'Shakespeare's significances', cited in *King Lear*, ed. Kenneth Muir, New Arden edition (1952), Act III, sc. i, 1, 45.
18 Baldwin, *Literary Genetics*, P. 262.
19 Leishman, *Themes and Variations*, *passim*.
20 ibid., p. 50.
21 cf. *2 Henry IV*, Act III, sc. i, ll, 45*ff*.

CHAPTER 4 COMMENTARY

1 Cf. above, pp. 35–7. Gerald Massey was apparently the first to point this out. The best analysis of the first six sonnets is by Winifred M. T. Nowottny, 'Formal elements in Shakespeare's Sonnets', *EC*, vol. II (1952), pp. 76–84.

2 One characteristic of the style of many of the Sonnets is to be found in the first – the use of internal rhyming. The first syllable of 'fairest' (1) is echoed in 'thereby' (2) and also in 'heir' and 'fear' (4); 'bright' (5) is echoed in 'light' (6); and there are less obvious assonances in 'flame' (5) and 'famine' (6), 'churl' (12) and 'world' (13). See below, p. 000. Stephen Booth, *An Essay on Shakespeare's Sonnets*, p. 43, points out that the 'division at line 9 is not only sharper logically and syntactically than that at line 5, it is also sharper phonetically. Line 9 begins with a trochee, and the rhyme between the stressed syllables of *Thou art now* emphasises the metrical variation and thereby emphasises the change of approach.' Booth has many interesting comments on formal, logical and syntactical patterns in the Sonnets.

3 Adams, cited by Rollins. Among Milton's references to this parable may be mentioned the letter to a friend, enclosing the sonnet written on his twenty-third birthday, the autobiographical digressions in his early pamphlets, and 'When I consider how my light is spent'.

4 In *Shakespeare's Sonnets*, ed. Stephen Booth (1977).

5 cf. J. E. Hankins, *Shakespeare's Derived Imagery* (1953), *passim*.

6 Perhaps a suggestion that the seminal fluid is a distillation of the man's beauty.

7 i.e., *traductio*.

8 Cited in Rollins.

9 ibid.

10 See above, p. 38.

11 Booth, *Essay*, p. 45, comments: 'The couplet sounds like a statement of the purpose of the poem, and it retroactively removes all formal and logical complexity from the first twelve lines. It reduces the whole body of the poem to a single unit easily comprehensible in the terms of the single argument the poem seems written to express.'

12 Anton M. Pirkhofer quotes Holofernes as an epigraph to his article on alliteration in the Sonnets, (*SQ*, vol. XIV (1963), pp. 3.14). Other valuable treatments will be found in Booth, *Essay*, pp. 193*ff*., and David Masson, *Neophilologus*, vol. XXXVIII (1954), pp. 277–89.

13 See above, p. 36.

14 Caroline Spurgeon, *Shakespeare's Imagery and What It Tells Us* (1935), pp. 68–9.

15 Booth, *Essay*, p. 27.

16 Sidney, *Astrophil and Stella*, XXVI.

17 J. Middleton Murry, *The Aryan Path* (1933).

18 Dover Wilson, p. c.

19 Maurice Morgann, *An Essay on the Dramatic Character of Sir John Falstaff* (1777).

20 Kenneth Muir, *The Singularity of Shakespeare* (1977), pp. 134*ff*.

21 *Shaw on Shakespeare*, ed. E. Wilson (1969), p. 45.

22 Booth, *Essay*, pp. 20*ff*.

23 Rollins, vol. I.

24 cf. G. Wilson Knight, *The Mutual Flame* (1955), Martin Seymour-Smith's chapter in Hilton Landry's *New Essays on Shakespeare's Sonnets* (1976), and Hubler, *The Sense of Shakespeare's Sonnets*, for divergent views.

25 Baldwin, *Literary Genetics*, p. 165.

26 Thus modifying the simple contrast between the Poet's two loves.

27 Tucker, cited in Rollins, vol. I, p. 60.

28 Sidney, *A Defence of Poetry*, ed. J. Van Dorsten (1966), p. 70; *Astrophil and Stella*, XV.

29 cf. *LLL*, Act II, sc. i, ll. 13–16.

30 This sonnet has internal rhyming on 'therefore': 'wary' (10), 'bearing', 'chary' (11), 'faring' (12).

31 Ficino, *Commentary on Plato's Banquet*, II, 8, trans. Kenneth Muir.

32 The emendation 'looks' (9) is certainly correct. There is a characteristic echo in line 11, and it alliterates with 'let' and 'eloquence'.

33 Sonnets XXIII and XXVI are linked by two rhymes ('stage', 'wit'); but as XXIII also has a rhyme common with XXIV we cannot deduce that XXIII and XXVI were written at the same time. As we have seen, some of Shakespeare's most effective strokes are the result of sudden contrasts and surprises.

34 There is a textual crux in the third quatrain. Q reads 'worth' as the rhyme-word of line 9. Some editors retain this not very expressive word and alter 'quite' (11) to 'forth'. Others alter 'worth' to 'flight', which alliterates with 'famoused' but is otherwise feeble. It may be suggested that 'might' is a more appropriate word.

35 The aubade sung before Imogen's window mentions the lark singing at heaven's gate.

36 Kenneth Muir, *Life and Letters of Sir Thomas Wyatt* (1963), p. 12.

37 Mark Van Doren, *Shakespeare* (1939), p. 8.

38 Martin Seymour-Smith (see above, note 24), p. 33, thinks it unlikely that XXXIII and XXXIV are related to XLI–XLIII. He suggests that the friend's fault 'seems to have consisted in allowing a person – a person not only reprehensible in the eyes of the world but actually reprehensible – to associate with him: this is a disgrace'.

39 Wyatt, *Collected Poems*, CCXLIV and n.

40 This sonnet shares two rhymes with XXXV and two (including the same four rhyming words) with XXXVII.

41 Booth, *Essay*, pp. 5–9.

42 Not, as some have supposed, literally lame: cf. LXXXIX 3.

43 cf. XXXV 14: 'Sweet thief'. This parallel supports the view that both sonnets refer to the same episode.

44 A formal flaw in this sonnet is the repitition of 'thought' as a rhyme.

45 Watson, *The Tears of Fancie*, XIX, XX: Constable, *Poems*, ed. Joan Grundy, p. 206; Drayton, XXXVII; Barnes, XX.

46 Sidney, *Astrophil and Stella*, XLIX.

47 Rollins cites Juvenal, IX 208, Florio's Montaigne, I.42, and *1 Henry IV*, Act I, sc. ii, ll. 228*ff*.

48 J. J. Chapman, cited by Rollins. Sonnet CVI is on a similar theme.

49 Booth, Essay, p. 107.

50 cf. Leishman, *Themes and Variations*, p. 76. G. Wilson Knight, *The Mutual Flame* (1955), p. 101, comments: 'The two ways of eternal understanding, poetry and religion, are happily balanced in our final juxtaposition of "judgment" and "lovers' eyes".'

51 There is an interesting sound-pattern in the third quatrain of LVII: 'dare' (9) is echoed by 'affairs' (10) and 'where' (12); 'may' (10) by 'stay' (11);

and 'slave' (11) by 'save' (12). C. K. Pooler (1918 edn.) comments on LVIII: 'complaint in the form of an assertion that he has no right to complain'.

52   Frederick Turner, *Shakespeare and the Nature of Time* (1971), p. 7.
53   cf. *TC*, Act IV, sc. iii, 1. 41: 'injurious Time'.
54   *SS23* (1970), p. 77.
55   See W. G. Ingram's essay in Landry (n. 24 above), pp. 58–9, for an admirable analysis of LXIV and LXV.
56   cf. *Shakespeare's Sonnets*, ed. W. G. Ingram and Theodore Redpath (1964).
57   On LXIX and LXX, Landry, *Interpretations*, p. 54, quotes Beeching's remark that Shakespeare was 'hoping the best and giving precept in the form of praise' as Bacon advised in 'Of Praise': 'Some praises come of good wishes and respects . . . when by telling men what they are, they represent to them what they should be'.
58   Ingram (n. 55 above), p. 61, commenting on the first quatrain, says that it 'reverberates its dirge-like tones, its long-drawn open vowels (some like "mourn", "dead" and "surly", longer and more lugubrious in conjunctive sequences in Shakespeare's pronounciation than in our own) heavily tolled out in alliterative stresses, like the passing bell itself. Then, suddenly ("in the space of a crotchet, in the turn of a semitone") the second quatrain leaps into a lighter music, tender with love and renunciation, with lighter vowels, lighter stresses, a swift tempo of exultant affection'. Apart from the epithet 'exultant' (which could not be conveyed in reading the sonnet) this analysis is excellent.
59   The phrase 'which thou must leave ere long' has caused some difficulty since the Poet has been talking of his own death. Ingram and Redpath gloss 'leave' as 'forgo'. It could mean that the Poet is thinking that when he dies his surviving friend will be leaving him – but both these explanations seem forced. Perhaps Massey was right to emend to 'lose'. Another proposed emendation is 'leese'.
60   Wyndham, cited by Rollins, vol. I p. 193.
61   e.g., Stirling, *Shakespeare Sonnet Order*, pp. 204ff.
62   Because of neo-Platonic anxiety about accusations of perversion.
63   Robert Gittings, *Shakespeare's Rival* (1960), p. 112, uses these lines in support of his theory that Markham was the rival poet. *Devoreux* has a stanza interpolated between 237 and 238 entitled 'THE TOMBE'.
64   For a longer discussion of XCIV, see above, p. 104.
65   Quoted in Rollins.
66   ibid.
67   Baldwin, *Literary Genetics*, pp. 171–6.
68   Hotson, *Mr W. H.*, p. 276.
69   Baldwin, *Literary Genetics*, p. 309.
70   L. C. Knights, *Explorations* (1946), p. 60.
71   Landry, *SSt*, vol. III (1967), p. 103, and *Interpretations*, pp. 17ff.
72   *TC*, Act III, sc. ii, 11. 158–9.
73   The point has been made by several critics who have been disturbed by the warmth of the poet's feelings of friendship.
74   Stirling, *Shakespeare Sonnet Order*, pp. 201ff.
75   Philip Edwards, *Shakespeare and the Confines of Art* (1968), p. 31; Michael Allen, *SS31* (1978), pp. 127–38.
76   *MV*, Act V, sc. i, 1. 237.
77   *Sonnets*, ed. Booth.
78   *2 Hen. IV*, Act. II, sc. ii, 11. 160–2.
79   See Chapter 1, note 2.
80   Melchiori, *Shakespeare's Dramatic Meditations*, p. 161, and p. 107 above.

CHAPTER 5   STYLE

1   cf. above, p. 29.
2   David Masson. See Chapter 4, note 12.
3   Baldwin, *Literary Genetics*, p. 350.
4   Rosalie Colie, *Shakespeare's Living Art* (1974), pp. 79*ff.*
5   Booth, *Essay*, p. 36.
6   There are some excellent examples of detailed analysis by Nowottny (Chapter 4, note 1) and Landry (Chapter 4, note 24).
7   *OHEL* (1954), p. 507.
8   Tennyson, *The Princess*, 1. 207; *Henry V*, Act I, sc. i, 1. 198.
9   *SQ*, vol. XIV (1963), pp. 3–14.
10   ibid.
11   Leishman, *Themes and Variations*, *passim*; cf. above, p. 42.
12   J. W. Lever, *The Elizabethan Love Sonnet* (1956), p. 271.
13   *Sonnets*, ed. Ingram and Redpath.
14   *Sonnets*, ed. Booth.
15   Hubler, *Sense of Shakespeare's Sonnets*, p. 103.
16   Melchiori, *Shakespeare's Tragic Meditations*, p. 50.
17   Robert Graves and Laura Riding, *A Survey of Modernist Poetry* (1927), pp. 63–82.
18   For the poem, see Chapter 2, note 3.
19   Romans 7, 14.
20   *Sonnets*, ed. Booth.
21   Booth, *Essay*, pp. 94–5.

CHAPTER 6   THE TRUEST POETRY

1   T. S. Eliot, *Selected Essays* (1932), pp. 21, 18.
2   *Tennyson*, ed. Christopher Ricks (1969), p. 847.
3   But Humbert Wolfe, reviewing Hotson's edition of *Shelley's Lost Letters to Harriet*, said that if he had discovered them he would have burnt them.
4   Dorothy Wordsworth, *Journals* (1958), p. 56.
5   Wilkinson used the phrase 'long after they were heard no more'.
6   The autobiographical inaccuracy of *The Prelude* has been discussed in the books of Harper, Meyer and Moorman.
7   Shelley, *Peter Bell the Third*, IV. 8.
8   In his copy of Hazlitt's *Characters from Shakespeare's Plays* (cited by Amy Lowell).
9   Robert Gittings, *John Keats: the Living Year* (1954), pp. 64*ff.*
10   Keats, *Poems*, ed. M. Allott, gives evidence collected from articles by J. Middleton Murry, B. Ifor Evans and others.
11   cf. Kenneth Muir, 'Personal involvement and appropriate form', *EA* (1974), pp. 425*ff.*
12   Una Ellis-Fermor, *Shakespeare the Dramatist*, ed. Kenneth Muir (1961), pp. 1–20.
13   Kenneth Muir, *Shakespeare the Professional* (1973), pp. 22*ff.*
14   *Keats*, Letters, 27 February 1818.
15   Sidney, *Defence of Poetry*, p. 52.
16   Marlowe, *1 Tamburlaine*, Act V, sc. ii, 11. 161*ff.*
17   Rollins, vol. II.
18   ibid., vol. II, p. 133 (*Sämmtliche Werke*).
19   ibid., p. 133 (*A Course of Lectures*, trans. Black and Morrison, 1846).

20 ibid., 134 (in his edition of Shakespeare's *Works*).
21 ibid., 135 (*Penelope Taschenbuch*, p. 315).
22 ibid., p. 135 (in his edition of Shakespeare's *Dramatic Works*).
23 ibid., pp. 135–6 (in his edition of 1832, p. lxxxvi).
24 ibid., p. 136 (*Table Talk*, 14 May 1833).
25 ibid., p. 137 (*Sämmtliche Werke* (1876), vol. III, p. 177).
26 Heine, *Letters*, 9 June 1819.
27 Rollins, vol. II, p. 137 ('M.R.' in *London and Westminster Review*, 1836).
28 ibid., p. 127 (*On Heroes and Hero-Worship*).
29 ibid., p. 138 (*ShJ*, vol. I (1865), pp. 55*ff*.)
30 ibid., p. 138 (*Shakespeare's Scholar* (1944), pp. 473*ff*.)
31 ibid., p. 139 (in his edition of Shakespeare, p. 152).
32 ibid., p. 139 (Essays, p. 12.)
33 ibid., p. 142 (in his edition of Shakespeare, p. lxiii).
34 ibid., p. 142 (*Fortnightly*, vol. XXXIV, p. 714; *Sonnets*, ed. Dowden (1881), pp. 16*ff*.).
35 ibid., p. 143 (*Nineteenth Century*, vol. XVI, p. 242).
36 ibid., p. 144; cf. above, p. 30.
37 ibid., p. 146 (*Shakespeare* (1907), pp. 87*ff*.).
38 ibid., p. 146 (*Oxford Lectures on Poetry* (1909), pp. 330*ff*.).
39 ibid, p. 156 (*Shakespeare* (1916), pp. 51*ff*.).
40 ibid., p. 240 (*EngSt*, vol. XLIX (1916), pp. 172–80.
41 *Sonnets*, ed. Wilson; A. L. Rowse, *William Shakespeare* (1963) and other works; Hotson, *Mr W. H.*
42 e.g., J. Dover Wilson.
43 Castiglione's *The Courtier*, trans. Sir Thomas Hoby (1561), was the most popular vehicle for neo-Platonic ideas.
44 e.g., *MA*, Act IV, sc. i, 1. 55; *Ham*, Act I, sc. ii, 11. 76*ff*.; *MM*, Act II, sc. iv, 1. 150.
45 'Tu mettrais l'univers . . .', *Les Fleurs du mal* (1926 ed.), no. 40: 'La nature . . . De toi se sert, ô femme, ôreine des pechés – De toi, vil animal – pour pétrir un genie?'
46 Two quotations may fitly close this chapter. J. Winny, *The Master-Mistress* (1968), p. 22, writes: 'The sonnets may be unconnected with Shakespeare's experience within this actual world, yet autobiographical in that they represent happenings inside the much more extensive private world which is the theme of his creative consciousness. If the events which they appear to describe did not actually take place, something corresponding to those events did happen within this imaginative field.' Northrop Frye, in an essay in *The Riddle of Shakespeare's Sonnets*, ed. E. Hubler (1962), pp. 31*ff*.: 'The experience of love and the writing of love poetry do not necessarily have any direct connection. One is experience, the other craftsmanship. . . . What has produced them [the Sonnets] is not an experience like ours, but a creative imagination very unlike ours.'

CHAPTER 7   LINKS WITH OTHER WORKS

1 cf. above, pp. 1–4.
2 Edward A. Armstrong, *Shakespeare's Imagination* (1946), *passim*.
3 F. E. Hardy, *The Life of Thomas Hardy 1840–1928* (1962), p. 378.
4 One would not expect parallels with *Julius Caesar, Macbeth* or *Coriolanus*.
5 Kenneth Muir, *Shakespeare as Collaborator* (1960), p. 44.
6 Schaar, *Elizabethan Sonnet Themes*, p. 148.
7 Sonnet CXXVI.

8   925*ff.*
9   cf. Kenneth Muir, *Shakespeare's Comic Sequence* (1979), p. 28.
10 This is one of the passages used by Lee to suggest that Shakespeare's own sonnets were 'insincere'.
11 e.g. Act I, sc. i, 11. 80–93.
12 See above, p. 55.
13 e.g. Baldwin, *Literary Genetics*, pp. 325*ff.*; M. M. Mahood, *SS15* (1962), pp. 50–61; *Sonnets*, ed. Wilson, p. lxxvii.
14 *Sonnets*, ed. Beeching (1904), p. xxvi.
15 Kenneth Muir, '*Troilus and Cressida*', *SS8* (1955), pp. 28*ff.*
16 Roger Warren, 'Why does it end well?', *SS22* (1969), pp. 79–92.
17 *AYLI*, Act III, sc. ii, pp. 128*ff.*
18 Eliot, *Selected Essays* (1932), p. 143. Eliot later recanted.

CHAPTER 8   CRITICAL HISTORY

1   Text from the Riverside Shakespeare.
2   *SS16* (1963), pp. 118–20.
3   J. Leslie Hotson, *I, William Shakespeare* (1937), p. 214.
4   Rollins, vol. II, p. 332.
5   ibid., p. 335.
6   ibid., p. 339.
7   ibid., p. 337.
8   ibid., p. 344.
9   ibid., p. 341.
10 Keats, *Letters*, November 1817. Shelley, *Collected Poems*, ed. Hutchinson (1925), p. 422; Coleridge, see below.
11 Rollins, vol. II, p. 347.
12 ibid. This and the preceding quotation are written in a copy of Anderson's Poets in the Folger Library.
13 Essay, Supplementary to the Preface, in *Collected Poems*, ed. Hutchinson, p. 947.
14 Rollins, vol. II, p. 341 (*Letters . . . Later Years*, vol. II, p. 587).
15 ibid., p. 353 (*Complete Works*, ed. Welby, vol. V, p. 181).
16 ibid. (*Complete Works*, ed. Welby, vol. V, p. 318).
17 Hazlitt, *Characters from Shakespeare's Plays* (1906 ed.), pp. 263*ff.*
18 Rollins, vol. 11, p. 355.
19 cf. above, Chapter 6.
20 *Collected Poems*, ed. Hutchinson, p. 260.
21 Rollins, vol. II, p. 343.
22 ibid., p. 356.
23 ibid., pp. 358, 343.
24 ibid., p. 343.
25 ibid., p. 359 (Hallam, vol. III, pp. 289*ff.*).
26 ibid., p. 364 (Hallam Tennyson, *Tennyson: a Memoir* (1899 edn), p. 660).
27 ibid., p. 364.
28 ibid., p. 362.
29 *CHEL*, vol. V, p. 263.
30 *OHEL*, vol. III, p. 505.
31 Rollins, vol. II, p 365.
32 ibid., p. 365.
33 ibid., p. 369.
34 ibid., p. 375.
35 cf. above, p. 50.

36   *Sonnets*, ed. Booth, pp. xiii, xii.
37   cf. XXXII.6, where 'pen' is not meant to suggest 'penis', and XXXI.3, where 'loving parts' should not convey the idea of 'private parts', and LIII.5, where 'counterfeit' does not represent 'a play on the bawdy potential in the first syllable' of the word.
38   Graves and Riding, *Survey of Modernist Poetry*.
39   See above, p. 104.
40   Mahood, *Shakespeare's Wordplay*, pp. 89*ff*.
41   ibid., p. 96.
42   See above, p. 92.
43   Booth, *Essay*, and his edition.
44   *TLS*, 28 May 1970. Richards based his article on *Shakespeare's Verbal Art in 'Th' Expense of Spirit'*, a pamphlet by Roman Jakobson and Lawrence G. Jones (1970). Although these writers give us an interesting analysis of the complex structure of the sonnet, and although they help to show that some interpretations ought to be rejected, they do not significantly modify the standard interpretation. They rely too much on the compositorial spelling and punctuation, and their suggestion that 'the letters and sounds of the first line seem to disclose the family name of the poet' (p. 30) is highly improbable.
45   The concordance is inconsistent in its choice of texts.
46   cf. above, p. 141.
47   cf. above, p. 88.
48   Schaar, *Elizabethan Sonnet Themes*, pp. 183*ff*.
49   Wilson, *Shakespeare's Sugared Sonnets*, p. 88.
50   ibid., pp. 83–8.
51   J. W. Lever, *The Elizabethan Love Sonnet* (1956), p. 58.
52   ibid., p. 60.
53   ibid., p. 107.
54   ibid., p. 216.
55   ibid., p. 217.
56   Although Leishman is more concerned with themes than with the analysis of individual sonnets.
57   Edward L. Hubler (ed.), *The Riddle of Shakespeare's Sonnets* (1962), p. 8.
58   See also an essay in Krieger's *The Play and Place of Criticism* (1967).

APPENDICES

1   But see I. R. W. Cook, 'William Hervey and Shakespeare's Sonnets', *SS21* (1968), pp. 96*ff*.
2   Hotson, *Mr W. H.* (1964), passim, and *Shakespeare by Hilliard* (1977).
3   Hotson, *Mr W. H.*, p. 159.
4   *TLS*, 2 October 1937, p. 715; 9 October 1937, p. 735 (where it is pointed out that the name was pronounced *Wrisley*).
5   Rollins, vol. II, pp. 303*ff*.
6   Hotson, *I, William Shakespeare*.
7   B. N. De Luna, *The Queen Declined* (1970).
8   But see *RES* (1971), pp. 335–40, for a criticism of De Luna's book.
9   Having found support for their candidates from events mentioned in the Sonnets, critics then use these events to justify their choice of candidate. But none of the topical references is certain.
10   Hotson, *Mr W. H.*, p. 245.
11   ibid., pp. 238*ff*.
12   Sonnet CXXXI.

13 cf. *Shakespeare the Man* (1973), pp. 106*ff.*, with *Simon Forman* (1974), pp. 99*ff.*

14 It is not absolutely certain that the consenting woman was Emilia, although probable.

15 Rowse, *William Shakespeare.*

16 So far as is known.

17 Hotson, *Mr W. H.*, p. 265.

18 Rowse, *Christopher Marlowe* (1964).

19 Hotson, *Mr W. H.*, p. 265.

20 *LLL*, Act II, sc. i, 1. 16.

21 Chapman, *Poems*, ed. P. Bartlett (1941), p. 19.

22 Gittings, *Shakespeare's Rival*, *passim.*

23 ibid.

24 In a paper she read at the Washington Congress of the International Shakespeare Association (1976).

25 M. P. Jackson, *A Lover's Complaint: Its Date and Authenticity* (1965).

26 Fowler, *Triumphal Forms.*

27 The title-page of the only extant copy of the first edition is missing.

28 The above section is greatly indebted to an article by C. H. Hobday, *SS26* (1973), pp. 103–10.

SELECT BIBLIOGRAPHY

I EDITIONS OF SHAKESPEARE'S SONNETS

1 *A New Variorum Edition of Shakespeare: The Sonnets*, edited by Hyder E. Rollins (1944) .

2 *Shakespeare's Sonnets*, edited by Martin Seymour-Smith (1963). (See above, p. 143.)

3 *Shakespeare's Sonnets*, edited by W. G. Ingram and Theodore Redpath (1964). (See above, p. 143.)

4 *The Sonnets*, edited by John Dover Wilson (1966; second edn, 1967). (See above, p. 144.)

5 *Shakespeare's Sonnets*, edited with an analytic commentary by Stephen Booth (1977). (See above, p. 144.)

II EDITIONS OF THE OTHER SONNETEERS

6 Barnabe Barnes, *Parthenophil and Parthenophe*, edited by Victor A. Doyno (1971).

7 Richard Barnfield, in *Some Longer Elizabethan Poems*, edited by A. H. Bullen (1903).

8 Henry Constable, *Poems*, edited by Joan Grundy (1960).

9 Samuel Daniel, *Poems and Defence of Ryme*, edited by A. C. Sprague (1950); *Works* (1623) .

10 Michael Drayton, *Poems* (1619), Scolar Press facsimile (1969).

11 Fulke Greville, *Poems and Dramas*, edited by Geoffrey Bullough (1939).

12 Philip Sidney, *Poems*, edited by William A. Ringler (1962).

13 Edmund Spenser, *Daphnaida and Other Poems*, edited by W. L. Renwick (1929).

14 Henry Howard, Earl of Surrey, *Poems*, edited by Emrys Jones (1964).

15 Thomas Watson, *Poems*, edited by E. Arber (1870).

16 Sir Thomas Wyatt, *Collected Poems*, edited by Kenneth Muir and Patricia Thomson (1969).

17 Sir Sidney Lee (ed.), *Elizabethan Sonnets* (1904). (Containing, *inter alia*, Lodge, Percy, Griffin, Linche, Smith, Tofte and *Zepheria*.)

III BOOKS ON SHAKESPEARE'S SONNETS

18 T. W. Baldwin, *On the Literary Genetics of Shakspeare's Poems and Sonnets* (1950).

19 Stephen Booth, *An Essay on Shakespeare's Sonnets* (1969).

20 Edward L. Hubler, *The Sense of Shakespeare's Sonnets* (1952).

21 Edward L. Hubler (ed.), *The Riddle of Shakespeare's Sonnets* (1962).

22 G. Wilson Knight, *The Mutual Flame* (1955).

23 Murray Krieger, *A Window to Criticism* (1964).

24 Hilton Landry, *Interpretations in Shakespeare's Sonnets* (1964).

25 Hilton Landry (ed.), *New Essays on Shakespeare's Sonnets* (1976).
26 J. B. Leishman, *Themes and Variations in Shakespeare's Sonnets* (1961).
27 Philip Martin, *Shakespeare's Sonnets: Self, Love and Art* (1972).
28 Giorgio Melchiori, *Shakespeare's Tragic Meditations* (1976).
29 Claes Schaar, *Elizabethan Sonnet Themes and the Dating of Shakspeare's Sonnets* (1962).
30 Brents Stirling, *The Shakespeare Sonnet Order* (1969).
31 James Winny, *The Master-Mistress* (1968).

IV CHAPTERS AND ARTICLES

32 Rosalie Colie, *Shakespeare's Living Art* (1974).
33 William Empson, *Seven Types of Ambiguity* (1930).
34 William Empson, *Some Versions of Pastoral* (1950).
35 Alastair Fowler, *Triumphal Forms* (1970).
36 Joan Grundy, 'Shakespeare's *Sonnets* and the Elizabethan sonneteers', *SS15* (1962), pp. 41–9.
37 G. K. Hunter, 'The dramatic technique of Shakespeare's Sonnets', *EC*, vol. III (1953), pp. 152–64.
38 L. C. Knights, *Explorations* (1946).
39 Murray Krieger, 'The innocent insinuations of wit', *The Play and Place of Criticism* (1967).
40 J. W. Lever, *The Elizabethan Love Sonnet* (1956).
41 Molly M. Mahood, *Shakespeare's Wordplay* (1957).
42 Molly M. Mahood, 'Love's confined doom', *SS15* (1962), pp. 50–61.
43 L. E. Pearson, *Elizabethan Love Conventions* (1933).
44 J. C. Ransom, *The World's Body* (1938).
45 I. A. Richards, 'Jakobson's Shakespeare: the subliminal structure of a Shakespeare sonnet', *TLS*, 28 May 1970.
46 J. G. Scott, *Les Sonnets élisabéthains* (1929).

V BIOGRAPHICAL THEORY AND FACT

47 Robert Gittings, *Shakespeare's Rival* (1960).
48 J. Leslie Hotson, *Mr W. H.* (1964).
49 J. Leslie Hotson, *Shakespeare's Sonnets Dated* (1949).
50 J. Leslie Hotson, *Shakespeare by Hilliard* (1977).
51 A. L. Rowse (ed.), *Shakespeare's Sonnets* (1964).
52 A. L. Rowse, *William Shakespeare* (1963).
53 A. L. Rowse, *Shakespeare the Man* (1973).
54 A. L. Rowse, *Christopher Marlowe* (1964).
55 A. L. Rowse, *Shakespeare's Southampton* (1965).
56 A. L. Rowse, *Simon Forman: Sex and Society in Shakespeare's Age* (1974).
57 S. Schoenbaum, *Shakespeare's Lives* (1970).
58 S. Schoenbaum, *William Shakespeare: a Compact Documentary Life* (1977).
59 R. J. C. Wait, *The Background of Shakespeare's Sonnets* (1972).

INDEX